WEST VIRGINIA POLITICS AND GOVERNMENT

RICHARD A. BRISBIN JR., ROBERT JAY DILGER,
ALLAN S. HAMMOCK, AND CHRISTOPHER Z. MOONEY

West Virginia
Politics &
Government

UNIVERSITY OF NEBRASKA PRESS
LINCOLN AND LONDON

⊛ The paper in this book
meets the minimum requirements of
American National Standard
for Information Sciences–Permanence of
Paper for Printed Library Materials,
ANSI Z39.48-1984.

Library of Congress
Cataloging-in-Publication Data
West Virginia politics and government/
Richard A. Brisbin Jr. . . . [et al.].
p.   cm.—(Politics and governments
of the American states)
Includes bibliographical references and index.
ISBN 0-8032-1271-2 (cl : alk. paper). —
ISBN 0-8032-6128-4 (pa : alk. paper)
 1. West Virginia—Politics and government.
I. Brisbin, Richard A.
II. Series.
JK4016.W47   1996
320.9754—dc20
96-14437   CIP

DANIEL J. ELAZAR

Series Introduction

West Virginia Politics and Government is the sixteenth book in the Center for the Study of Federalism and University of Nebraska Press series, Politics and Governments of the American States. The aim of the series is to provide books on the politics and government of the individual states that appeal to political scientists, their students, and the public. Each volume in the series examines the state's political culture, traditions and practices, constituencies and interest groups, and constitutional and institutional frameworks. They also review the state's political development to demonstrate how its political institutions and characteristics have evolved from the first settlement to the present, presenting the state in the context of the nation and section of which it is a part, and reviewing the state's role and relations vis-à-vis its sister states and the federal government. The state's constitutional history, its traditions of constitution making and constitutional change, is examined and related to the workings of the state's political institutions and processes. State-local relations, local government, and community politics are examined. Finally, each volume reviews the state's major policy concerns and their implementation and concludes by summarizing its principal themes and findings and drawing conclusions about the current state of the state, its continuing traditions, and emerging issues. Each volume also contains a bibliographic survey of the existing literature on the state and a guide to the use of that literature and state government documents to assist the reader in learning more about the state and its political system. Although the books in the series are not expected to be uniform, all focus on the common themes of federalism, constitutionalism, political culture, and the continuing American frontier to provide a framework within which to consider the institutions, routines, and processes of state government and politics.

FEDERALISM

Both the greatest conflicts of American history and the most prosaic day-to-day operations of American government are closely intertwined with American federalism. American federalism has been characterized by several basic tensions. One is between state sovereignty—the view that in a proper federal system, authority and power over most domestic affairs should be in the hands of the states—and national supremacy—the view that the federal government has a significant role to play in domestic matters affecting the national interest. The other tension is between dual federalism—the idea that a federal system functions best when the federal government and the states function as separately as possible, each in its own sphere—and cooperative federalism—the view that federalism works best when the federal government and the states, while preserving their own institutions, cooperate closely on the implementation of joint or shared programs.

West Virginia can be considered a product of the most difficult aspects of federalism—civil war, secession, and, in the case of American federalism, the use of federalism as the basis for trying to protect slavery and the slave system. As it turned out, West Virginia benefited from these difficulties since it would not have become independent had they not existed. Beyond that, the state has occupied an unexceptional position in the federal union. As a poor state it has benefited from federal largess, but not as much as other poor states in the South. By and large it has had to take the lead in its own development, which has been shaped by the character of its population far more than by any outside governmental influence. On the other hand, West Virginia has not much run afoul of the federal government either. It has had some problems in the Civil Rights field and more attention-grabbing ones in the field of legal activities, especially federal investigations of state officials for corruption.

CONSTITUTIONALISM

The American constitutional tradition grows out of the Whig understanding that civil societies are founded by political covenant, through which the powers of government are delineated and limited and the rights of the constituting members are clearly proclaimed in such a way as to provide moral and practical restraints on governmental institutions. That constitutional tradition was modified by the federalists, who accepted its fundamental principals but strengthened the institutional framework designed to provide energy in government while maintaining the checks and balances they saw as needed to preserve liberty and republican government. At the same time, they turned nonbinding declarations of rights into enforceable constitutional articles.

American state constitutions reflect a melding of these two traditions. Under the U.S. Constitution, each state is free to adopt its own constitution, provided that it establishes a republican form of government. Some states have adopted highly succinct constitutions, such as the Vermont Constitution of 1793, with 6,600 words, that is still in effect with only fifty-two amendments. Others are just the opposite—for example, Georgia's Ninth Constitution, adopted in 1976, which has 583,000 words.

Overall, six different state constitutional patterns have developed. The commonwealth pattern, developed in New England, emphasizes Whig ideas of the constitution as a philosophic document designed first and foremost to set a direction for civil society and to express and institutionalize a theory of republican government. The commercial republic pattern reflects a series of compromises required by the conflict of many strong ethnic groups and commercial interests. The southern contractual pattern sets explicit terms governing the relationship between polity and society, such as those that protected slavery or racial segregation, or those that sought to diffuse the formal allocation of authority in order to accommodate the swings between oligarchy and factionalism characteristic of southern state politics. Of all the southern states, only Louisiana stands somewhat outside this pattern, since its legal system was founded on the French civil code. Its constitutions have been codes—long, highly explicit documents that form a pattern in and of themselves.

A fifth pattern is found in the states of the Far West, where the state constitution is primarily a frame of government explicitly reflecting the republican and democratic principles dominant in the nation in the late nineteenth century, but emphasizing the structure of state government and the distribution of powers within that structure in a direct, businesslike manner. Finally, the two newest states, Alaska and Hawaii, have adopted constitutions following the managerial pattern developed and promoted by twentieth-century constitutional reform movements in the United States. Those constitutions are characterized by conciseness, broad grants of power to the executive branch, and relatively few structural restrictions on the legislature. They emphasize natural resource conservation and social legislation.

West Virginia's constitutional development seems to place it in the commercial republic pattern, reflecting the state's strong cultural character and historic circumstances. Since West Virginia became a state because its people remained loyal to the Union, it did not have to go through the processes of constitution making and unmaking that the Confederate states did, first to incorporate secession and then to find their way back into the Union. Nevertheless, West Virginia has had two constitutions and numerous amendments, reflecting a certain penchant for making extensive formal constitutional changes to accommodate new situations.

THE CONTINUING AMERICAN FRONTIER

For Americans, the very word *frontier* conjures up the images of the rural-land frontier of yesteryear—of explorers and mountain men, of cowboys and Indians, of brave pioneers pushing their way west in the face of natural obstacles. Later, Americans' picture of the frontier was expanded to include the inventors, the railroad builders, and the captains of industry who created the urban-industrial frontier. Recently, television has begun to celebrate the entrepreneurial ventures of the automobile and oil industries, portraying the magnates of those industries and their families in the same larger-than-life frame as once was done for the heroes of that first frontier.

The United States was founded with a rural-land frontier that persisted until World War I, more or less, spreading farms, ranches, mines, and towns across the land. Early in the nineteenth century, the rural-land frontier generated the urban frontier based on industrial development. The generation of new wealth through industrialization transformed cities from mere regional service centers into generators of wealth in their own right. That frontier persisted for more than one hundred years as a major force in American society as a whole and perhaps another sixty years as a major force in various parts of the country. The population movements and attendant growth on the urban-industrial frontier brought about the effective settlement of the United States in freestanding cities from coast to coast.

Between the world wars, the urban-industrial frontier gave birth in turn to a third frontier stage, one based on the new technologies of electronic communication, the internal combustion engine, the airplane, synthetics, and petrochemicals. These new technologies transformed every aspect of life and turned urbanization into metropolitanization. This third frontier stage generated a third settlement of the United States, this time in metropolitan regions from coast to coast, involving a mass migration of tens of millions of Americans in search of opportunity on the suburban frontier.

In the 1970s, despite the widespread "limits of growth" rhetoric, a fourth frontier stage was opened in the form of the rurban, or citybelt-cybernetic, frontier generated by the metropolitan-technological frontier just as the latter had been generated by its predecessor. It first emerged in the Northeast, as the Atlantic Coast metropolitan regions merged into one another to form a six-hundred-mile-long megalopolis—a matrix of urban and suburban settlements in which the older central cities yielded importance if not prominence to smaller ones.

The spreading use of computer technology is the most direct manifestation of the cybernetic tools that make such citybelts possible. Both the revival of small cities and the shifting of population growth into rural areas are as much a product of long-distance direct dialing, the fax, and Internet as they are of the continued American longing for small-town or country living.

The new rurban-cybernetic frontier is finding its true form in the South and West, where these citybelt matrices are not being built on the collapse of earlier forms but are developing as an original form. The present sunbelt frontier—strung out along the Gulf Coast, the southwestern desert, and the fringes of the California mountains—is classically megalopolitan in citybelt form and cybernetic with its aerospace-related industries and sunbelt living made possible by air conditioning and the new telecommunications.

West Virginia was initially settled while it was still part of Virginia. Because it was also off the beaten track of the national westward movement, it was less of a frontier for the mainstream of the rural-land frontier and more a catch basin for those who sought new lands but who brought with them more limited horizons and expectations. As a result, except for some Indian conflicts, it has no mythic history of its original frontier. But at the same time, the frontier way of life persisted well into the twentieth century in many areas of the state.

West Virginia was more prominent and even reached the height of its prominence on the urban-industrial frontier, primarily as part of the eastern industrial system to which it contributed its coal and other minerals. Some industrial plants were built in the state to be even closer to sources of energy and raw materials. The difference was that most Americans elsewhere moved from rural areas or from overseas to newly developed cities and became industrial workers. In West Virginia the mines and plants generally went to where the workers were, allowing them to continue to live in their small communities while entering the urban-industrial labor force. The result was a combination of traditionalistic styles of organization with individualistic styles of enterprise—the famous industrial plantation system that W. J. Cash wrote about in *The Mind of the South*, whereby large numbers of

low-wage and unskilled workers served in the mines and in the factories almost as if they were plantation hands in the antebellum days.

The urban-industrial frontier was West Virginia's economic heyday, although West Virginians themselves benefited only modestly from it. By the
time that the metropolitan-technological frontier engulfed the Northeast,
West Virginia's economy was on the decline because its resources were becoming less needed. The state was in no position to capitalize on the metropolitan-technological frontier except as its back door and, in some cases,
backwater.

What this third frontier stage did bring, aside from pockets of third-stage
settlement along the state's principal transportation routes, was a federal effort to improve local economic and social conditions through the Appalachian Regional Commission, a product of the Great Society in the 1960s. All
of West Virginia was included within the commission's territory, which em-
braced all or parts of thirteen states from Alabama to Maine. ARC brought in
seed money for development and attracted a few more industries to the state.
But as the authors of this volume indicate, despite all of its promise, ARC did
not change the state very much.

Meanwhile, the medium-size and small cities that had grown up in the
wake of the urban-industrial frontier began to lose population. West Virginia
returned to being a rural state but this time in the rurban mode. Its climate
and terrain allowed rurban development even before the cybernetic frontier
was added to it. In this way it was like much of the South. It remains to be
seen to what extent the cybernetic dimension will be added to the rurban
character of West Virginia and what its consequences will be.

THE PERSISTENCE OF SECTIONALISM

Sectionalism—the expression of social, economic, and especially political
differences along geographic lines—is part and parcel of American political
life. The more or less permanent political ties that link groups of contiguous
states together as sections reflect the ways in which local conditions and differences in political culture modify the impact of the frontier. This overall
sectional pattern reflects the interaction of three basic factors. The original
sections were produced by the variations in the impact of the rural-land frontier on different geographic segments of the country. They, in turn, have
been modified by the pressures generated by the various frontier stages. As a

result, sectionalism is not the same as regionalism. The latter is essentially a phenomenon—often transient—that brings adjacent state, substate, or interstate areas together because of immediate and specific common interests. The sections are not homogeneous socioeconomic units sharing a common character across state lines but are complex entities combining highly diverse states and communities with common political interests that generally complement one another socially and economically.

West Virginia is in a sectionally ambiguous position, perhaps uniquely so among the American states. As part of Virginia it was part of the greater South, specifically the Upper South, but the clear identification that came from being connected to that larger entity, whose own sectional position was clear-cut, was significantly diminished when West Virginia became a separate state. Of all the states of the Upper South, it was the only one that chose to remain in the Union. Virginia and Tennessee reluctantly seceded rather than go to war against their sister states in the South, while Kentucky was divided and had its own internal civil war. West Virginia, though, was largely, except perhaps at its peripheries, Union. Moreover, its boundaries were established, in part, for strategic reasons; that is to say, to assist the Union in waging the war. For example, its easternmost counties were detached from Virginia despite their secessionist sentiments in order to protect the main line of the Baltimore and Ohio Railroad through Harper's Ferry, one of the Union lifelines for moving troops and supplies east and west. Thus, we can think of West Virginia as a borderline state, between the greater Northeast and the greater South, and between the Upper South, Near West, and Middle Atlantic states.

A perennial problem of the states, hardly less important than that of direct federal-state relationships, is how to bend sectional and regional demands to fit their own needs for self-maintenance as political systems. One of the ways in which the states are able to overcome this problem is through the use of their formal political institutions since no problems can be handled governmentally without making use of those formal institutions. Some would argue that the use of formal political institutions to deflect sectional patterns on behalf of the states is 'artificial,' interference with the "natural" flow of the nation's social and economic system. Partisans of the states would respond by arguing that the history of civilization is the record of human efforts to harness their environment by means of their inventions, all artificial in the literal and real sense of the term. It need not be pointed out that political institutions are among the foremost of those inventions.

THE VITAL ROLE OF POLITICAL CULTURE

The United States as a whole shares a general political culture that is rooted in two contrasting conceptions of the American polity that can be traced back to the country's earliest settlement. In the first, the polity is conceived as a marketplace in which the primary public relationships are products of bargaining among individuals and groups acting primarily out of self-interest. In the second, the polity is conceived to be a commonwealth, in which the whole people have an undivided interest, and the citizens cooperate in an effort to create and maintain the best government in order to implement certain shared moral principles. The influence of these two conceptions can be felt through American political history, sometimes in conflict and sometimes complementing each other.

This general political culture is a synthesis of three major political subcultures—individualistic, moralistic, and traditionalistic. Each reflects its own particular synthesis of the marketplace and the commonwealth. All three are of nationwide proportions, having spread, in the course of time, from coast to coast. At the same time, each subculture is strongly tied to specific sections of the country, reflecting the streams and currents of migration that have carried people of different origins and backgrounds across the continent in more or less orderly patterns. The individualistic political culture emphasizes the democratic order as a marketplace in which government is instituted for strictly utilitarian reasons, to handle those functions demanded by the people it is established to serve. Beyond the commitment to an open market, a government need not have any direct concern with questions of the good society, except insofar as it may be used to advance some common view formulated outside the political arena, just as it serves other functions. Since the individualistic political culture emphasizes the centrality of private concerns, it places a premium on limiting community intervention—whether governmental or nongovernmental—into private activities to the minimum necessary to keep the marketplace in proper working order.

The moralistic political culture emphasizes the commonwealth as the basis for democratic government. Politics is considered one of the great activities of humanity in its search for the good society—a struggle for power, it is true, but also an effort to exercise power for the betterment of the commonwealth. Consequently, both the general public and the politicians conceive of politics as a public activity centered on some notion of the public good and properly devoted to the advancement of the public interest.

There is a general commitment to utilizing communal—preferably nongovernmental, but governmental if necessary—power to intervene in the sphere of private activities when it is considered necessary, to do so for the public good or for the community's well-being. Accordingly, issues have an important place in the moralistic style of politics, functioning to set the tone for political concern. Government is considered a positive instrument with a responsibility to promote the general welfare, though definitions of what its positive role should be may vary considerably from era to era.

The traditionalistic political culture is rooted in an ambivalent attitude toward the marketplace, coupled with a paternalistic and elitist conception of the commonwealth. It reflects an older attitude that accepts a substantially hierarchical society as part of the ordered nature of things, authorizing and expecting those at the top of the social structure to take a special and dominant role in government. The traditionalistic political culture accepts government as an actor with a positive role in the community, but it tries to limit that role to securing the continued maintenance of the existing social order. To do so, it functions to confine real political power to a relatively small and self-perpetuating group drawn from an established elite who often inherit their right to govern through family ties or social position. Those who do not have a definite role to play in politics are not expected to be even minimally active as citizens. In many cases, they are not even expected to vote.

West Virginians' political culture has historically been traditionalistic with an individualistic leaven, no doubt derived from the general culture. Moreover, given the state's poverty, its politics and government have been among the better career opportunities in many of its counties, further encouraging individualistic behavior on the part of those who enter West Virginia politics. The state's moralistic elements, strongest in the Eastern Panhandle counties, have, until recently, been rather thoroughly submerged in this combination of a more powerful traditionalistic culture and straitened economic circumstances.

WEST VIRGINIA: THE EFFECT OF SO MANY MOUNTAINS

As this book shows, not only has West Virginia had to live in the backwash of the South and the Northeast, but its people have prided themselves on conquering that remote area, which, with a different topography, would still be too close to the centers of those great sections to maintain its own distinctiveness and very distinctive patterns of social, economic, and political life. Those patterns may not appeal to most other Americans, but they are authentically West Virginian. If federalism has any meaning, West Virginia is part of that meaning, namely, the ability of particular populations settled in particular politically defined territories, especially states, to live as they want to live.

It may be that West Virginia's way of life is not everyone's cup of tea. It is also true that as the fourth stage of the continuing American frontier carries momentum, West Virginia's position at the southwestern back end of the Northeastern megalopolis opens it far more to penetration from the outside. Moreover, the development of common federal standards in areas previously left to the states means the likelihood of more federal intervention and imposition of those standards on what is likely to be a reluctant population in many cases (though it should be noted in other cases it may give West Virginians who want change and who have been unable to dislodge local elites wedded to old systems the boost they need to achieve that change). Thus there finally may be a frontier that transforms West Virginia as significantly as it was transformed after the Civil War by the urban-industrial frontier.

Acknowledgments

This introductory study of West Virginia politics and government is a collegial effort of four members of the Political Science Department at West Virginia University, each of whom has an abiding interest in various aspects of West Virginia politics and government. Each author initially drafted chapters in his areas of expertise and then solicited comments from the others. The final product thus reflects the ideas and research of all four authors. Richard Brisbin wrote the initial draft for the introduction and chapters 1, 5, and 9; Robert Dilger wrote the initial draft for chapters 4, 7, and 10; Allan Hammock wrote the initial draft for chapter 3; and Christopher Mooney wrote the initial draft for chapters 6 and 8. Richard Brisbin, Robert Dilger, and Allan Hammock drafted sections of chapter 2. Richard Brisbin and Robert Dilger codrafted chapter 11.

We would like to acknowledge the extensive support provided by the Institute for Public Affairs at West Virginia University for research related to parts of the chapters on political culture, the legislature, the executive, the budgetary process, and the judiciary. Randy Moffett, a research assistant at the institute, performed various vital tasks with great efficiency, including management of the statewide survey of political attitudes cited by the authors in several chapters. Also, early drafts of portions of chapters 2, 4, 6, 7, 8, and 9 were delivered as papers by the authors at the 1991 and 1992 meetings of the West Virginia Political Science Association. We would like to acknowledge the comments and suggestions we received at these meetings from various political scientists and public officials in the state.

The authors also have specific individual acknowledgments. Richard Brisbin thanks Joseph Patten, his former graduate assistant, for managing the surveys of judicial officials reported in chapter 9 and for performing other tasks related to the book. Thanks are also extended to his colleagues Professor John C. Kilwein, who joined in gathering data and drafting the publications from which much of the information on the judiciary was derived, and Professor Neil Berch for comments on drafts of several chapters. Chapter 9 was improved substantially by the advice and assistance of Judge Frank Jolliffe, Magistrate Carol Wolfe, and especially Ted Philyaw and the staff of the Supreme Court of Appeals Administrator's Office. Michael Goldcamp and Deborah Wituski, graduate assistants to the department, gathered information on education and health policy for chapter 11. Finally, Professor Brisbin acknowledges Professor Robert L. Hunt, his tutor in West Virginia history and politics at West Virginia Wesleyan College. Robert Dilger thanks Randy Moffett for his assistance in gathering data on gubernatorial powers and for reading and commenting on several chapters. Also, John Hoff, director of the West Virginia Association of Counties, Elizabeth Arbuckle, executive director of the County Commissioners Association of West Virginia, and Stephen Zoeller, Kanawha County administrator, provided many useful suggestions for improving chapter 10. Allan Hammock would like to thank Professor James Oxendale of the West Virginia Institute of Technology for assistance in gathering, analyzing, and reporting some of the data in chapter 3. Christopher Mooney thanks his graduate assistant Mei-Hsien Lee for excellent research assistance in gathering data for chapters 6 and 8. Susan Tewksbury, David Brown, Laura Mooney, and Maude Shunk also provided important suggestions and assistance. Finally, all of the authors express appreciation to the many current and former state elected and civil service officials who provided insights during interviews and discussions about West Virginia politics.

This book is dedicated to the memory of our colleague David G. Temple. Dave, who taught and wrote about West Virginia politics for nearly three decades, participated in the planning of this volume. We miss his gentle counsel and good humor.

WEST VIRGINIA POLITICS AND GOVERNMENT

Introduction

From an airliner West Virginia appears to be one vast mountainous forest broken by an occasional cleared valley and with a vista marred only by whiffs of smoke from distant power plants. From an auto West Virginia is again the forest of beech, yellow poplar, sugar maple, oak, and hemlock, either sparkling with dogwood and redbud blossoms in the spring or daubed with gilded maple leaves in the autumn. The forest has made a glorious recovery from the early decades of this century when timber companies and farmers reduced it to a burned stubble.[1] Today, West Virginia is the third most heavily forested state in the nation.[2] Driving through this forest demands skill and care, for the narrow, twisting roads laid out in hollow bottoms and over gnarled ridges confront the driver with the dangers of the road and the danger from a frequent companion on the road—the triaxle coal truck. Moreover, the driver is likely to be distracted from the beauty of the forest by the abandoned refuse of industrial civilization—piles of coal tailings or "gob" and the strewn remnants of rusted metal around former glassmaking, mining, and refining facilities that once processed the coal, sand, limestone, natural gas, and oil abundant in the state.

The people encountered are exceedingly friendly, helpful, and eager to invite our traveler to a local ramps supper.[3] Most of them love West Virginia and are proud to call themselves Mountaineers. However, they are realists. They know that historically the state's economy has been one of the weakest in the nation, that incomes are relatively low, and that their children will most likely have to leave the state to find good-paying jobs.[4] Often, they blame out-of-state business interests for the state's economic woes and complain that their elected officials do little to curb the influence of out-of-state coal, timber, and natural gas firms. Also, in the past they have experienced widespread corruption of the public sector. Frequently they wonder, is government my friend and acting for me? Or is it in the employ of powerful interests?

West Virginians suffer from more than just a weak economy. The state's rates of teenage pregnancy, maternal health problems, occupational injury, obesity, and deaths from heart disease, cancer, lung diseases, and accidents are all above the national average.[5] Also, many state citizens are not prepared for employment in white-collar jobs. The state's college attendance rate is last among the states. Recently, however, the state has focused additional resources on primary and secondary education by building new schools, increasing teacher pay, and introducing computer-assisted instruction. The dropout rate of high school students, once among the highest in the nation, is now among the lowest. Although once at the bottom of national rankings in teacher pay, teacher compensation has been increased to only slightly below the national average. Also, West Virginia has an exceptionally low crime rate, a fact not lost on its citizens.[6]

West Virginia is primarily a rural state. Only 41 percent of the state's 1.8 million people live in Standard Metropolitan Statistical Areas, far less than the national average of 79 percent. Only eight other states have a more rural population. There are no large cities; indeed, Charleston, the state capital, is the largest city in the state and it has fewer than fifty-nine thousand residents. West Virginia's population is overwhelmingly white (96 percent) and ethnically homogeneous. The population is largely descended from North Briton stock, including Lowland Scots, Ulster Scots (Scotch-Irish), and English from the northern shires. Contributing to this homogeneity is the second lowest percentage of foreign-born population in the nation and the state's small and decreasing African American population.[7] Fewer than fifty-six thousand African Americans reside in the state, less than 3 percent of the state's population.[8]

INTERPRETING WEST VIRGINIA POLITICS

This book explores how West Virginians cope with life in the Mountain State—how they use politics, govern themselves, and seek collective responses to their problems. Although we use the methodologies of contemporary political science to examine West Virginia state and local politics, we trust that the book will be of interest both to scholars and to the state's citizens. Whereas West Virginia achieved separate statehood in 1863, few scholars have chronicled its politics and government.[9] Moreover, the available literature on its politics and society typically lacks data or confirmable factual information about its politics, or erroneously leaps to conclusions about the state's political life from a single set of facts or a single factor.

This book challenges four of the more popular and traditional explanations of West Virginia's political life. These explanations are incomplete because each employs a single category of social or economic factors to explain state politics and governance. Such explanations fail to capture all dimensions of the state's political life and tend to overstate the importance of the unique aspects of West Virginia's politics and to understate recent changes within the state's economy and government, which have brought the state closer to national norms. Our explanation is built on a model of the multiple linkages among various aspects of the state's political culture, economy, and organized political demands, and the centrality of its political capacity, especially the government's institutional capacity to generate resources and make political decisions responsive to popular demands.

Appalachian Regional Consciousness

The first of the four incomplete explanations of West Virginia politics is Appalachian regionalism. A reductionist argument, it holds that political activity is a function of, or can be "reduced" to the results of, the geography, climate, resources, or other physical characteristics of West Virginia's location in Appalachia. The notion of Appalachia as an intellectual construct emerged in the late nineteenth and early twentieth centuries.[10] It was viewed as a peripheral region, unique in its natural environment, folk culture, and economic life. The region's political meaning emerged during President John F. Kennedy's administration. A combination of his political experiences during the 1960 presidential primary campaign in West Virginia, his general social welfare concerns, and the attention intellectuals and journalists focused on Appalachian life led to the creation of a regional development strategy for the area. After Kennedy's assassination, the Appalachian Regional Development Act of 1965 codified the region's boundaries. Whereas previous definitions had included much of West Virginia within Appalachia, the act liberally defined the region to include all of West Virginia.[11]

West Virginia's official designation as Appalachian portended both positive and negative political consequences. Positively, it made the state's organizations and people eligible for any special economic largess that the federal government might devote to the region's development. Negatively, it assigned a label to the state and associated its residents with derogatory economic and cultural stereotypes (barefoot hillbillies, the Hatfields and McCoys, etc.) marking its provincialism. Politically, however, the official designation as Appalachian did not have significant secondary effects on the state. Indeed, there is little evidence that being designated as Appalachian has had much effect on West Virginia's politics. Other than grants for infrastructure from the Appalachian Regional Commission (ARC), being in Appalachia has not meant the state receives great sums of money from Washington. For example, there are no large federal military installations in the state to help stimulate its economy.

Moreover, the perception of being Appalachian has not stimulated political action by West Virginia's population or its elites. Additionally, during the past two decades altruism or even attention toward Appalachian residents, and West Virginians in particular, by external political interests has paled, even to the point of eliminating most of the funding for the Appalachian Regional Commission. Finally, there is little evidence to suggest that being in Appalachia has affected West Virginians' political behavior. Less than one-third (29 percent) of the respondents to a recent survey of West Virginia residents said they lived in Appalachia. Nearly the same number (26 percent) said that they lived in the Northeast.[12] If West Virginians do not view themselves as being part of Appalachia, it is difficult to believe that they could develop a uniquely Appalachian set of attitudes about economic and social policies, or a distinctively regional sense of political malaise. Consequently, both as an intellectual and official construct, the idea of Appalachian regionalism as an explanation of West Virginia politics remains problematic at best.

Economic Dependency

Another explanation of West Virginia politics, often referred to as economic dependency theory, assumes that political activity is a function of an economy that is dependent on out-of-state corporate decisions. Economic dependency explanations of West Virginia politics have two variations. The first draws on the concept of "internal colonization," while the second uses the broader logic of socialist political economic theory. The idea of internal colonization sprang from observations about the absentee ownership of the mineral and timber resources in Appalachian states. According to colonial theorists, during the late nineteenth century West Virginia became a "colony" as external capitalists forced their way into the region and bought up its resources from "illiterate, simple mountain farmers." The capitalists then redesigned the region's social life by creating company towns designed to control the labor needed for resource extraction. The capitalists further secured their control of labor and resources by controlling local political organizations that could legislate on community and labor order, mineral rights, taxation, and land use. Their control was abetted by political corruption and the creation of a local clientele class. Finally, the external capitalists symbolically dominated the indigenous population by defining it as culturally and intellectually inferior.[13]

The evidence to support the internal colonization theory is thin. Unlike the internal colonies defined in the comparative politics literature, West Virginia has not been dominated by a foreign conqueror or a linguistically dissimilar group. Moreover, while the control of labor by capital was fairly strong in many of the state's coal company towns during the early 1900s, that control was never as total as the explanation implies throughout the rest of the state, and it quickly eroded after the federal government passed the National Industrial Recovery Act (1933) and after the United Mine Workers of America (UMWA) increased its power following the passage of the Wagner Act (1935). Moreover, control of local politics by external capital in contemporary West Virginia politics is unsubstantiated by any empirical study. Thus, the internal colonization theory may have had some validity as a partial explanation of West Virginia's politics during the early 1900s, but it is not a valid explanation of West Virginia's contemporary politics.

According to the second variation of the dependent political economy explanation, politics in West Virginia, and Appalachia more generally, is a product of advanced capitalism's hegemonic power in the political economy.[14] External corporate capitalists use their control of property in West Virginia to direct the state's governmental policies toward the subordination and exploitation of the working class. Also, these external capitalists drain the state of its capital, labor, and resources to improve their economic advantages in the nation's urban centers.

As with most studies in the socialist tradition, it is difficult to test the assertions of the colonial and political economic dependency explanations through the methods of empirical social science. For example, research on out-of-state land ownership in West Virginia is inconclusive.[15] Even the most extensive ownership study claiming external control of West Virginia land, the Appalachian land ownership study conducted in 1979, had numerous methodological problems.[16] For example, it equated political power with acreage owned, not with the market value of the land or its resources. Moreover, the proponents of the colonial and political economic dependency explanations of West Virginia politics have not convincingly illustrated how external corporate domination of land enables external capitalists to control labor, establish corporate hegemony, and dominate day-to-day West Virginia politics.

The economic dependency explanations of West Virginia politics might have had some validity in the past, when many West Virginians lived in company housing and worked in industries owned by out-of-state interests, but its utility as a summary explanation for contemporary West Virginia politics is dubious. Corporate interests are influential in the state, but they do not always present a united front, and they compete for political power with many other organizations and interests, including unions, professional organizations, and government workers.

Labor-Management Conflict

The third explanation of West Virginia politics, the instrumentalist explanation, assumes that West Virginia's state policy outcomes are determined by a bipolar conflict between coal-mining and allied industry groups, such as the Bituminous Coal Operators Association (BCOA), and the UMWA and associated labor groups.[17] According to this explanation, these interests attempt to secure discrete outcomes from state politics through instrumental action designed to provide material and solidary rewards for their members.[18]

Today, for several reasons, this explanation of West Virginia politics is incomplete. First, coal mining has become significantly less central to the state's economy. Employment in mining and its allied industry groups has dropped sharply. Therefore, miners are far less of a force in elections. Second, the number of active interest groups in West Virginia has increased. The coal industry and the unions now compete with other occupational groups, such as educators, health-care workers, and other service workers, with environmental and public interest groups, and with the demands of the federal government in shaping the state's public policies. Finally, the BCOA and UMWA are no longer the unified organizations they were at midcentury.[19] Thus, although coal companies and labor unions remain influential and important participants in contemporary West Virginia politics, the state's political environment is far more factional than suggested by the bipolar model.

Backcountry Culture

The backcountry culture explanation of West Virginia politics argues that the state's political choices are the product of the state's particular rural mind-set

and folkways.[20] It suggests that people in the backcountry political culture
are apolitical or antagonistic toward political authority and law, concern
themselves with only short-term personal gains through infrequent political
action, concern themselves more with the sociability aspects of political participation, use social control mechanisms other than political institutions,
and reluctantly engage in organized political activity with long-term goals.[21]
Although it can be argued that such political behavior is irrational because
poor people should use political action to alleviate their economic plight,
this political behavior has been hypothesized to be an "analgesic" response
to a political environment that continually frustrates their interests and fos-
ters their distrust of the ability of political institutions to address their
plight.[22] A distrust of politics conditions individuals to rely on tradition, de-
fer to leaders, and isolate themselves from political leaders. Such behavior
encourages policy stasis because elected officials never feel pressure to respond to unarticulated popular preferences.

There has been considerable academic criticism of the backcountry culture explanation.[23] For example, empirical evidence gathered in two West
Virginia counties questions the explanation's overall viability, and other
studies have suggested that Appalachian culture is but a minor variation of
the culture of poorer rural Americans.[24] Moreover, there is evidence that the
Appalachian backcountry is experiencing significant change in cultural preferences and in normative orientations toward national norms.[25] Because of
the paucity of convincing empirical data, serious doubt remains about the
validity of the backcountry political culture explanation of contemporary
West Virginia politics.[26]

POLITICAL CAPACITY AND POLITICAL PRACTICE IN WEST VIRGINIA

Although there is some validity to aspects of the regional, dependent political economy, bipolar conflict, and backcountry cultural explanations of
West Virginia politics, each shares a common fault. Without providing reliable empirical evidence, these explanations assume that elected and appointed officeholders and bureaucrats are controlled by either a regional perception, cultural values, corporate power, or dominant groups. Nothing is
said about the officeholders' and bureaucrats' influence on the content of
public policy and its implementation or their influence on public preferences. Moreover, nothing is said concerning the impact of the government's
institutional structure and operating procedures on the outcome of public
policies. We argue in chapters 1 through 4 that the state's political agenda is

influenced by the public's regional, historical, economic, and cultural concerns, but that public and nongovernmental organizations, including political parties and organized interest groups, further define the political agenda. Additionally, the structure of intergovernmental relations in the American federal system greatly affects which issues are included or excluded from the state's political agenda. In chapters 5 through 10 we discuss the state's political institutions—focusing on the three branches of the state government and the formation of the state's budget. These institutions set the parameters of action and help define politicians' perception of feasible political choices. Collectively, these chapters enable us to evaluate the capacity of West Virginia politics and government to address problems considered significant by state residents. In assessing the outcomes of institutional rules and organizational activity, we employ comparisons with other state governments and a broad definition of capacity.[27] Capacity is defined as the extent to which West Virginia's state and local governments can represent or "act for" the public and attempt to respond to their expressed needs, interests, and demands. Thus, public officials should not be "persistently at odds with the wishes of the represented" but should normally be responsive to a represented public "capable of independent action and judgment."[28]

We conclude that the construction of West Virginia's political agenda and the specific operation of its state political institutions have some unique procedural aspects, but they are not exceptionally different from the political and governmental processes found in other states. West Virginia's political agenda and institutions are not driven primarily by a unique Appalachian consciousness, economic dependency, the coal industry, or backcountry values. Instead, West Virginia state politics features rather typical American political processes and institutions but is subject to two distinctive limitations on its capacity to respond to citizens' demands—an anemic economy subject to several structural impediments to economic growth, which restricts government's ability to generate revenue, and severe constitutional restrictions on local governments' policymaking power.

PART ONE

The Construction of
the Political Agenda

Sources of the Political Agenda: Geography, History and Economy, and Political Culture

This chapter explores the geographical, historical, economic, and cultural factors that condition and constrain West Virginia's political agenda and the alternative policy choices facing the state. These factors are elements of what has been called the "primeval policy soup."[1]

GEOGRAPHY AND THE POLITICAL AGENDA

Federal and state politicians defined West Virginia's boundary during the first years of the Civil War with little regard to what, in retrospect, makes any political or economic sense. Instead of trying to maintain the state's topographical, social, political, or economic integrity, they included several distinctive geographical regions that were more closely bound to economic markets beyond the state than to one another. The politicians did this for several reasons. First, they were more interested in including specific counties loyal to the Union than in creating a viable political and economic entity. Second, they were very aware of the extent of Union military control in each county. Finally, the political machinations of Copperhead (pro-Southern) elements also played a role in defining the state's boundary.[2]

Geographical Regions

West Virginia's physical geography divides the state into several distinct regions (see map 1).[3] Although there are some differences among the regions, the overall ruggedness of the state's terrain cannot be overemphasized. West Virginia is mostly steep hill and mountainside with little flat land avail-

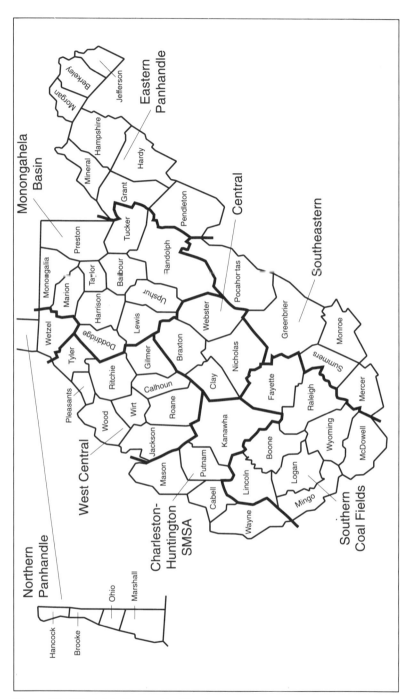

Map 1. West Virginia's Geographical Regions.

able for either extensive commercial agriculture or large manufacturing enterprises.

The state's Eastern Panhandle counties feature separated rolling valleys but also contain some of the highest mountain ridges in the East. Its most famous town is picturesque Harper's Ferry, where John Brown's insurrection in 1859 was a pivotal factor in the outbreak of the Civil War. The Eastern Panhandle's valleys are devoted primarily to orchards and, further to the west, to chicken and cattle raising. The counties at the eastern end of the Panhandle are rapidly being transformed into the western suburbs of the Washington DC metropolitan area, and the entire region, with nearly two hundred thousand residents, is growing in population more rapidly than any other region in the state.[4] The region's relatively rapid growth makes its local politics somewhat unique in West Virginia. Like most other counties, the Eastern Panhandle counties are concerned about attracting high-paying jobs, but they have also been forced to deal with problems of rapid growth, such as overextended water and sewer systems, that threaten their quality of life and their rural heritage.

The rest of the state's counties, with rare exceptions, feature deep, narrow creek and river valleys or "hollows" and twisted ridges of sandstone and limestone usually five hundred to more than fifteen hundred feet above the valley bottom. Flat lands or "levels" of more than a few dozen acres are nearly impossible to locate. Within these counties are areas geographically identifiable in large part by their association with river valleys. These river valleys have served as continuous avenues of commerce and orient most of the state north and west toward the Ohio River.

The Monongahela Basin counties are among the national leaders in bituminous coal production and electricity generation. The Monongahela River, many of its tributaries, and rail and road connections direct most of this region's commerce northward toward Pittsburgh, Pennsylvania. The region includes three small cities, Clarksburg, Fairmont, and Morgantown, and its population of 350,000 is growing at a slow but steady pace as various businesses continue to locate in and around the Morgantown area to take advantage of the resources available at West Virginia University's main campus and its hospital complex. The region was once famous for its glass industry, but international competition has nearly eliminated that industry.

The Northern Panhandle counties are located along the Ohio River in the area west of Pittsburgh. The region's economy is dominated by steel production and related industries. Marshall County is also a major coal production area. The region's population of 167,000 has been declining slowly in recent years as international competition has weakened employment opportunities in steel and other heavy manufacturing industries. Wheeling is the region's largest city (thirty-four thousand residents). It was once known as just another grimy steel town but now boasts one of the finest municipal parks in the nation, and its winter Festival of Lights attracts hundreds of thousands of visitors annually.

Although Lewis and Upshur Counties in the Monongahela Basin also produce considerable natural gas, the West Central counties remain the center of the state's natural gas and oil industry. The region's population of 178,000 has remained fairly stable in recent years.

The Charleston and Huntington Metropolitan Statistical Areas and Mason County lead the state in manufacturing employment. The region's population of 420,000 is growing once again after suffering substantial losses during the 1980s. Charleston, the state capital, and Kanawha County, the state's most populous county, serve as the center of state government, state banking, and related service employment. Kanawha County is also a coal producer and, along the Kanawha River, is home to an extensive and economically important chemical industry. West of Charleston are Cabell and Wayne Counties in the Ashland (Kentucky)–Huntington Metropolitan Statistical Area. Once a railroad center, Huntington is now primarily a manufacturing center with an increasingly diverse economy.

To the northeast of Charleston are the sparsely populated counties (sixty-two thousand residents) of Central West Virginia. Isolated until the completion of new highways during the past two decades, these counties have rapidly expanding coal-mining and timber operations. Tourist enterprises are also appearing along the many reservoirs located in this region.

The Southern Coal Field counties are fabled as the site of mine wars, deadly family feuds, and coal company towns. The economy is based on coal production, with Mingo County leading the state in underground mining production and Logan County leading in surface mining production. Only in Fayette and Raleigh Counties, especially around the city of Beckley, have service firms and more diverse sources of employment begun to appear. The region's population has been declining for over a decade as employment opportunities in the coal industry have weakened, primarily due to technological innovations in coal extraction. Fewer than 313,000 residents remain in the region, down from nearly 400,000 in 1980. Resurrecting this region's coal-dependent economy remains one of the most perplexing and difficult problems facing the state today.

Finally, the state's Southeastern counties have approximately 137,000 residents. The Southeastern economy is dominated by coal production and timbering, with cattle raising and tourism being small but growing parts of its economy. The region is home to the Greenbrier Hotel in Greenbrier County, a world-class resort hotel that attracts tourists from all over the world, and the Monongahela National Forest, which stretches across ten West Virginia counties, attracts visitors from throughout the Mid-Atlantic region.

Economic Regions

West Virginia's topography has created different areas with different resources separated by physical barriers like escarpments and steep ridges. This led to the emergence of independent regional economies throughout the state. For example, during the 1700s the economies of the Monongahela Basin and Northern Panhandle counties became tied to the Pittsburgh market. The Charleston-Huntington and West Central area economies became oriented toward Cincinnati. The Southern Coal Field and Central counties remained undeveloped until the last two decades of the century, but the Southeastern counties found markets in Virginia. The Eastern Panhandle counties found markets for their products in Maryland, especially in Baltimore.

The completion of the Baltimore and Ohio Railroad (B&O) from Baltimore to Wheeling in 1853 and to Parkersburg in 1857 provided better connections among the Eastern Panhandle, Monongahela Basin, West Central, and Northern Panhandle counties. However, it linked those areas to markets in Baltimore, Pennsylvania, and Ohio, not to each other.[5] The Chesapeake and Ohio Railway (C&O), completed in 1873 through the Southeastern counties, Charleston, and Huntington, reinforced these areas' connections to external markets in the Virginia Tidewater and Cincinnati. To the south, the Norfolk and Western Railway, completed into the Southeastern counties in 1883 and into the Southern Coal Fields counties in 1892–95, tied them to markets in the Midwest and the Tidewater of Virginia. It was not until 1906 that a north-south railway connection linked the separate areas of the state serviced by the B&O and C&O Railroads. Moreover, it was not until the completion of interstate highways and much of the proposed system of Appalachian corridor highways in the late 1970s that automobile travel averaging more than forty miles per hour became common in the state. North-south travel, historically extremely slow or requiring round-about routes, improved radically during the 1970s. The driving time from the Monongahela Basin and the Eastern Panhandle to the Charleston-Huntington area and the Southeastern counties was cut nearly in half.[6]

Even with improvements in transportation and communication, the historical patterns of economic regionalism remain intact in contemporary West Virginia. For example, the Rand McNally Company regularly publishes information on trading areas in the United States. In 1992 it listed the Southeastern, Central, Southern Coal Field, and metropolitan Charleston-Huntington areas as part of the Cincinnati trading area; the Monongahela Basin and Northern Panhandle counties as part of the Pittsburgh trading area; and the Eastern Panhandle as part of the Washington DC trading area. Most of West Central West Virginia fell into the Columbus trading area, with Jackson and Roane Counties listed as part of the Cincinnati area, and Gilmer and Tyler counties listed in the Pittsburgh area.[7] This suggests that not only is West Virginia divided into distinct economic regions, but it lacks its own core urban center. Unlike most states, West Virginia lacks a central city in which trade is centered, in which investment capital accumulates, and from which economic and related political information flows to adjacent towns and rural areas. This has, no doubt, played a significant role in the state's economic difficulties over the years.

Cultural Regions

West Virginia's topography is also associated with a degree of cultural regionalism. Although some of the alleged cultural differences in the state are either curiosities, like the penchant of southern West Virginia restaurants to offer coleslaw on hot dogs and barbecue sandwiches, or probably spurious, like the supposed "sophistication" of northern West Virginians, some cultural differences among the various regions deserve attention.

West Virginia's settlement proceeded in two historical phases. First, before the American Revolution, settlers arrived in the Eastern Panhandle from south central Pennsylvania. These emigrants, largely of North Briton and especially Ulster Scots ancestry, occupied the region's valleys and gradually began to import slaves for labor. Second, in the post-Revolution era, emigrants from south central Pennsylvania, composed primarily of North Britons and Germans, moved into the Monongahela Basin, West Central, and Northern Panhandle counties. Crossing the mountains on roads through Pennsylvania or via the National Road from Cumberland in western Maryland, emigrants also moved into nearly all parts of the state's northern and western counties and, by means of the Ohio River, to the Kanawha basin. Another, less extensive, stream of North Briton and German emigrants from the Shenandoah Valley of Virginia and the Virginia Piedmont moved into the Southeastern counties.[8]

By the Civil War all parts of the state had been settled, but most areas in Central West Virginia and the Southern Coal Fields remained in near frontier conditions. When the coal industry began its rapid growth after 1880, industrialists sought labor from out-of-state sources. They recruited British, Italian, Hungarian, Polish, Slovak, and Ukrainian workers for the northern and southern coal fields, Italians for the Monongahela Basin's glass industry, and various Eastern European ethnic groups for the Northern Panhandle's steel industry. They also induced African Americans to emigrate from Virginia and the Carolinas to the mines of the Southern and Southeastern coal fields. Emigration and changes in the demand for labor led to rapid growth in the formerly lightly populated counties in the southern half of the state. Yet, the emigration did not have much effect on local elites anywhere in the state into the late twentieth century. They remained representative of the dominant early emigrant streams.[9]

Emigration greatly affected the state's religious affiliation. The Ulster Scots and other North Britons were predominately Presbyterian, but the lack of strong allegiance to the church, the dearth of ministers, and the lack of towns where stable congregations could emerge and support an educated pastorate inclined most of them to elect membership in more evangelical denominations. Historically, the Northern Panhandle, West Central, Monongahela Basin, and Eastern Panhandle counties were affiliated with three of the predecessors of the modern United Methodist Church—the Methodist Episcopal Church, Methodist Protestant Church, and Evangelical United Brethren Church.[10] American Baptist congregants predominated in the Southeastern, metropolitan Charleston-Huntington, and the Southern Coal Fields areas. A few counties featured large numbers of members of the Disciples of Christ, a church founded in the Northern Panhandle in 1826 and rooted in the evangelical Presbyterian and Baptist traditions.[11] A census of religions in 1980 revealed that United Methodists or American Baptists were one of the two largest denominations in every county of the state.[12] Most important, both of these denominations affiliated with denominational leadership in northern rather than southern states.

Regions and Political Agendas

Although settlement patterns and religion do not determine political values, they can reinforce the distinctiveness of topographical areas and economic market areas.[13] This is true especially when, as in West Virginia, some settlement and religious patterns largely cut across the state in directions akin to topography and economic divisions. The importance of these differences must not be pushed to extremes, however. It is important to remember that most West Virginians practice religions with roots in the evangelical Protestant tradition, live in areas where the processing of natural resources is economically important, and live in a rugged land distant from the economic diversity, racial and class divisions, and amenities of major metropolitan centers. West Virginia is mostly a rural, white, and Protestant society without distinctive class divisions. Consequently, it is not surprising that a recent study found little regional variation in political values or policy concerns among the states's regions.[14]

HISTORY, ECONOMY, AND THE POLITICAL AGENDA

West Virginia's political institutions originated in the political environment of antebellum Virginia. At that time, Virginia's political leadership hailed from a class with economic ties to the slave labor system. To protect slave labor, they had to protect their control of the state government. Therefore, they supported property requirements for suffrage in order to reduce the number of voters not owning slaves, and they required that slaves be included in legislative apportionments to increase representation in the state legislature from counties with large numbers of slaves. They also opposed internal improvements, including the construction of roads and canals vital to the economic development of the western counties, because improvements required taxes on property and slaves. The inability of western leaders to change these unfavorable constitutional and legislative provisions became a source of intense political resentment. Although Pennsylvania, New York, Ohio, and the other Old Northwest states spent state money on canals and roads, provided widespread public education, and subsidized private railways and industries in their undeveloped regions, Virginia's western counties did not have these public goods. Consequently, their economic and educational development suffered.[15]

Unionists and Secessionists, 1860–1872

The Civil War divided western Virginia. The referendum on Virginia's secession from the Union won mixed support in the Eastern Panhandle. Secessionists predominated in the Southeastern counties, Central West Virginia, and in the Southern Coal Field counties. The Northern Panhandle, Monongahela Basin (except Barbour, Randolph, and Tucker Counties), West Central counties (except Calhoun, Gilmer, and Roane Counties), and Charleston-Huntington area voted for allegiance to the Union. Yet, even in the Unionist counties, secessionists and southern sympathizers known as "Copperheads" comprised approximately 40 percent of the population. The movement for separate statehood for West Virginia began in the Unionist counties, and its supporters originally sought separate statehood for only those counties. However, the state's boundaries resulted from an accommodation of demands from Congress for a larger state with more area under Union political control and, curiously, Copperhead maneuvers for a proposed state with more southern sympathizers who could vote against separation from Virginia or at least against the pursuit of the war. Nonetheless, in part because the referendum on statehood took place only in areas under Union military control and because secessionists wanted to avoid the viva voce (oral) method of voting used at the polls, West Virginia achieved statehood in 1863.[16]

During the Civil War, approximately thirty-six thousand West Virginians served in the Union Army and approximately twelve thousand served in the Confederate Army. After the war, the mix of sentiments about statehood and the war merged into partisan divisions. The Republican party became dominant in strongly Unionist areas, and Copperheads, Peace Democrats, and secessionists moved into the Democratic party. Once the federal government eliminated restrictions on the former secessionists' political activities, the Democrats gradually emerged as the majority party in West Virginia. In 1872 they replaced the state's first constitution, written by Unionists in 1863, with a new one featuring a states' rights philosophy, a Jacksonian penchant for popular election of officials, and restrictions on state and especially local policymaking powers. The result was a state government that lacked the time, expertise, and fiscal resources to be an aggressive policymaker.[17]

Industrialists and the Control of Labor, 1873–1935

From the end of the Civil War (1865) through the New Deal (1933–45), the state government's minimalist approach to policymaking permitted large economic enterprises to dominate the state's economy.[18] Unfortunately, nearly all of the investments made by West Virginia entrepreneurs—such as Johnson N. Camden (oil refining and railroads), Henry Gassaway Davis and his son-in-law Stephen B. Elkins (coal and railroads), A. Brooks Fleming (oil), and James O. Watson (coal)—and by out-of-state corporations focused on the exploitation of the state's natural resources. Except for investment in chemical plants, glass manufacturing, and coke and steel production for the initial conversion of raw materials into semifinished products, the corporate investment centered on building railroads to isolated mines or forests, developing the mines, or cutting timber. These economic activities did not demand a skilled work force essential to produce finished goods, a centralized pool of labor in a large urban center, or, because of the development of the company store in isolated mine towns, a local commercial district. Consequently, government officials confronted few demands to invest in public education, supply public services, regulate an urban population, or develop market towns in which people could live and do business.[19]

Industrialists needed reliable but unsophisticated workers who were willing to accept employment in these dangerous occupations for low pay. They found some in the state's existing pool of rural agricultural workers who were being displaced by more efficient farms elsewhere in the world,[20] and they imported European immigrant and African American laborers. Especially in the Southern Coal Fields, employers liked a "judicious mixture" of these workers so that cultural and language differences and racism would prevent unified opposition to management practices. To further control workers, companies throughout the state forced workers to rent company-owned housing in the hollows near the mines. Limited transportation meant that miners had to shop at the company store. In some towns miners were paid in scrip redeemable only at the company store. The company store also gave credit to miners, encouraging debt and a legal obligation to their employer. The mine owners employed detectives or mine guards, frequently a force of thugs, to control labor unrest. In many counties, the mine owners supported or paid local politicians to use their authority in support of their hegemony. Together with local lawyers and small businessmen who did business with the mining companies, the local politicians protected the exploitation of labor. Some of the same forms of control over labor emerged in the towns where steel, glass, and chemicals were produced.[21]

From 1873 to 1935, as in many contemporary modernizing nations around the world, industrialists, land speculators, and resource-exploitation firms, especially coal companies, used organized political corruption to control the state's resources and labor for their own private gain. These practices were used throughout the state but were particularly prevalent in the Southern Coal Field counties. Payments to local officeholders helped to control labor and also helped the industrialists secure title to land and obtain favorable judicial rulings on their resource-exploitation activities. Sometimes the money or related economic favors were funneled through a county political machine or "courthouse gang." Whatever the arrangement, the money secured cheap labor for the company because the officeholders ejected troublesome laborers and union organizers from company housing, deputized mine guards with salaries contributed by mine owners, legitimated anti-union yellow dog contracts with laborers, and enjoined strikes. Money and other favors like railway passes also went to state legislators as an inducement for pro-industrialist legislation on the ownership of mineral lands, injuries to industrial and mining workers, and labor regulation. Before the ratification of the Seventeenth Amendment to the U.S. Constitution in 1913, which provided for the popular election of U.S. senators, the state legislature also selected U.S. senators, like Stephen B. Elkins, who used their personal money to help them obtain office and to influence federal laws and policies that affected the exploitation of resources and labor.[22] Over time the acceptance of the gift, or the habit of expecting it, became a legitimate political norm as generations of politicians learned it was acceptable behavior.[23]

Labor-management conflicts rarely flared in this environment. The United Mine Workers of America (UMWA) began to organize miners about 1897, but unionization took hold slowly because of anti-union injunctions from the federal judiciary and threats from mine managers and guards. When the UMWA tried to organize or, when organized, tried to strike, mine management and the guards normally took extreme action: blacklisting strikers, firing them, or using physical coercion. The result was outbreaks of extreme violence, as during the Paint Creek strike in Kanawha County in 1912–13, the shootout between mine detectives and local officials friendly to miners in Matewan (Mingo County) in 1920, and the Battle of Blair Mountain in 1921. At Blair Mountain, untold thousands of UMWA members, in an attempt to march into Logan County to rally miners, engaged in armed conflict against a force of mine guards, deputy sheriffs, and state police until federal troops and aircraft forced the miners to abandon the march.[24] All of these events contributed to the popular, and somewhat undeserved, image of West Virginia as a place of extreme violence and continuous confrontation between labor and management.

Following the adoption of the federal National Labor Relations Act of 1935, which guaranteed unions certain organizational rights, West Virginia labor overwhelmingly unionized. Suddenly the UMWA and, to a far lesser extent, unions for steel workers, glass workers, and chemical workers, became powerful organized political interests in the state.[25] However, the previous years of oppression had created deep-seated hostility between the state's corporate and labor interests that spilled over into the political arena, particularly on issues concerning worker health and safety legislation, the regulation of the largely nonunion surface mining industry, and workers' compensation. Besides these tensions, the years of industrialist hegemony left the state with an economy dependent on a few industries, a poor and poorly educated work force, and a legacy of political corruption.

Economic Troubles and Transformation

Although West Virginia's economy, boosted by the demand for coal following the Arab Oil Embargo, fared moderately well during the latter half of the 1970s, the state's economy has been in serious trouble since World War II.[26] At that time coal mining changed for both technical and economic reasons. The flow of capital to mine owners, especially those with interests in steel and other businesses during the war, permitted them to purchase mechanical deep-mining equipment. The equipment had been invented earlier but was not deployed because of cost considerations. During the war the labor-intensive mode of coal seam undercutting by hand followed by blasting and hand loading gave way to the use of heavy equipment, like long-wall mining machines, in underground mines.[27] Moreover, the invention and improvement of earthmoving equipment made possible much more efficient surface or "strip" mining. Meanwhile, the development of strip mining caused severe environmental damage as unregulated, mostly local entrepreneurs cut the hillsides for coal. Finally, the demand for coal began to level off as natural gas became a more competitive energy source. Mine owners thus were in a position where they could and perhaps had to reduce labor costs. UMWA leaders recognized these technical and economic trends. By 1950 UMWA President John L. Lewis agreed to the mechanization of deep mining and layoffs in exchange for higher wages and benefits for the remaining miners, a policy that was continued by his successor, Tony Boyle. Thus, the UMWA and the coal companies made an uneasy and sometimes quarrelsome marriage of convenience.

The reduction of West Virginia's mine labor from approximately 120,000 workers in 1948 to 43,000 in 1962 and 24,200 in 1994,[28] together with related reductions in railway, coal-processing, and service employment created persistent unemployment in the state and led to a steady exodus of people from the mining counties to other parts of the nation. At the same time, productivity per miner increased nearly sixfold, and the miner became a technician, operating costly earthmoving equipment like huge draglines, long-wall seam-cutting machines, and mechanical loading equipment. Also, the miner became the best paid category of nonprofessional worker in West Virginia, averaging nearly $20 an hour plus benefits in 1996.[29] Miners moved into the middle class, perhaps affecting the old policy agenda with its overtones of antagonism between owners and miners.

Mining (27,800 employees), construction (34,600 employees) and manufacturing (81,800 employees) together employ approximately 21 percent of West Virginia's 674,800 nonfarm workers, whereas service industries (174,100 employees) account for 26 percent, wholesale and retail workers (154,400 employees) 23 percent, and government (136,500 employees) 20 percent of all nonfarm workers in the state. The remaining 10 percent (65,600 employees) are employed in the finance, insurance, and real estate industries and in the transportation, communication, and public utilities industries. These employment figures clearly demonstrate that the state is no longer as dependent on the whims of external corporations engaged in resource exploitation as it was just a generation ago.[30] Change in the West Virginia economy has made the current employment mix between mining, manufacturing, and service industries much more similar to the national employment mix. The state's employment growth rate, however, continues to lag behind the national average, primarily because the state suffers from several structural impediments to economic growth.[31] The state has one of the lowest percentages of college graduates in the nation and relatively few young adults in the labor force. Moreover, although the state has increased its investment in water and sewer infrastructure and in highway construction, the condition of these fundamental building blocks of economic growth continue to lag behind those in surrounding states. The state's low population density also precludes the development of a major international airport, considered by many to be critical to sustained economic growth in an increasingly global economy. These impediments to economic growth are compounded by the pollution of the state's waterways by acid mine drainage and the lack of developable flatland for plant sites. Together, these economic impediments mean that the state is not in an advantageous position to attract high-technology industries, corporate headquarters, or service industries offering high-paying jobs. Additionally, financial institutions with large amounts of investment capital do not exist in the state. Consequently, West Virginia's new economy has become increasingly dependent on government employment and on employment in industries that are, at least in part, subsidized by federal or state government, as in tourism and health services.[32]

Economic forecasts predict only slow growth in most sectors of the state's economy and negative growth in mining and some transportation industries. However, as the state's economy becomes more like the national economy, the forecasts indicate that income growth and economic change will become more like that in the nation as a whole.[33]

West Virginia's economic difficulties have been the top priority on the state's political agenda for more than a decade. The technological changes in mining pressed West Virginia's state government to establish new economic development policies, to increase dramatically its spending on Medicaid and other welfare programs to care for the unemployed and poor, and to develop new revenue sources, such as the increased severance tax on coal and natural gas, to cope with the expense of caring for an increasingly aged and government-dependent population. The initial infusion of funds from the federal Great Society programs of the 1960s, like the Appalachian Regional Commission that helped upgrade the state's highway infrastructure, found a warm reception in the state.[34] However, despite federal and state government assistance, the state's economy was not capable of generating a significant expansion in employment.

In the past two decades, West Virginia's government has attempted to address its economic woes, but it has never developed an enduring consensus on exactly what to do about the state's economic difficulties. Instead, it adopted a series of initiatives, one after the other, with relatively little thought or analysis given to their cumulative impact on the state's economy or on the state government's budget. Each initiative, however, did provide state elected officials with political support from those who benefited from the initiative and with an opportunity to tell the electorate that they were responding to demands for jobs. During the 1970s, the state's economic development policy focused on business tax credits and increased funding for highway construction. During the 1980s, the state began to address its water and sewer needs, essential for attracting private investment to the state, and continued to expand its business tax credit programs and its highway budget. During the 1990s, the state continued to offer business tax credits (amounting to more than $100 million annually), raised the state's gasoline tax to finance even more highway construction (more than $700 million annually), issued approximately $500 million in state bonds to finance the construction of elementary and secondary schools, and authorized the issuance of $300 million for water and sewer construction. However, despite all of this activity, most of the economic development initiatives paled in comparison to the efforts in surrounding states.[35]

Besides affecting economic development policy, the state's economic plight has another impact on the political agenda. Slow or no growth and low incomes restrict government revenue generation. Lower incomes produce smaller revenues from income taxes and consumption taxes like the sales tax. Consequently, West Virginia's governments confront a very difficult economic policy agenda. Government investment in the economy and related infrastructure and education policies are necessary to improve the economy, but the state's economy does not generate the revenue necessary to pursue such policies. This "Catch 22" dilemma (where A depends on B, but B depends on A) has left West Virginia economically far behind most other states, and even behind the nation's other rural, mountainous states.

During the post-1935 era of economic transformation, West Virginia also underwent important but gradual change in its institutional politics. Some of the changes included greater federal participation in the construction of the state's political agenda, discussed at length in chapter 4, and changes in legislative, executive, judicial, and budgetary procedures, discussed in chapters 5 through 9. Also, West Virginia struggled with the control of political corruption. During the administrations of Governor W. W. Barron (1961–65) and the third administration of Governor Arch A. Moore Jr. (1985–89), the governors, many of their administrators, and state legislators either associated with their schemes or involved in individual acts of corruption were convicted of various offenses by the federal government and served time in federal correctional facilities. There also were disclosures and prosecutions of several dozen corrupt local officials, mostly in Logan and Mingo counties in the Southern Coal Fields.[36]

These acts of corruption differed in significant ways from those occurring earlier in the century. The use of systematic corruption by resource-exploitation firms disappeared with the onset of collective bargaining and the change in coal-mining technology. Most of the political corruption became individualized illegal acts by officeholders or the abuse of the law to secure votes and money for reelection.

The federal government, armed with new legal tools like the Racketeer Influenced Criminal Organizations Act (RICO), has led the attack on corruption, generating nearly a hundred recent convictions of state and local officials and the parties with whom they exchanged favors. Noteworthy federal convictions included Governor Arch Moore and other executive branch officials for extortion, mail fraud, and tax evasion,[37] two presidents of the state senate for the receipt of money in exchange for the support of gambling legislation,[38] several lobbyists, and the top assistant to former state treasurer

A. James Manchin for the criminal mismanagement of state investments.[39] Manchin resigned rather than face trial before the Senate after his impeachment by the House of Delegates.[40] Federal prosecutions resulted in the correction of some of the worst examples of corruption or conflict of interest in state politics and in several counties, including Hancock, Logan, and Mingo.[41] Interventions by state agencies, such as the State Board of Education, attacked corruption in the administration of schools and special districts. Finally, both the state and its local governments have gradually expanded the civil service recruitment of employees, and federal judicial decisions about patronage hiring and firing have reduced opportunities for rewarding or selling government jobs for political gain.[42]

In 1989 the state adopted the West Virginia Governmental Ethics Act, which requires yearly financial disclosure by state, county, and school board officials and by candidates for office. It prohibits a variety of activities, such as the giving and receiving of gifts, clarifies conflicts of interest, and regulates the contacts between officials and private interests and lobbyists. The act also created the state Ethics Commission and granted it the power to adopt additional rules, to give advice about government ethics, to investigate allegations of impropriety, and to seek the appointment of a special prosecutor.[43] Although the state's ability to police lobbying remains weak, these recent efforts suggest that the values of legal authority and honesty are replacing gift giving, favoritism, and nepotism in West Virginia's state and local politics.

POLITICAL CULTURE

The concept of political culture can be defined as the shared "set of attitudes, beliefs, and sentiments which give order and meaning to a political process and which provide the underlying assumptions and rules that govern behavior in the political system."[44] Thus, political culture is something of a summation of the general meaning of politics for a people. Political culture is important because community values shape, at least in part, the political agenda. A unified political culture might ignore some potential agenda items or policy alternatives, while a fragmented culture might encourage debate and the consideration of more policy alternatives.[45]

The literature on political culture in the American states has relied extensively on a typology set forth by Daniel J. Elazar that defines three types of political subculture in the American states: individualistic, moralistic, and traditionalistic. The individualistic culture emphasizes the centrality of private concerns and limited government intervention in private affairs. The moralistic culture emphasizes community solidarity and communal well-being. Government is a "positive instrument with a responsibility to promote the general welfare" through appropriate social and economic regulatory powers. The citizenry has a duty to serve and assist in public affairs. The traditionalistic culture emphasizes the retention of the existing political order and its governing elite. It is critical of depersonalized, bureaucratic government that devalues social and family ties. Instead, government is to be custodial and to act on policies that maintain the stability of an "elite-oriented political order."[46]

In 1984 Elazar categorized West Virginia as traditionalistic, with most regions having strong individualistic undertones and with the Eastern Panhandle having strong moralistic undertones.[47] Elazar cautioned, however, that the passage of time and the impact of events can alter cultural patterns. Given the rather dramatic population shifts that have taken place within the state since 1984, with population growth in the northern counties and Eastern Panhandle and population decline in the southern counties, we conducted a statewide survey in 1992 that asked West Virginians to respond to sets of statements drawn from Elazar's definitions of political culture to look for any evidence of changes in the state's political culture.[48] Although the results of a single survey, no matter how well done, cannot be judged as being conclusive one way or the other, the survey results suggest that West Virginians as a whole, particularly those located in the northern counties and in the Eastern Panhandle, hold values associated with the moralistic political culture, with a strong undercurrent of values associated with the traditionalistic political culture.

Given our discussion of geography and state political and economic history, the expression of values consistent with the moralistic political culture in northern West Virginia and in the Eastern Panhandle is not so surprising. As indicated earlier, prior to the Civil War and during the population boom of the late nineteenth century, immigration into northern and central West Virginia came primarily from northern states that were not dominated by traditionalistic views. As Elazar noted, the Appalachian Mountains deflected the immigration of the moralistic Ulster Scots (Scotch-Irish) southward from Pennsylvania into West Virginia, the Carolinas, and Georgia.[49] Immigration into southern West Virginia, on the other hand, came primarily from traditionalistic Virginia. Moreover, the alignment of the state's major religious denominations with northern rather than southern denominational leadership and the development of a rural industrial and resource extractive economy not quite like any political economy in the traditionalistic states of the South may also help to explain the moralistic views evidenced in the survey. Also, the economies of the northern counties have always been oriented toward Pennsylvania and Ohio and those of the Eastern Panhandle counties toward the Baltimore-Washington metropolitan region. None of these regions have traditionalistic political cultures.

Another factor that may help to explain West Virginians' moralistic responses to the survey is the nature of the labor-management conflict that has marked the state's politics since the early 1900s. UMWA members, in their calls for worker solidarity and in their willingness to include persons regardless of their racial or religious identities, often express moralistic themes, such as the "exercise of power for the pursuit of justice in public affairs or the betterment of the commonwealth"; they have long advocated active participation in politics and "active government intervention into the economic and social life of the community."[50] The expression of these moralistic themes became particularly strong once the reform movement gained control of the UMWA during the 1970s. Consequently, unlike the situation in traditionalistic political cultures, where personal ties outweigh ties to collectives like unions, West Virginia has a long history of collective action. Additionally, West Virginia did not have the kind of racial politics that encouraged deference to traditional elites and induced the strong regional conflict that once marked the relationship between the northern and southern states.

Today many West Virginians, particularly those residing in the northern part of the state and in the Eastern Panhandle, desire a more policy-oriented leadership than suggested by the state's past association with the traditionalistic-individualistic political culture. Also, more West Virginians envision themselves as being from the Northeast or from the North than from the South. However, despite this orientation toward the North, the state's contemporary political culture has not shaken off all vestiges of its past connections to Virginia's traditionalistic political culture. As indicated earlier, the state's constitution contains provisions derived from traditional Virginia politics and nineteenth-century Jacksonian political thought. These provisions severely limit county, municipal, and other local governments' capacity to act. Although some of the constitutional restraints on the West Virginia state government have been removed by constitutional amendments ratified by the people, some still remain in force and limit the state government's capacity to act. Therefore, political cultural tensions—rather than a single, dominant political culture—influence the formation of the state's political agenda and the capacity of the state's political institutions to act on that agenda.

Although West Virginia's political culture is not as traditionalistic as some southern states, during most of its history its governments acted as if it were located in a state with a strong traditionalistic political culture. Powerful commercial elites used their influence to minimize government activity, especially when it involved controlling natural resource exploitation and labor. They recognized that it was not in their interest to allow a broad range of items to reach the policy agenda. Now that the economy has diversified and the coal wars are history, West Virginians are beginning to express values consistent with a more active government. Consequently, although geography, history, and economics have closed windows for state and local policymaking in the past, the contemporary political agenda is not constrained by deep-seated, one-dimensional regional cultural patterns of belief or behavior. This may help to explain the significant expansion of state government spending, much of it authorized by the voters through the approval of state constitutional amendments authorizing the issuance of state government bonds, during the early and mid-1990s. Moreover, as highway construction and innovations in telecommunication technology continue to overcome the isolation brought about by the state's rugged topography, the historical legacies of minimal government and labor-management conflict are being replaced by beliefs in the need for government to address the policy problems facing the state, especially the need to encourage economic growth, provide access to adequate health care, improve education, and protect the environment.

Public Contributions to the Political Agenda: Political Values, Participation, Parties, and Elections

This chapter describes the status of the linkages between the government and people of West Virginia by examining the extent of West Virginians' political knowledge, their views on the state's political agenda, and their participation in political affairs. It also evaluates West Virginians' perception of the legitimacy of their state government as a force in their lives. Some information reported in this chapter comes from a survey of West Virginia residents conducted by the West Virginia University Institute for Public Affairs (IPA) in May 1992.[1] Other data are from various polls conducted by the Ryan-McGinn-Samples survey research organization and released to the press as *The West Virginia Poll*. These surveys provide the only contemporary and empirically reliable evidence about the political values and attitudes of contemporary West Virginians.

POLITICAL KNOWLEDGE AND GOVERNMENTAL LEGITIMACY

A representative government presupposes that the public pays at least some attention to political events and demonstrates at least some confidence in its political leaders. If the public ignores political events entirely, it cannot make informed choices on election day. This, in turn, strains the connection between the citizens and their elected representatives and raises serious questions about the political system's legitimacy. The IPA survey results suggest that most West Virginians pay enough attention to political events to make at least partially informed choices on election day. Nearly all of the respondents indicated that they followed what was going on in West Virginia's government and public affairs either some of the time (46.2 percent) or most of the time (44.7 percent). Only 7.7 percent indicated that they paid hardly any attention at all to West Virginia's government and public affairs.

The IPA survey also revealed that West Virginians' knowledge of the names of their key state elected officials is about the same as Americans in other states. Ninety-two percent of the respondents in 1992 correctly named Gaston Caperton as governor, 13.7 percent correctly named Robert "Chuck" Chambers as the Speaker of the West Virginia House of Delegates, and 7.4 percent correctly named Keith Burdette as the president of the West Virginia Senate. Nationally, 90 percent of Americans can correctly name their governor, and 10 percent can correctly name their state legislative leaders.[2]

The Performance of West Virginia's Elected Officials

Most West Virginians do not think that their state and local elected officials do a very good job. Only 26.1 percent of the respondents to the IPA survey were willing to give the governor a good (23.6 percent) or excellent (2.5 percent) rating. The state legislature received even lower marks (1.0 percent excellent and 15.5 percent good). Although state judges (1.9 percent excellent and 36.6 percent good) and local government officials (.8 percent excellent and 30.0 percent good) received somewhat higher job ratings, overall most West Virginians rated their political organizations as doing either a fair or poor job.

Trust in Government

The IPA survey also indicated that West Virginians do not trust their state government officials. Only 2.5 percent of the respondents stated that they trusted West Virginia's state government to do what is right just about always, and only 16.2 percent felt confidence in state officials most of the time. More than half (53.8 percent) indicated that they trusted their state government to do what is right only some of the time, and 24.8 percent said they trusted the government almost never.

Although local government officials fared slightly better than state government officials, the survey revealed that West Virginians have relatively little trust in their local government officials as well. Only 3.9 percent of the respondents indicated that local government officials could be trusted to do what is right just about always, and 15.5 percent indicated they could be trusted to do what is right most of the time. A majority indicated that they could trust their local government officials to do what is right some of the time (52.2 percent), and 16.6 percent said local government officials could be trusted to do right almost never.

Influence over Government

West Virginians' lack of trust in the state's political organizations was also reflected in the responses to the question, "Would you say that West Virginia's government is pretty much run by a few big interests looking out for themselves or that it is run for the benefit of the people?" More than three-quarters of the respondents (77 percent) indicated that West Virginia's government was run by a few big interests looking out for themselves. Only 16 percent indicated that it was run for the benefit of the people. The IPA survey also asked, "Who has the most influence on your state legislators in Charleston?" Respondents could choose from among the governor and his staff, special-interest lobbyists, the media, the voters who elected him or her, and other legislators. More than one out of every three respondents indicated special-interest lobbyists (34.6 percent) had the most influence, followed by the governor and his staff (20.1 percent), the media (13.2 percent), the voters who elected him or her (11.6 percent), and other legislators (10.6 percent). Just under 10 percent did not respond to the question. The responses to these two questions suggest public mistrust of West Virginia's state government because it is perceived as being controlled by special interests.

POLITICAL VALUES: THE POPULAR POLITICAL AGENDA

Although West Virginians lack faith in their state and local government officials, they still have a political agenda that they want the government to address.

The Policy Agenda

West Virginia has one of the highest unemployment rates and one of the lowest labor participation rates in the nation. As a result, it was not surprising to find that more than half of the respondents to the IPA survey (54.7 percent) indicated that the lack of jobs was the most important problem facing West Virginia's government. Education (6.6 percent) and state finances (5.6 percent) lagged far behind as the next most frequently cited concerns. Other issues of major concern were government leadership and integrity and health care. Given the state's long history of economic deprivation, it is not surprising that economic issues are the public's most important concern. On the other hand, national polling data show the same concerns among all Americans and at about the same percentages. The popular agenda in West Virginia, then, is similar to the agenda in most other states.

Which Level of Government Should Respond to the Popular Agenda?

The U.S. Advisory Commission on Intergovernmental Relations (ACIR) conducts a national survey each year to determine public attitudes toward government performance and taxes. In the most recent ACIR poll, Americans indicated that they have a general skepticism about government performance at all levels of government. Yet, when they were forced to choose the level of government with which they were most satisfied, they picked local governments.[3]

The IPA survey results suggest that West Virginians, like most other Americans, are somewhat skeptical about government performance. Unlike most Americans, however, they have more confidence in their state government than in either the federal government or local government. When asked, ''What level of government, federal, state, or local, is best suited to solve West Virginia's economic problems and provide jobs?'' more than half (56.7 percent) chose state government, 14.3 percent chose the federal government, and 11.6 percent chose local government (17.4 percent did not respond to the question). When asked to identify which level of government was best suited to improve education in West Virginia, 61.7 percent of the respondents chose state government, 17 percent chose local government, and 10.3 percent chose the federal government (11 percent did not respond). Finally, when asked to identify which level of government was best suited to improve the environment and provide clean air and water in West Virginia, 43.0 percent chose state government, 33.5 percent chose the federal government, and 8.1 percent chose local government (14.5 percent did not respond). Despite their distrust of state government, the responses to these questions suggest that West Virginians believe that their state government is better able to deal with the state's problems than other levels of government.

POLITICAL PARTICIPATION

Ideally, democratic politics is characterized by the full involvement of its citizens in the nation's political life. Nevertheless, few citizens actually live up to such expectations. According to national surveys, only about 10 percent of Americans perform all of the political acts associated with the ideal democratic citizen, from paying attention to the news to voting to running for or accepting appointment to public office.[4] The IPA survey revealed that West Virginians engage in political activities, such as working for a candidate (9.7 percent) and making a campaign contribution (12.8 percent), at about the same rate as most other Americans. Voting participation, however, is slightly lower, primarily because voting is correlated with income, and West Virginia is a poor state.[5] West Virginia's 50.6 percent voter-turnout rate in the 1992 presidential election was forty-second in the nation, well below the national average of 55.2 percent.

Turnout, however, cannot be explained solely by socioeconomic conditions. Other factors affect voter turnout, including the saliency of an election.[6] For example, when John D. "Jay" Rockefeller IV, great-grandson of the founder of Standard Oil Company, and Arch A. Moore Jr., a West Virginia native whose public career spanned three decades, squared off in close, heated governorship contests in 1972 and 1980, the state's turnout rate exceeded 70 percent. Another factor affecting voter turnout in West Virginia is the level of political party competition for local offices.[7] Virtually every county with a turnout rate below 60 percent in 1992 had low party competition. For counties with relatively strong party competition, almost all had a relatively high percentage of voter turnout.

POLITICAL PARTIES AND ELECTIONS

Political parties are the single most important organization for the mobilization of voters.[8] The parties' role in modern-day policymaking is widely recognized. They provide the public with an opportunity to affect the agenda-setting process through the expression of the electorate's policy preferences, they provide a continuing organization to recruit political leaders, they define policy alternatives, and they make it possible for political institutions to deal with conflict about public policies in an organized and peaceful fashion.[9]

Party Competition in West Virginia since 1932

Few propositions advanced by political scientists, commentators, and political observers have found greater acceptance than the notion that political competition among parties promotes good government.[10] Although the Democratic and Republican parties have dominated American politics for more than a century, the degree of competitiveness between them has varied considerably. Both nationally and at the state level, there have been long periods of one-party rule or domination. Although there were occasional victories by the nonmajority party at various times, American politics was dominated from 1789 to 1800 by the Federalists, from 1800 to 1860 by the Democrats, from 1860 to 1932 by the Republicans, and finally, from 1932 to the early 1990s by the Democrats. During each of these periods, the dominant party won most national and state offices and was able to command the loyalty of a majority of the electorate over an extended period of time. With rare exception, West Virginia followed these national trends. From 1863 to 1872 the Unionist/Republican Party was the dominant party, between 1872 and 1896 the Democrats were dominant, and between 1896 and 1932 the Republicans controlled the state. Beginning in 1932, the Democratic party became dominant once again, continuing its control of most state and local offices to the present day.

The extent and depth of the Democratic party's dominance in the state is demonstrated by an analysis of the party's electoral successes, office by office, since 1932. Of the 121 terms of statewide public offices filled by election from 1932 to 1994, all but seven were captured by Democrats, and three of these seven Republican terms were won by Arch A. Moore Jr. Moreover, Democrats have constituted a majority in both houses of the state legislature since 1930 and currently are the majority party in all but nine lightly populated counties (Morgan, Grant, Preston, Upshur, Doddridge, Tyler, Ritchie, Jackson, and Roane); the Republican majorities in these nine counties are relatively slim.

West Virginians almost always support the Democratic candidates for national office. Since 1932 they voted for the Democratic candidate for president in every election except 1956, 1972, and 1984 and have sent only two Republicans to the U.S. Senate, in 1942 and 1956. Moreover, of the 168 contests for the U.S. House of Representatives between 1932 and 1994, Republicans have won just twenty-three times. Six of those victories were secured by Arch A. Moore Jr., the state's only elected Republican politician to major statewide or national office for many years.

Party Identification

Almost 95 percent of West Virginia's registered voters have registered with either the Democratic or Republican parties. This high rate of party registration, however, exists because West Virginia's electoral laws discourage people from registering as Independents. For example, state law not only provides for a closed primary, excluding independents from participation, but it also prohibits anyone who signs a petition to place an independent candidate on the general election ballot from voting in the primary election. In addition, because the Democrats almost always win the general election, the voters recognize that it is not in their interest to register as an Independent and exclude themselves from the "real" election that takes place in the Democratic primary.

A better indicator of party identification in West Virginia, therefore, is self-identification. Nearly half of the respondents to the IPA survey (46.8 percent) identified themselves as either a strong or weak Democrat, 24.6 percent identified themselves as an independent Democrat, an Independent, or an independent Republican, and 26 percent identified themselves as either a strong or weak Republican. Nationally, only 35.3 percent identify themselves as either a strong or weak Democrat, 38 percent identify themselves as an independent Democrat, an Independent, or an independent Republican, and 37.5 percent identify themselves as either a strong or weak Republican.[11]

Republican Party Atrophy

The Republican party's prospects for ending the top-to-bottom Democratic domination of politics in West Virginia remains slim. The party's weakness is largely a function of what political scientist V. O. Key calls the "atrophy of party organization."[12] In many counties and even in some statewide races, for example, the Republicans do not even nominate someone to run for office. During the 1992 general election, the Republicans contested only five of the seven statewide elective offices (governor, treasurer, secretary of state, attorney general, auditor, agriculture commissioner, and justice of the Supreme Court of Appeals), seven of the seventeen open state senate seats, and sixteen of the fifty-three circuit judgeships. They did contest seventy-two of the one hundred seats in the House of Delegates but won only twenty-five of those races. This pattern continued during the 1994 state legislative races. The Republicans contested nine of the seventeen open state senate seats and seventy-seven of the one hundred seats in the House of Delegates.

If the quantity of GOP candidates is a problem in making West Virginia a more competitive two-party state, the quality of Republican candidates is no less a problem. As *Charleston Daily Mail* business editor Philip Nussell wrote after the 1992 general election, "neither the business community nor the Republicans offered quality candidates. Cleve Benedict [candidate for governor] was probably the best candidate the Republicans put up, and he got thumped. He's a nice guy and a good agriculture commissioner, but he didn't inspire. His call for tax cuts sounded like an old GOP broken record."[13]

Part of the Republican party's failure to become competitive must be attributed to the party's organizational leadership, which has for years been either too dependent on a single personality, such as former governor Arch A. Moore Jr., or rife with intraparty divisions. In recent years, for example, there have been sharp divisions between two former state chairmen of the party, Edgar F. "Hike" Heiskell, secretary of state while Moore was governor and a longtime supporter of Moore, and John Raese, an anti-Moore Morgantown businessman. The Heiskell-Raese feud spilled over into the media, with each accusing the other of destroying the party. Although Heiskell has since stepped down as chairman, the party continues to be severely divided, with the most recent manifestation being a dispute over whether to locate the GOP headquarters in Charleston or Wheeling.[14] Although a minor matter, the party headquarters controversy is symptomatic of the schisms within the party. Even after making some gains in legislative seats in 1994 (thirty-one out of one hundred seats in the House of Delegates and eight out of thirty-four seats in the Senate), divisions continued to surface in the Republican party, particularly between Republican legislators committed to a low-tax, anti-regulatory policy agenda and those who wanted to focus on social issues like abortion and school prayer.

The Reasons for Democratic Party Majorities

There are two other explanations for the failure of two-party competitiveness to appear in recent West Virginia politics. First, the state's demography makes it unlikely that it will become strongly two-party competitive. In comparison to other states, West Virginia's population has a relatively large proportion of older citizens; given that older citizens are more likely than younger citizens to demand greater government services, such as health-care and supplemental income programs, they, in turn, are more likely to support the Democratic party because it more nearly conforms to their social and economic needs. Also, these older citizens took on their party loyalties during the New Deal, when the Democratic party emerged as the majority party, thus making them even more likely to continue to support the Democratic party over the Republican party.

Second, a recent study indicated that West Virginia was "the most liberal" of all states relative to its demographic composition,[15] and a recent statewide survey found that even with all the recent negative connotations associated with the terms *liberal* and *liberalism* nationally, almost 22 percent of West Virginians are willing to classify themselves as "Liberal" or "Very Strong Liberal." Likewise, the survey revealed that 37.9 percent of West Virginians believe that "the proper role of government is to bring about what it believes is good," whereas only 8.3 percent believe that "the proper role of government is to interfere as little as possible with the way things are." Thus, it would appear that West Virginians are ideologically inclined to demand or accept an activist government, and since the Democratic party is the most likely to respond to such demands, it is the Democrats who benefit the most from the electorate's "liberal" propensities.

Candidate Recruitment and Democratic Factionalism

A major function of political parties is the recruitment of candidates for public office. Scholarly research suggests, however, that both Democratic and Republican county chairpersons in West Virginia spend only a modest amount of time actively recruiting candidates to seek public office.[16] Most candidates are self-recruited.

According to John Fenton, once on the campaign trail, the Democratic candidates for statewide office have had to contend with three main factions.[17] The first, the liberal and organized labor faction headed by the UMWA, was located principally in the Southern Coal Fields. The second, the traditional "Bourbon" or conservative faction, was located primarily in the state's more rural areas, including Central West Virginia and the Eastern Panhandle. The third, the statehouse faction, was based largely on political patronage in the local county courthouses and the statehouse. Although each of these factions has had its ups and downs, until the late 1980s popular support for each faction was about equal. During the 1988 and 1992 primaries, however, the factions began to weaken as Gaston Caperton, the winner on both occasions, received the support of labor, some conservative business interests, and some reform liberals. Then a new and intriguing alignment appeared in the 1992 election. State senator Charlotte Pritt, recognized as a reform candidate, challenged Caperton. Although Caperton held on to most of the Bourbon counties and the statehouse group, he was unable to fully retain his labor support, losing some counties in the Southern Coal Fields to Pritt. Pritt also took advantage of Caperton's vulnerability on the issue of taxes, appealing to those who were angry over tax increases during his first term. Still, Caperton managed to do what most other Democratic incumbent governors failed to do, gain support from all three of the party's main factions.

Although Pritt's emergence as a viable gubernatorial candidate in the 1992 primary was a surprise to many, and not in keeping with the tripartite divisions within the Democratic party, it was, in another sense, a mainstream phenomenon in the Democratic primary. In the past, the traditional power centers have fought over the nomination until an established politician with the backing of enough voters from one of the party's three wings prevailed. In the last several elections, however, successful candidates have emerged who have not had long traditions of working their way up on one or more of the party's wings. John D. Rockefeller, for example, became a viable candidate for governor in 1972 more because of his name and money than for any long accomplishments within the party, though he did hold a number of lesser offices along the way. Caperton also became a viable candidate for governor more as an "outsider" with money than because of his previous support of the Democratic party. Thus, Pritt's emergence as an outsider is not so surprising. Her uniqueness comes not from her name or money but because she served as a coalescing point for a number of disgruntled groups and others upset at an incumbent governor who had raised taxes after promising not to increase them.

There is additional evidence of change in the recruitment of state political leaders. The statehouse faction within the Democratic party does not have the strength that it once possessed primarily because state and local patronage is no longer readily available. Moreover, Pritt's emergence reveals the party's vulnerability to substantive change. Perhaps as a consequence, politics in the state's primary system is likely to be a bit more episodic and unstructured than in the past, with many factions entering into temporary alliances to further their policy positions or ideologies. If the past is any indication of the future, however, the influence of the traditional factions within the Democratic party will continue to play a significant role in the outcome of Democratic primary elections.

Party Organization, Policy Leadership, and the Political Agenda

Another major function of political parties is to develop a policy agenda. The extent to which political parties convey a policy agenda into the wider political arena not only depends on the degree of party competition but also on the viability of the parties as organizations. West Virginia's parties, particularly the Republican party, leave much to be desired in terms of leadership and organizational viability. In 1990, thirty-one of the fifty-five counties in West Virginia did not have full memberships on one or the other county party executive committees. Sixteen county committees had no secretary, and eighteen had no treasurer as required by law. In some cases, the county committee hardly existed at all, such as the Republican committee in Hampshire County, which had no secretary or treasurer and twelve vacancies out of a committee of fourteen. Other counties, such as Wood, had as many as fourteen Democratic and fifteen Republican vacancies on their respective committees. In Kanawha County, the center of state government, the Republican party had eleven committee vacancies out of a total of seventy-two positions. In general, a lack of organizational viability is more clearly a problem with the Republican party than with the Democratic party. Democrats had only twenty-eight vacancies of one sort or another throughout the state, whereas the Republicans had ninety-two, with one-fifth of those vacancies occurring in top leadership positions.

Despite the weakness of local party leadership, West Virginia's Democratic and Republican party platforms reveal major philosophical and policy differences between the parties. Democrats favor a much more activist role for government than Republicans. Republicans favor cutting taxes; the Democrats' platform does not mention taxes. Republicans oppose public funding of abortions; Democrats favor it. Republicans want to reduce state control of education; Democrats favor state involvement in a host of education activities. The platforms also reveal major differences on health, education, human rights, labor issues, and government reform. The only areas of general agreement concern the need to increase teachers' salaries, improve economic development, and increase tourism. Clearly, the parties offer the electorate a clear choice on election day. In this sense, West Virginia's parties have developed a responsible party system in which the parties offer citizens an opportunity to make clear policy choices. In the recent past, however, these differences have not necessarily been evidenced by the behavior of state elected officials. The policy agenda pursued by the two Republicans elected to the governor's office since 1956 was almost indistinguishable from the agenda pursued by recent Democratic governors. Governors Underwood and Moore emphasized road construction and improvement, education, public employee and teacher salary increases, economic development, workers' compensation and unemployment benefits, labor relations, and government reorganization. Democrats emphasized the same things. Indeed, rhetoric set aside, every governor since Rockefeller has proposed and usually obtained tax increases of one sort or another for social and economic programs during one or more of their administrations. Rockefeller, the lone exception, reduced taxes by having the sales tax removed from food. Still, the similarities in administrations are remarkable. It made little difference in state policy outcomes whether a Democratic or a Republican held the governorship.[18] This is explained, at least in part, by the state's Democratically dominated political party system, which only partially facilitates citizen control over the agenda-setting process.

CHAPTER THREE

Interest-Group Politics

Interest groups have a strong effect on the state's political agenda by communicating ideas to state political leaders, providing them with incentives to support the group's goals, mobilizing mass support for their policy positions, and influencing the outcome of elections.[1] Occasionally, they even go to court to affect governmental decisions. This chapter presents an introduction to the history of interest-group power in West Virginia and examines their impact on the state's politics.

THE LEGACY OF KING COAL

Historically, the coal industry has dominated West Virginia politics. Although coal may no longer be king, coal's impact on the state's economy and on its political and social institutions cannot be denied. In fact, the West Virginia Coal Association boasts in its advertisements that "Coal *is* West Virginia."

The coal industry has not been the only economic interest active in West Virginia. Chemicals, timbering, and oil and gas interests have also played a role in shaping the state's political life. Moreover, the fundamental restructuring of the state's economy during the 1980s resulted in a more diversified economy and a diffusion of interest-group power toward public employee unions, environmental groups, health-care associations, and representatives of other service industries. Nevertheless, the coal industry, with its exploitative character and its economic influence, has molded the state's political image.[2] To many people, West Virginia is viewed as the site of one tragic episode after another: leading the nation in unemployment, enduring yet another bitter mine strike, cleaning up after a devastating flood, or, worst of all, suffering still another tragedy of death in the mines. All of these devastating circumstances are commonly linked to the economic power or the political activity of West Virginia's coal industry. Therefore, the present interest-group system cannot be understood without some familiarity with the history of the coal industry's political influence in the state.[3]

The coal interest has shaped West Virginia politics in at least five ways. First, following the discovery of large tracts of coal and gas in West Virginia in the latter half of the nineteenth century, representatives from numerous eastern firms purchased title to millions of acres in the state's coal fields or, at a minimum, the mineral rights to such lands.[4] Because West Virginia did not have a sufficient population to mine all the coal needed by industry, the coal companies imported miners from southern Europe.[5] They also constructed entire communities in which the company owned everything, including churches, homes, stores, medical services, and law enforcement. In 1920, 80 percent of West Virginia coal miners lived in company-owned houses.[6] This had an enormous impact on West Virginia's state and local politics. Coal company power in the company towns and coal field counties was not seriously challenged until the New Deal, when unions were permitted to organize the state's coal miners.

Second, until fairly recently the coal industry was able to use its influence to preclude state regulations that increased the cost of doing business and, therefore, cut into their profits. For example, the coal industry has historically opposed environmental and safety regulations, including ones concerning the omnipresent slag pile or slate dump, which is aesthetically unpleasing and slowly releases poisonous fumes into the atmosphere. In some instances these slag piles pose even more immediate danger. In 1972, at Buffalo Creek, an eighty-thousand-ton slag pile created by the Pittston Company released 21 million cubic feet of water, which killed 125 people, destroyed a thousand homes, and caused $50 million in property damage.[7] The slag pile was unregulated. Indeed, the West Virginia Department of Energy at the time was not noted for its vigorous enforcement of even the most lenient of state regulatory laws. At the time of the Buffalo Creek disaster, there were hundreds of such piles in the coal fields, and most continue to exist today.

Third, the coal-mining industry has historically been able to secure favorable tax treatment from the state government. For example, most states and nations impose severance taxes on their extractive industries to generate the revenue necessary to restore the land to its previous condition once the natural resource is depleted and the industry moves on, and to deal with such issues as acid mine drainage and the industry's adverse impact on public health. Even with all these known destructive consequences of mining, there was no serious move to impose a severance tax in West Virginia until 1953. That year Governor William Marland proposed a 10-cent a ton tax on coal in his first address to the legislature. It never got out of committee. A modest severance tax was not imposed until 1970.

Fourth, until fairly recently both political parties have been closely tied to the extractive industries, and both were dominated by and had officeholders closely associated with mining, railroads, and oil and gas exploration.[8] Instead of advocating policy change, the primary purpose of both parties was to gain and remain in power, which they did through an extended patronage system and by placating both of the main players in state politics, labor and management.

Fifth, the coal-mining industry remained influential because, in state politics, it faced a quiescent union. The UMWA had a conservative leadership that became increasingly friendly to management. For the most part, the political concerns of its leaders were unemployment compensation and workers' compensation laws.[9] The UMWA took little action to promote reform, such as reducing the environmental impact of mining, counteracting the industry's extremely low tax rates, modifying the state's regressive tax system, or pushing for basic public services and education facilities in the coal fields. This is not to say that such issues were not occasionally raised in the *UMW Journal*, but they were not top political priorities either in lobbying the legislature or in extracting promises from candidates.

After 1965 coal industry and UMWA influence over state politics began to recede, and major changes in interest-group activity took place. Like much of the nation, West Virginia was in the midst of significant social and political change. It was an era characterized by consumerism, environmentalism, and populism. The UMWA especially was unprepared for the reform movements that hit the state in the late 1960s and early 1970s. The two major reform groups were the Miners for Democracy and the Black Lung Association, which sought state legislation to compensate the victims of pneumoconiosis, a chronic lung disease among coal miners.

The change in interest-group politics began subtly. In 1967 the legislature passed a relatively strong strip-mining bill. Then, in 1967 and 1968 there was agitation for environmental legislation, stronger coal-mining safety standards, and compensation for disability. The critical point in the movement was the Farmington disaster in November 1968. An explosion killed seventy-eight miners, generating hostility against mine operators and UMWA president Tony Boyle, who supported the claims of mine owners on safety issues, including exposure to coal dust and the origins of black lung disease. In 1969 strikes backed by the Black Lung Association closed virtually every coal mine in the state and filled the state capital with coal miners while the legislature debated the black lung bill. Out of fear of political repercussions, the legislature passed the bill. Later in the year, Tony Boyle ordered the assassination of Jock Yablonsky, his reform rival in the union. The disclosure of Boyle's role in Yablonsky's death ended Boyle's leadership and the UMWA's close working relationship with the state business and political establishment. A reform leadership under Arnold Miller, more hostile to the coal firms, gained control of the union.

During the next three years, coal and other business interests suffered three costly defeats in the legislature. New laws imposed a moratorium on surface mining in counties that had no stripmines, stringent and punitive standards for surface mining, and a severance tax on coal. These were unambiguous losses in a legislature that for decades largely shared the same political views as the coal interests. The business community in general, but especially the coal industry, reacted to these defeats by using the tools that helped them function efficiently and profitably in their business environment. They mobilized their organizational skills and money to counter future onslaughts by the state's populist groups. The result was the emergence of a much more pluralist interest-group system in the state, similar to the interest-group systems in most other states.

LEGISLATIVE LOBBYING

Since the coal industry's political losses in the early 1970s, there has been significant growth in both the number and types of groups operating in the state. In 1977 there were 121 organizations represented by registered lobbyists in Charleston. In 1993 that number had increased to 581. The largest increases were among business groups (increasing from 21 to 101), oil, gas, coal, and timber groups (increasing from 13 to 71), and the health-care industry (increasing from 8 to 57). Other dramatic increases occurred in insurance (increasing from 7 to 54), manufacturing (increasing from 12 to 45), utilities (increasing from 5 to 41), and labor (increasing from 9 to 35).

In the past, the undisputed interest-group leaders were the representatives from the West Virginia Coal Association, West Virginia Railroad Association, West Virginia Oil and Gas Association, and West Virginia Manufacturers Association. These business representatives had a close relationship with the Speaker of the House of Delegates and president of the Senate, through whom policies satisfactory to these interests were worked out.[10] Labor unions also had permanent representation in the legislative chambers, and according to most observers, their impact was significant. Over the years, the AFL-CIO and the UMWA were the dominant labor groups in the state.

More recently, the West Virginia Education Association (WVEA) and, to a lesser extent, the West Virginia Public Employees Union have emerged as important labor organizations. As a result, there is a much greater variety of interests at work in the legislative arena than ever before. The once dominant coal, oil, gas, and timber industries now share the business influence picture with the insurance industry, the health-care industry, solid-waste enterprises, utilities, various trade associations, and gambling interests. Consequently, the state's interest-group system is much more pluralistic than ever before, and the emergence of countervailing groups, such as organized labor, the WVEA, and environmentalists, makes for a much more fluid and dynamic system than was the case just a decade ago.

Expenditures by Lobbyists

Just as the number of active interest groups has increased, so has the cost of lobbying the legislature. In 1977 registered lobbyists spent $30,478. In 1993 they spent $210,203.[11] Business increased its expenditures sixfold (from $25,391 in 1977 to $159,946 in 1993). These amounts, however, might be even larger if the disclosure requirements included the lobbyists' salaries or living expenses. Still, no other groups approximate the amounts spent by business.

An interesting development in the past decade has been the emergence of the health-care industry as a major player among professional lobbyists. For example, of the $159,946 spent by business lobbies in 1993, $25,065 was spent by this industry, exceeding that of organized labor and professional associations. Thus, the new "big four" in the interest-group equation in West Virginia are business, health care, labor, and teachers.

Relative Influence of Lobbyists

In December 1987 each legislator was asked to rate the degree of influence that selected interest groups had on politics and policy in the West Virginia House of Delegates and Senate. Only three of the top fifteen most influential groups were directly involved in the mining industry: the UMWA, the Appalachian Power Company, which controls numerous coal mines and purchases vast quantities of coal under contract, and the West Virginia Coal Association. The UMWA ranked seventh, Appalachian Power ninth, and the Coal Association tenth; they were surpassed in perceived influence by such organizations as the National Rifle Association (NRA), West Virginia School Service Personnel Association, and the West Virginia Federation of Labor. Of the top fifteen organizations, seven represented business interests, six lobbied for organized labor, and two worked on behalf of single-issue groups, the NRA and the Hospital Association. (The Hospital Association is interested in more than a single issue, but its focus rarely roams beyond issues that directly affect hospital operations.)

The results of the 1987 survey are confirmed to some extent by a *Charleston Daily Mail* survey of the 1993 legislature, which showed that the three most powerful lobbies were the West Virginia Coal Association, the WVEA, and the AFL-CIO. The survey also found two of the four most powerful individual lobbyists to be Joe Powell of the AFL-CIO and Perry Bryant of the WVEA, thus reinforcing the perception that organized labor is powerful. The other two top individual lobbyists named were Tom Winner of the West Virginia Bankers Association and Ken Legg of the West Virginia School Services Personnel Association, both associated with top-named lobbying groups identified in the 1987 survey.[12] The data thus indicate that the top groups are associated with either business or labor, with an indeterminate advantage being given to labor, which has five of the top ten groups. The survey results, however, probably overstate labor's influence in the state legislature. Throughout the last two decades labor's top legislative priority was collective bargaining rights for public employees. The WVEA, and the State Federation of Labor (AFL-CIO), and, more recently, the West Virginia State Employees Union have expended considerable amounts of their political resources in an attempt to get collective bargaining rights passed. Yet, the legislature has never come close to passing such a bill, even without a right-to-strike clause. On the other hand, labor has had some legislative successes. The WVEA, for example, is a major force to contend with in contemporary legislative and executive politics, a fact brought home by its successful effort in 1990 to force a $5,000 pay raise for teachers over three years. Therefore, the influence configuration among contemporary interest groups in West Virginia appears muddied. The legislative survey indicates that labor is a significant force in legislative policymaking, and this is undoubtedly true. However, the results probably understate the influence of business interests in legislative politics and certainly shed little light on the real activities of the private sector in extra-legislative politics.

Who Are the Lobbyists?

The diverse array of lobbyists in and around the West Virginia legislature includes five types of lobbyists: contract lobbyists who are hired on contract specifically to lobby; in-house lobbyists who are employees of an association, organization, or business and who act as lobbyists; government lobbyists and legislative liaisons who are employees of state, local, and federal agencies and represent their agency to the legislative and executive branches of state government; citizen or volunteer lobbyists who represent citizen and community organizations or informal groups, usually on an ad hoc and unpaid basis; and private individual, "hobbyist," or self-styled lobbyists who act on their own behalf and who are not designated by any organization as an official representative.[13] All five types of lobbyists exist in West Virginia, but neither hobbyist nor volunteer lobbyists are particularly effective. Hobbyists are essentially treated as cranks, and volunteers receive little acceptance unless they clearly represent a large mobilized constituency, as with the black lung uprising of the 1960s, the public school teachers' strike in 1990, or perhaps the out-of-state trash demonstrations of the late 1980s and early 1990s. Government officials do not register as lobbyists, but nearly every major department assigns someone as legislative liaison. Their effectiveness is largely a function of gubernatorial support, and the governor has his own legislative liaison.

The most effective lobbyists in West Virginia are the contract and in-house lobbyists. The major interest groups in the state have long hired lawyers, former legislators, and former members of the executive as lobbyists. They recognize that successful lobbying, like success in any endeavor, requires both skill and experience. Clearly, prior experience in the state legislature or in the state executive branch enhances the lobbyists' prospects for success. Moreover, many scholars of American politics have noted that training as a lawyer is most compatible with success in politics and, hence, success as a lobbyist.[14] In 1993, for example, more than three dozen lawyers were hired as lobbyists to represent seventy-six individual clients. During the same session, numerous former legislators and executive officials worked as lobbyists.

One recent trend in contract lobbying is the hiring of public relations or consulting firms as lobbyists. Although most contract lobbyists are lawyers, since the mid-1970s corporations have gradually increased the use of public relations firms to represent them. Many of these firms were created by former gubernatorial staff, such as Linda Arnold of Willard and Arnold. In 1993 Arnold, a former staff member of Governor John D. Rockefeller IV, represented communications, gas, and natural resource interests at the legislature. In the 1993 session, at least six separate public relations firms represented twenty clients. Characteristically, most of these firms' clients were businesses. Only one public relations firm represented labor, education, or environmental interests.

Lobbyist Tactics

The lobbying tactics employed by West Virginia interest groups are typical of those employed everywhere in the United States. Until the passage of public ethics legislation in 1989, lobbyists routinely wined and dined legislators at legislative "buffets" almost nightly throughout the session, provided tickets and transportation to sporting events, and delivered beer or whiskey to legislators, in addition to their more respected, although not necessarily more effective, job of supplying information to legislators. Most larger groups employed one or more of the these tactics. For example, the West Virginia Coal Association had five lobbyists working during the 1988 legislative session. The senior Coal Association lobbyist was Carmine Cann, a former Judiciary Committee chairman, who for years operated the "Coal Suite" with his fellow Coal Association contract lobbyist, Ned "Big Daddy" Watson, descendent of the Consolidation Coal founders and former chairman of the House Judiciary Committee. The suite apparently never closed during the legislative session. It was fitted with a well-stocked bar, food, card tables, a wide variety of electronic games, and private areas for legislators to escape from the legislature's activities. The other four Coal Association lobbyists were permanent employees of the association who specialized in health, tax, and operational aspects of mining. In interviews with lobbyists representing both management and labor, the coal lobby was mentioned by all as being especially effective. Clearly, the Coal Association's financial resources have been a major factor in its ability to provide a complete panoply of activities in its lobbying efforts. Probably no other group can come close to the expertise and resources marshaled by this organization over the years.

Today, a common interest-group activity is the hiring of staff and the use of outside counsel to draft legislation. West Virginia's legislature has relatively few full-time employees, and its committees had no permanent legal staff until 1993, when only the House and Senate Judiciary Committees were granted a permanent legal staff member. Therefore, the legislature routinely hires dozens of lawyers during the legislative session to serve as committee counsel or to work for the leadership. Frequently, these attorneys represent major interests in the state and thus are in strategic positions to influence the language of legislation that might affect their clients. For example, the most important law firm involved in influencing the legislature is Jackson and Kelly, whose attorneys have served as clerks for both chambers' Judiciary Committees. Jackson and Kelly is the state's largest, most prestigious, and most powerful law firm. Among its clients are West Virginia–American Water Company, GTE, Cabot Corporation, Johns-Manville, Union Carbide, West Virginia Coal Association, Beth Energy, Arch Mines, Ashland Oil, Consolidation Coal, General Motors, and Ford Motor Company.[15]

One relatively recent lobbying tactic has been the institutionalization of formal interest-group alliances or coalitions. Beginning with the protest activities of the late 1960s, organized labor formed a loose coalition of labor groups known as the United Labor Committee (UNLC). It has since become a formal organization, meeting every Monday morning when the legislature is in session. During these meetings the coalition members formulate their legislative agenda, map out their lobbying strategies, and share perspectives on legislators and legislation. They meet quarterly when the legislature is not in session.

The United Labor Committee has its business counterpart in the Business and Industry Council (BIC), which is composed of the state's twenty major trade associations, including the West Virginia Builders Supply Association, West Virginia Contractors Association, West Virginia Independent Oil and Gas Association, West Virginia Chamber of Commerce, West Virginia Coal Association, West Virginia Manufacturers Association, West Virginia Retailers Association, and West Virginia Mining and Reclamation Association (strip-mining firms). BIC was formed in 1981 under the leadership of the West Virginia Coal Association and the West Virginia Chamber of Commerce to provide "a means for business and the industrial community to consolidate and coordinate efforts regarding legislative, governmental, and regulatory matters in this state."[16] The BIC founders had two immediate goals: to provide a united business front to the legislature and governor, and to give recognition to those who supported the business philosophy.[17]

BIC fulfills these goals in two ways. During the session BIC members, who are lobbyists for their individual trade associations, meet weekly to plan strategy and to decide issues around which to cooperate. Occasionally they assign individual lobbyists to selected legislators to make friendships, rally campaign supporters, or solidify constituency relationships. Clearly such a strategy gives the business community, at least those in BIC, another important contact in regard to issues and personalities in every legislative session. BIC's second major function is to rate legislators on major legislative policy issues. Devised in 1981, the rating system is important because it is used by the business community to determine organizational as well as individual contributions to political campaigns. According to a former BIC chairman, when the ratings first came out in 1981 several legislators called to find out why they had scored so low. Since then, members sometimes call to ask if a given vote will be included in the ratings.

Although business interest groups often cooperate and form alliances like BIC, divisions do occur among them. One of the more fascinating divisions occurred in 1985 between two groups that are ordinarily allies, the coal and railroad industries. Coal companies, which face stiff competition in both their domestic and foreign sales, charged that the railroads were abusing the rail bed monopoly they enjoyed in delivering coal to the eastern seaboard by charging rates far beyond the cost of haulage. To remedy this, the coal companies proposed that competition be permitted on tracks that pass through the coal fields. Obviously, the railroads did not want to share an extremely lucrative market. Such a profound split between these two giants is rare; some would say it was unprecedented. Given the reputation of these two groups, it was thought that this dispute would produce a major confrontation in the legislature. In the end, there was no contest. The railroads, facing united opposition from all groups interested in the mining industry's health, lost in the Senate, 34-0, and in the House, 71-27.

Lobbying Regulation

For years, West Virginia had no lobby registration law. In 1976, however, the Senate modified its rules to mandate registration of lobbyists with the clerk of the Senate. The Senate rules did not require government or political party personnel to register, but all others were required to do so. Lobbyists were expected to identify the groups they represented, issues with which they were concerned, and their expenditures. However, failure to comply with the rules did not entail criminal sanctions because no statute was involved, and, indeed, the Joint Rules Committee, which oversaw lobbying regulations, never dealt with the subject.

In 1989 the legislature passed the historically significant Governmental

Ethics Act, which mandates a new code of conduct for legislative lobby-ists.[18] Lobbyists now are required to register with the Ethics Commission and to place on file the identity and business of their employer, the general subject of the lobbying activity, and a statement of the contract agreement between the lobbyist and employer. They also must file copies of their regis-tration with the clerks of the two houses along with a recent photograph and biography to be included with others in a booklet published by the Ethics Commission and must file an annual report of lobbying activities. Lobbyists must file reports during and after the legislative session that list total expen-ditures, including meals, travel, accommodations, gifts, and contributions and any expenditures made to or on behalf of government officers or em-ployees that exceed $25. The penalty for violating the act is a public repri-mand and a civil fine up to $1,000.

The Governmental Ethics Act also prohibits certain practices. Public em-ployees or appointed or elected public officials may not use their office for private gain nor use subordinates to work on personal projects or activities, such as campaigns, during work hours. Public employees may not have a fi-nancial interest in any contract or purchase over which their job gives them control, and with some exceptions (meals, beverages, and ceremonial gifts), public officials may not accept or solicit gifts from lobbyists or other "inter-ested persons." Thus, the laws on lobbying went from negligible to a fairly comprehensive system of accountability. However, a year after the act's pas-sage the legislature stripped the Ethics Commission of its investigative powers.[19] Therefore, the ethics law's potential impact was diminished al-most immediately. Nevertheless, with rare exception, most analysts have concluded that the law, coupled with major prosecutions of wrongdoers by the U.S. Attorney's Office, has been moderately successful. Lobbyists have become more circumspect in offering meals and beverages to lawmakers,[20] and the famous "Coal Suite" has now been shut down.[21] In 1994, moreover, the West Virginia Ethics Commission forced the dismissal and fine of a pub-lic highway official who had abused the Ethics Act's private gain provisions, an action that was upheld by the West Virginia Supreme Court of Appeals.[22]

CONTEMPORARY INTEREST-GROUP ACTIVITY: INFLUENCE ON THE EXECUTIVE BRANCH

Interest groups also have significant influence on policymaking in West Vir-ginia's executive branch, primarily because it lacks experienced executive officers. This occurs for two reasons. First, West Virginia's public salaries are among the lowest in the nation, thus leading to high turnover in state government employment. Frequently perceiving state government as a training ground for employment in private enterprise, many public employees move into the private sector where salaries are higher. For example, there has been a steady flow of employees from the Department of Natural Resources and the Bureau of Mines into the mining industry and of young lawyers from the Office of Attorney General into private law firms. These former state employees then lobby their former co-workers on behalf of their new employers.

Second, significant regulatory power has been delegated to a large number of citizen boards and commissions. In many cases the legislature requires these boards and commissions to include representatives from the groups being regulated. Even if the legislature does not require such representation, the governor invariably follows the practice. Two of the appointed members of the Air Pollution Control Commission, for example, must be representatives of industries engaged in business in the state and four of the six members of the Board of Banking and Financial Institutions must be executives of banking and financial institutions.

THE ELECTORAL INFLUENCE OF INTEREST GROUPS

In 1993, 427 political action committees (PACs) were registered in West Virginia. About 60 percent of them (256) were affiliated with a national organization, and about 40 percent (171) were affiliated with an organization based in West Virginia. A PAC is the electoral assistance and funding arm of an interest group or alliance of interest groups. Most of the state entities were local political party PACs in the counties (34), education PACs (34), or labor PACs (31). Among national PACs, the greatest concentration was in business and industry (fifty-seven), followed by labor (28) and professional groups (22). The degree to which PACs influence West Virginia's politics and policies is a matter of dispute. For example, Speaker of the House Robert "Chuck" Chambers, a public official who has taken no PAC contributions, minimizes PAC influence: "I don't see much of a connection between the decisions we have made and their [PAC] contributions to campaigns." On the other hand, George Rider, executive director of the West Virginia State Medical Association, acknowledges the "access" derived from PAC contributions: "Basically it's an éntree that you might not otherwise have."[23]

The number of PACs operating in West Virginia can be viewed both positively and negatively. On the positive side, the large number of PACs means that many players compete for the attention of lawmakers and executive officials, making it less likely that any one group or set of actors will prevail on any given issue. Still, the potential for the exercise of excessive PAC power is illustrated by the role that PACs played in contributing funds to Governor Gaston Caperton's reelection campaign in 1992. In the Democratic primary and the general election, moneyed interests contributed $2.7 million to the Caperton campaign while the Democratic primary runner-up and later the write-in general election candidate, Charlotte Pritt, received only $127,000. Caperton's contributions included $350,000 from individuals working in coal and other energy-related industries, $334,000 from doctors, hospital administrators, and others employed in the health-care industry, $274,000 from investment bankers, real estate brokers, and others in the financial industry, and $194,000 from lawyers. Common Cause concluded that "the flood of special interest money in West Virginia politics imperils the health of our democratic system of government."[24]

The fact that Caperton received the great bulk of money expended in the 1992 campaign does not in and of itself mean that PACs have undue influence with the chief executive or with anyone else. Caperton's primary race, for example, was extremely close even though he was the recipient of most of the PAC money and the support of the party apparatus. Moreover, Caperton came right back after the election and proposed an increase in the coal severance tax, strongly opposed the development of massive landfills to accommodate out-of-state garbage, and proposed regulation of the logging industry.

THE FUTURE OF THE NEW PLURALISM IN INTEREST-GROUP POLITICS

Although coal is no longer the dominant force in West Virginia's political life, business organizations remain very influential on many issues. The UMWA, the State Federation of Labor (AFL-CIO), the WVEA, and, to a lesser extent, the West Virginia State Employees Union also are active, but the extent of their influence is constrained by a number of factors. Mine employment in the state (down to 24,200 in 1994) and union membership have declined in recent years. Moreover, West Virginia's economic difficulties during the 1980s led to a significant migration of young adults from the state in search of jobs, which means that the number of school children in the state is not expected to grow appreciably over the next decade.[25] Thus, the need for additional teachers in the state is not great. In 1993, for example, over sixteen hundred new teaching certificates were awarded by West Virginia's colleges and universities to state residents, who competed for fewer than two hundred job openings. Therefore, although labor and the WVEA will most likely continue to be important players in West Virginia's political system, it is unlikely that either group has the resources necessary to be as dominant a force in West Virginia politics as coal once was in the past.

Although business, labor, the WVEA, and health-care associations now highlight West Virginia's interest-group system, certain groups have built a niche for themselves in the interest-group configuration and, within a narrow range of issues, are powerful. The National Rifle Association (NRA), for example, while having only one lobbyist at the legislature, is extremely influential on issues involving guns because its "right to bear arms" philosophy appeals to many West Virginians. The School Service Personnel Association, representing staff workers, has also been quite successful on the one issue with which it is concerned, the pay and benefits of its members. In addition, the West Virginia Environmental Council has emerged as another important niche group. During the early 1990s the council was instrumental in the passage of landfill regulations designed to control the flow of garbage from other states into West Virginia, a ban on waste incineration, the regulation of sludge, and a study of water quality with an eye toward reducing the dumping of contaminants.[26] Although the council's efforts have not always been successful, it has emerged as an important countervailing interest to the business community on an increasing range of issues. Thus, West Virginia's interest-group system now has more participants than ever before, and while various business interests hold the upper hand on many issues, these firms are facing increased competition over the shaping of the political agenda, especially from those representing environmental concerns, teachers, and health-care providers.

CHAPTER FOUR

Intergovernmental Relations and
West Virginia Politics

There are 708 governments in West Virginia, including the state government, 55 county governments, 55 school districts, 231 municipal governments, and 366 special districts.[1] With so many governments providing public goods and services in the state and with 361 state elected officials, 442 county elected officials, 275 school board members, 231 mayors, 231 city clerks/recorders, and 1,273 city council members all "in charge," the extent and complexity of the relationships between and among these governments and elected officials is relatively great. However, not all of these participants have an equal role in defining the state's policy choices. The state constitution, for example, clearly identifies the state government as the dominant partner in West Virginia's state-local government relations, and in recent years, the federal government has emerged as the dominant partner in West Virginia's federal-state-local government relations.

FEDERAL-STATE-LOCAL GOVERNMENT RELATIONS

The federal government has always played an active role in West Virginia's political system. During the nineteenth century it worked closely with West Virginia's state and local governments to promote the state's economic development. The U.S. Army Corps of Engineers, for example, worked with the state to improve navigation along the Ohio, Monongahela, Kanawha, Little Kanawha, and Big Sandy Rivers. These improvements were critical for the development of the state's coal, timber, and petroleum products industries.[2] The federal government also paid for the construction of the Cumberland Road. Completed in 1811, the road connected Cumberland, Maryland, with Wheeling and the Ohio River, turning Wheeling from a small frontier town into the nation's gateway to the West. In 1867 the federal government granted the state 150,000 acres of land, located mostly in the present states of Minnesota and Iowa, to establish a land-grant college that offered instruction in agricultural and mechanical arts. The state used the proceeds from the auction of the land to establish West Virginia University.[3]

Near the turn of the century, and especially following the adoption in 1913 of the Sixteenth Amendment legalizing the federal income tax, the federal government began to offer states intergovernmental grant-in-aid programs to help them pay for such activities as the paving of roads in rural areas used by the U.S. Postal Service to deliver the mail and the establishment of agricultural experiment stations.[4] West Virginia aggressively pursued federal money whenever it became available, primarily because it was a poor state that needed the money to provide services that its elected officials considered both necessary and desirable.[5] Between 1922 and 1929, for example, the federal government spent over $125 million to establish a series of locks and dams along the Ohio River that were critical to the continued development of West Virginia's economy. West Virginia also benefited from the adoption of federal grant-in-aid programs during the Great Depression of the 1930s that were designed to combat unemployment by hiring people to build public service projects, such as dams and bridges. Federal funding in West Virginia jumped from just $3.2 million in 1932 to $31.6 million in 1934, and the federal government's Federal Emergency Relief Administration and Works Progress Administration provided jobs for more than one hundred thousand unemployed West Virginians between 1933 and 1936.[6]

The number of federal grant-in-aid programs continued to increase after the depression ended, reaching 132 in 1960. Their cost increased as well, reaching $6.8 billion. Most of the funds were used for relatively noncontroversial projects having widespread bipartisan support at all levels of government, primarily road construction ($3 billion) and income maintenance ($2.6 billion). West Virginia aggressively pursued federal grants whenever available because they were used for noncontroversial purposes, they had relatively few administrative requirements, and they provided the states with wide latitude of authority concerning project selection and eligibility requirements.[7]

The relatively permissive, noncontroversial nature of federal grant-in-aid programs changed during the 1960s and 1970s. Convinced that state and local governments were either fiscally unable or politically unwilling to address the needs of the poor, combat racial discrimination, or clean up the nation's water and air, large Democratic majorities in the Congress, committed to Keynesian economics and its advocacy of federal government spending, decided to take action. They attacked poverty and racial discrimination by encouraging the states to take a more proactive position in the areas of health, education, welfare, transportation, and job training by offering intergovernmental grants in each of these areas. This, in turn, led to a dramatic increase in the number of grants offered to the states and localities. Between 1960 and 1968 the number of federal grant-in-aid programs increased from 132 to 387. Moreover, the number of grants continued to increase throughout the 1970s, reaching 539 in 1980. Funding also increased dramatically, reaching $18 billion in 1968 and $90 billion by 1980. These new programs expanded the federal government's involvement in many areas of domestic policy that formerly were handled almost exclusively by state and local government officials, including health care (particularly through the adoption of Medicaid in 1965, which provides medical assistance for the poor), education (primarily through the expansion of assistance for educating the economically disadvantaged and for school construction), welfare (particularly through the expansion of the food stamp program and additional funding for the Aid to Families with Dependent Children program), and job training. Federal programs also supplemented state and local efforts in such areas as highway and mass transit construction.

At the insistence of Senator Jennings Randolph of West Virginia, the federal government also made a special effort to combat poverty in West Virginia and other Appalachian states by forming the Appalachian Regional Commission (ARC) in 1965. Since the early 1970s it has spent approximately $300 million annually to improve the region's economic infrastructure, focusing on the construction of highways to provide Appalachian businesses with access to eastern markets. ARC has also funded the construction of water and sewer lines, industrial parks, primary-care clinics, and vocational schools.[8] ARC's future, however, is currently in doubt. Its budget was reduced to $100 million annually in 1995, and several congresspeople from other regions have attacked its funding as political pork that should be eliminated.

The federal government also forced the states to take a more proactive position in the areas of racial discrimination and water and air pollution during the 1960s and 1970s by issuing intergovernmental regulations and mandates. Unlike the grant-in-aid programs, these regulations and mandates were not voluntary. State and local government officials who did not abide by the regulations and mandates would either suffer the withdrawal of federal funds for their jurisdiction or, in some instances, be subject to criminal prosecution.

The federal government's goal was to create what President Lyndon Baines Johnson called "The Great Society" with the promise of giving all Americans an opportunity to compete successfully for gainful employment by providing them with the finances and health care necessary to survive while they were in school or enrolled in a program that was designed to provide them with marketable job skills.

The federal government's expansion into domestic affairs has continued. Today, its annual expenditure of $1.6 trillion accounts for nearly 23 percent of the gross national product. In addition, the federal government outspends the states and localities by over $200 billion annually, and its fiscal and monetary policies, coupled with its regulatory powers, shape the national economy. Moreover, it now has 634 grant-in-aid programs, thousands of intergovernmental regulations, and hundreds of mandates that collectively have a strong impact on the behavior of state and local governments across the nation.[9] For example, the federal government is credited or blamed for stimulating state and local expenditures in the areas of income maintenance (primarily through the Aid to Families with Dependent Children's cost-matching requirements), health care (primarily through Medicaid's cost-matching requirements), highways and mass transit (primarily through the Federal-Aid to Highways' cost-matching requirements), and environmental protection (primarily through intergovernmental mandates concerning the attainment of specific air and water pollution standards and the low-interest loan program for the construction of wastewater-treatment facilities). The federal government also supplements state and local efforts in many areas of domestic policy, including school construction and provision of remedial education services (primarily through the Compensatory Education for the Disadvantaged program), the feeding of the poor (primarily through the school lunch and food stamps programs), the provision of social services such as day care and drug- and alcohol-abuse counseling (primarily through the Social Services Block Grant), and job training (primarily through the Job Training Partnership program). Nationally, the Medicaid program alone accounted for more than 19 percent of all state government expenditures in 1995 and was the single largest budgetary item in West Virginia's 1995 state budget. West Virginia currently spends over $1.3 billion on Medicaid (over $1 billion in federal funds and over $300 million in state funds), 21 percent of the state government's total expenditures of $6.1 billion.[10]

The federal government's expansion into domestic affairs has had a profound impact on West Virginia and its state government. West Virginia has always lagged behind the national averages on most economic indexes, such as per capita income and employment rates. Because these indexes are often used as criteria for grant allocation, West Virginia has profited greatly from the federal government's efforts to combat poverty. Although it receives relatively little money from the Defense Department and has not profited, as other states have, from the presence of large federal military bases and defense industries, the federal government still spends approximately $2 billion more in West Virginia each year than its residents pay in federal taxes and fees.[11] Most of that economic profit has been provided by the federal government's anti-poverty programs, highway construction grants, and federal contracts and jobs that have been brought to the state through the efforts of West Virginia's congressional delegation, especially Senator Robert Byrd, who served as chairman of the Senate Appropriations Committee from 1988 to 1994. Byrd played a major role in bringing the FBI Fingerprinting Identification Center to Clarksburg (nearly three thousand jobs), the Treasury Department's Bureau of Public Debt to Harper's Ferry, a NASA Research Center to Wheeling, a National Occupational Safety and Health Laboratory to Morgantown, and the Coast Guard National Computer Operations Center and the Bureau of Alcohol, Tobacco, and Firearms to Martinsburg.[12]

The federal government currently spends over $9 billion annually in West Virginia, or 24 percent of the state's entire gross state product (the national average is 19 percent). Included in this amount is over $6 billion paid to West Virginians who receive direct payments from the federal government through such programs as Social Security, Medicare, unemployment compensation, Supplemental Security Income, and food stamps; $788 million for salaries and wages earned by federal government employees who reside in West Virginia; and $445 million in federal procurement contracts paid to companies based in West Virginia. The federal government also provides the state government with over $2 billion annually in intergovernmental grants, or about one-third of the state government's total revenue of $6 billion.[13] The magnitude of these funds makes the federal government a major player in West Virginia's governmental system.

As much as West Virginia has profited from the federal government's largess, it has done so at a cost to its autonomy. Although the state continues to make many important policy decisions on a wide range of issues, including capital punishment, riverboat gambling, workers' compensation, gun control, and year-round schooling, by accepting the federal government's money, it must abide by the federal government's rules and regulations. As a result, the federal government now plays a leading role in determining what West Virginia's state and local governments do in the areas of health, welfare, and environmental protection and an increasingly important role in determining what they do in education, transportation, and job training.

West Virginia's economic survival is largely dependent on its ability to sell its coal and other products to other states. The federal government's control over interstate commerce, coupled with the U.S. Constitution's prohibitions against interstate trade barriers, has made interstate relations a nonissue in contemporary West Virginia politics. The state, for example, currently belongs to only five interstate compacts or agreements: the Interstate Commission on the Potomac River Basin (with Maryland, Pennsylvania, Virginia, and the District of Columbia), the Ohio River Valley Water Sanitation Commission (with New York, Pennsylvania, Ohio, and Virginia), the Southern States Energy Compact (with eight other states), the Wheeling Creek Watershed Protection and Flood Prevention District Compact (with Pennsylvania), and the Appalachian States Low-Level Radioactive Waste Compact (with Delaware, Maryland, and Pennsylvania).[14] The national average is twenty.[15] West Virginia has established standing committees in both the House of Delegates and the Senate to deal with interstate matters, but neither committee meets on a regular basis. Also, in its entire history West Virginia has been involved in only a few major interstate disputes that had to be settled by the U.S. Supreme Court. For example, the Supreme Court settled the dispute between Maryland and West Virginia concerning their boundaries along the Potomac River (1909 and 1911); denied Virginia's effort to reclaim Berkeley and Jefferson Counties (1870); and, in one of the nation's longest-running court battles ever, settled the dispute over West Virginia's share of Virginia's state debt that existed at the time of the state's formation (rulings in 1907, 1908, 1911, 1913, 1914, 1915, 1916, and 1918). This last dispute started in 1866 and was not resolved to the satisfaction of both states until West Virginia made its final payment on the debt in 1939.

Although West Virginia has had relatively few formal agreements or litigated disputes with other states in recent years, its state and local government officials do interact with their counterparts in other states through their participation in national organizations, such as the National Governors' Association, National Conference of State Legislatures, National Association of Counties, National League of Cities, and Council of State Governments. Arch Moore, for example, served as chair of the National Governors' Association in 1971.[16] For the most part though, West Virginia's public officials have relatively few interactions with public officials in other states, primarily because they view them more as competitors for economic development and job creation than as individuals to work with in the pursuit of common goals.

One issue that has elevated interstate relations to the top of the state's political agenda in the recent past, and could do so again, is garbage. During the late 1980s and early 1990s, there were several proposals to build very large landfills in West Virginia to accommodate New Jersey's garbage and that from other eastern seaboard states. The debate over the landfill issue generated a great deal of controversy. It was finally resolved when the state mandated a thirty-thousand-ton-per-month volume cap on all landfills located in the state and required countywide referendums on new landfill construction. The cap made the proposed megalandfills economically infeasible. In 1995 the volume cap was ruled invalid by a U.S. district judge on the grounds that it violated the U.S. Constitution's prohibition against state interference in interstate commerce. The federal court upheld the state's provision allowing citizens to vote on new landfill construction. As a result, the landfill issue could become, once again, one of the state's most controversial policy issues.

STATE-LOCAL GOVERNMENT RELATIONS

The relationship between West Virginia's state and local governments is a unitary one. Under unitary systems, all government power is vested in the central government. To expedite the delivery of government services, the central government in a unitary system routinely delegates specific powers and responsibilities to constituent units of government. It retains, however, the authority to alter those powers and responsibilities and even to dissolve its constituent units at its discretion. As a result, the state government determines the local governments' functions, finances, and organizational structures. Article IX of the West Virginia Constitution, for example, details how counties are formed and governed. It specifies the number, term of office, and powers of county commissioners. It also determines the election, term, and duties of the county clerk, surveyor of lands, prosecuting attorney, sheriff, and assessor.

To expedite the provision of government services, about three-fifths of the states, including West Virginia, have adopted home rule provisions that provide at least some of their local governments with the authority to make their own decisions on certain issues without interference from state officials. West Virginia's home rule provision was adopted as a state constitutional amendment in 1936. It grants electors in municipalities with populations of at least two thousand the power and authority "to pass all laws and ordinances relating to municipal affairs." However, most mayors and city council members would argue that home rule is basically meaningless in West Virginia because municipalities cannot enact ordinances or laws that are inconsistent or conflict with the state constitution or with the general laws of the state. This is a severe limitation. State statutes determine local government functions and operational procedures, and constitutional provisions place limits on local property tax rates as well as grant the state the authority to determine a local government's other taxing powers. An ongoing intergovernmental tension between the state and local governments has been the state's refusal to grant local governments the authority to expand their taxing powers, especially the right to impose local sales and income taxes. The state government has also repeatedly refused the counties' request to have the authority, like municipalities, to impose business and occupation taxes and utility taxes.[17]

Despite its home rule provision, West Virginia's state government has a strong unitary relationship with its localities. The lack of local autonomy was illustrated in 1992 when the state Board of Education took control of the Logan County school system. An unannounced state audit of the county school district by a Board of Education accreditation team revealed that the district had over a hundred uncertified teachers, had dozens of other teachers who were teaching classes for which they were not qualified, and, among other problems, had altered records to receive $50 million more in state funding than it deserved. The Board of Education subsequently fired the Logan County superintendent of schools, hired a replacement, and informed the local school board that it no longer had the power to hire or fire workers, spend money, set academic standards, or establish a school calendar.[18]

The state government has also issued a number of mandates that have preempted local government authority in several areas. For example, the Regional Jail and Prison Act of 1985 preempted local autonomy in corrections policy by establishing a state Regional Jail and Prison Authority to oversee the operation, maintenance, and construction of a newly designated system of regional jails.[19] Although local government officials constitute a majority of the members of the regional jail commissions that make recommendations to the state's Regional Jail and Prison Authority, and the authority has generally followed the advice provided by the regional jail commissions, the act preempts local government control over the operation and maintenance of existing jails and the location and financing of new ones. Similarly, the state has preempted local government authority in the solid-waste-disposal area by requiring counties to prepare landfill location plans, specifying landfill capacity limits and mandating that all landfills meet specific criteria concerning the collection, removal, and treatment of landfill leachate to protect the state's groundwater from possible contamination.[20]

Although state statutes and constitutional provisions have a direct and significant impact on the structures, functions, and operations of the state's local governments, the state government also indirectly influences the behavior of local government officials by offering intergovernmental grants-in-aid that encourage them to undertake certain activities and provide certain types of public services. In FY 1996 the state government provided its local governments with over $1.3 billion in grants, which accounts for nearly half of all local government expenditures in West Virginia. Most of the state assistance ($1.2 billion) went to school districts.[21] This assistance provides the state government with a tremendous amount of financial "clout" over its local governments, particularly its school districts.

Like the federal government's intergovernmental grant-in-aid programs, West Virginia's intergovernmental grants-in-aid have numerous rules and regulations attached to them. Local government officials throughout the United States as well as in West Virginia often react to their state's intergovernmental grant-in-aid rules and regulations in the same negative manner that they and state government officials react to the federal government's intergovernmental grant-in-aid rules and regulations. However, given their lack of fiscal resources, local government officials throughout the United States as well as in West Virginia rarely refuse state or federal intergovernmental assistance. This is particularly true in West Virginia because its local governments do not have the authority to impose local sales or income taxes, and the adoption of the Tax Limitation Amendment of 1933 placed severe limits on property tax rates.[22]

LOCAL GOVERNMENT INTERACTION

The West Virginia Association of Counties, West Virginia Association of County Commissioners, West Virginia Assessors Association, West Virginia Association of County and Circuit Clerks, West Virginia Sheriffs Association, and West Virginia Municipal League are all sponsored by West Virginia's local governments to foster better communication and cooperation among themselves. They provide a forum for the exchange of ideas for improving local government performance and a vehicle to exchange information with state officials.

The state government has also established a number of formal organizational structures to foster greater communication and cooperation among local governments. For example, regional planning and development councils facilitate intergovernmental cooperation and promote the "orderly growth and development of the State." Also, local governments are allowed to enter into written intergovernmental agreements to provide services or to construct facilities jointly to take advantage of economies of scale. The state has also mandated local government cooperation and interaction in a number of policy areas. As mentioned previously, the West Virginia Regional Jail and Correctional Facility Authority mandates the creation of regional jail commissions that are composed of members drawn from various local governments. This forces the local governments to interact to produce a corrections policy recommendation for their region. Also, the state has enacted legislation that authorizes and encourages counties to form regional solid-waste-disposal authorities to take advantage of economies of scale when dealing with solid-waste-disposal issues.

Despite the existence of these regional planning councils, state mandates for cooperation, and the efforts of professional associations to facilitate cooperation, West Virginia's local governments do not interact with each other on a regular basis. Some notable exceptions to this general rule include the recent action of seven counties in northern West Virginia to establish a regional system for dealing with health-care issues, and the sponsorship by the West Virginia County Commissioners Association and the Institute for Public Affairs at West Virginia University of an ongoing series of training and education programs for county commissioners. However, despite these efforts, interlocal agreements, cooperation, and interaction remain the exception in West Virginia rather than the rule.

Thus, federal regulations, mandates, and funding strongly influence the state's political agenda and its action on those agenda items, and state regulations, mandates, and funding strongly influence local government's political agenda and their action on those agenda items. Although interstate and interlocal interactions play a relatively minor role in West Virginia's intergovernmental system, they also affect the political agenda. Consequently, the political agendas at the state and especially at the local level are often shaped by individuals and influences that are, at least in part and sometimes mostly, outside of their direct control.

PART TWO

Political Institutions

CHAPTER FIVE

Constitutional Politics

West Virginia's origin as a part of Virginia had special significance for the history of constitutional politics in the Mountain State. When West Virginia became a separate state, it retained many of Virginia's constitutional structures and practices that emphasized distrust of political leaders and government. The legacy of these institutional features continues to restrain the use of power and limits the government's capacity to "act for" citizens' demands.

WEST VIRGINIA AND THE FIRST CONSTITUTION OF 1863

From 1775 to 1861 West Virginia was governed under three different constitutions of Virginia. The Constitution of 1776 created a government dominated by the legislative branch. It was accompanied by a Declaration of Rights, the first lengthy legal protection of rights in America. As mentioned in chapter 1, the Constitution of 1776 generated sectional controversy in Virginia because it included slaves in the population figures used to apportion the state legislature. It also limited suffrage to white males in possession of at least fifty acres of improved land. These provisions ensured that the legislature would be dominated by eastern counties. The Constitution of 1830 continued the property-holding restrictions on suffrage and retained an apportionment scheme that favored the eastern counties. In 1850 Virginians held another constitutional convention, but the results differed dramatically from those of the 1829–30 convention. The maturation and diffusion of Jacksonian ideology in the two intervening decades made it difficult for any elites to oppose direct popular election of public officials. The Jacksonian desire for universal white male suffrage cast aside the politics of deference to the landed interest and had become the new norm. Also, Jacksonian thought meant efforts to limit legislative and corporate power and ensure the election of most state and local officers. The Constitution of 1851 included universal white male suffrage but continued to a later date any debate concerning the counting of slaves during the legislature's apportionment. Although the extension of suffrage did provide western counties with more influence in the legislature, the state's history of sectional conflict set the stage for the west's secession during the Civil War.

Following President Abraham Lincoln's inauguration in March 1861, Virginia convened a convention to consider secession from the Union. On 16 April 1861, the convention voted for secession and resolved to hold a statewide referendum on the issue. Western delegates at the convention opposed secession by narrow margins, and mass rallies against secession occurred in the western counties. On 13 May 1861, 436 irregularly selected delegates met in Wheeling to oppose secession, but they withheld action until the statewide referendum was held in late May. After the election, Union supporters in the Wheeling area covertly arranged the intervention of Ohio and Indiana militia. During June and July 1861, these troops, with loyal Virginia militia from the Ohio valley counties, secured Union control of counties along the northern border and in the Ohio, Monongahela, and Kanawha valleys. Nearly all of these counties had voted against secession. With security assured, one hundred delegates from thirty-four counties in northwestern Virginia were elected to attend a second convention in Wheeling. The Second Wheeling Convention created a "Reorganized Government of Virginia" loyal to the Union and elected delegates to a constitutional convention.[1]

The constitutional convention, or Third Wheeling Convention, initially met from 26 November 1861 to 18 February 1862. The foremost issue was the question of state boundaries. Union support was strongest in counties roughly northwest of a line running diagonally across contemporary West Virginia from the western end of Maryland through Charleston and on to the Kentucky border, and in Morgan and Berkeley Counties in the Eastern Panhandle. After ten days of debate, the convention fixed the state's boundaries in all regions except the Eastern Panhandle. Those counties were given the option of joining the new state by election. All of these counties, except Frederick County (Winchester, Virginia), subsequently voted to join the state.

The other critical issue before the convention was slavery. After debating for over a month, the convention, by one vote (24-23), tabled a proposal for the gradual emancipation of slaves. Instead, they adopted a section prohibiting slaves and free blacks from entering and establishing residence in the state.[2]

The convention delegates debated the remainder of the proposed constitution more briefly but made several changes in Virginian practices. The Bill of Rights concentrated on free speech, press, and religion, and criminal procedural rights. Gone were the broad statements of individual liberty contained in the Virginia Declaration of Rights that were incorporated into the Virginia Constitution of 1851 and the Ohio Constitution of 1851. However, the new constitution contained language about religious freedom taken from the Virginia Statute for Religious Freedom. After much debate about black representation, the convention provided for universal white male suffrage, except for felons, paupers, and the mentally unsound, as in the Virginia Constitution of 1851. Viva voce (oral) voting, used in Virginia, was replaced by the exclusive use of ballots, as in Ohio.[3]

State senators were given two-year terms, with one-half of the body elected yearly from multimember districts. Delegates served one-year terms. Both houses were apportioned on the basis of white population. The constitution limited the annual legislative sessions to forty-five days unless three-fourths of the members voted to extend the session. Also, the governor was given a two-year term and was responsible for ensuring the faithful execution of the laws. Two features of the Virginia executive, the lieutenant governor and the Board of Public Works, were eliminated. As in Virginia, the voters elected three other executive officers—the secretary of state, treasurer, and auditor—to two-year terms.[4]

The judicial article provided for three Supreme Court of Appeals justices elected for staggered twelve-year terms and circuit court judges elected for six-year terms. Unlike Virginia, circuit judges did not serve in an appellate capacity.[5] Except for the Supreme Court of Appeals, the terms of executive and judicial offices were shorter than in the Virginia Constitution of 1851 to provide the public an opportunity to remove public officials more quickly should they abuse their powers.

Breaking with Virginia's practice, the 1863 Constitution provided for governmental subunits in the counties called townships. At a yearly township meeting, the voters were to transact township business, a variation on the New England town meeting, and elect a supervisor, clerk, surveyor of roads, overseer of the poor, and, every four years, a justice of the peace. Although Ohio also elected township officers annually, none of West Virginia's neighboring states elaborated township offices in the same fashion as did the West Virginia Convention.[6] County government, managed by a board of supervisors composed of the township supervisors, also assigned duties to a sheriff, prosecuting attorney, surveyor of lands, recorder, assessor, and other officers elected for two-year terms. The 1863 West Virginia Constitution also included articles on taxation and finance, forfeited and unappropriated lands, education, corporate charters, and the legality of Virginia laws, legal precedents, and legal actions. Supplemented by township taxes, state funds were to provide for a "thorough and efficient system of free schools." The "thorough and efficient" language drew in part on Article VI of the Ohio Constitution of 1851, but the West Virginia Constitution included a different form of school management. Finally, amendments had to be proposed and approved by the legislature and then bound over to the next legislative session for a second vote of approval by both houses before submission to a popular referendum.

Several hurdles had to be passed before the first West Virginia Constitution became effective. First, in May 1862 the "Reorganized" government of Virginia, also meeting in Wheeling, voted to permit the dismemberment of their state. Then, the U.S. Senate took action on a statehood bill. It rejected a proposal to expand the state's boundaries into the Shenandoah Valley and insisted that the state constitution provide for the gradual emancipation of slaves. The House and President Lincoln gave tentative approval to the amended statehood proposal. Despite some Unionist Democrat opposition, the emancipation amendment, known as the Willey Amendment, was later approved by a recalled session of the state constitutional convention and a referendum. The vote led to federal approval of statehood as of 20 June 1863.[7]

THE CONSTITUTION OF 1872

Factionalism and instability marked West Virginia politics in the decade after statehood. The new state contained about 250,000 persons in its northern and western half, the majority of whom supported the Union. The state's southern and eastern half, and most of the Eastern Panhandle, contained about 110,000 persons, the majority of whom were secessionists or Copperheads.[8] Until 1870 the Unionists, renamed the Republican party, controlled the state government. In 1866 they passed a constitutional amendment denying state citizenship and the right to vote to persons giving voluntary aid or assistance to the rebellion. They also passed legislation creating test oaths and political disabilities for the large number of secessionists and Copperheads who were dissatisfied with the conditions of statehood or the Lincoln administration's policies. However, the Fourteenth Amendment to the U.S. Constitution in 1868 let former secessionists reenter electoral politics. Coupled with divisions in Republican ranks and controversy over the proposed "Flick Amendment" to enfranchise black males, the Democrats gained control of the state government in the election of 1870.[9]

One of the first acts of the new Democratic leadership was to call for a new constitution. The constitutional convention, held in Charleston in early 1872, had sixty-six Democrat and twelve Republican members. It created the state's current constitution.[10]

Throughout its original text, the Constitution of 1872 echoed Jacksonian themes. The initial section rejected secession and recognized federal supremacy, but the second section attempted to curtail federal power. Using language from the federal Constitution's Tenth Amendment, it stated that the federal government has only enumerated powers and not implied powers, a "states' rights" theme.[11] The following section challenged Lincoln's restriction of constitutional rights during the Civil War by suggesting that any similar actions would be deemed "subversive of good government and tend to anarchy and despotism." Article II established the state's boundaries and defined state citizenship and treason.

The West Virginia Constitution's Bill of Rights restated the broad guarantees of liberty found in the Virginia Declaration of Rights. However, it used different language and included additional rights. For example, it included warrant requirements for unreasonable searches and seizures, a ban on hereditary emoluments, honors, and privileges, and a sentence on the quartering of troops in homes that almost exactly duplicated sections of the Ohio Constitution of 1851. The other sections of the Bill of Rights retained language from the 1863 Constitution or relied on federal or Pennsylvania constitutional language. Only the section that prohibited political and religious test oaths, a reaction to the test oaths required of former secessionists, was a wholly new creation.

The 1872 Constitution established universal male suffrage and contained provisions about the age of officeholders, reasons for removal from office, impeachment processes, and the operation of electoral processes. In a resurgence of Virginian concepts of government, voters could choose between viva voce or ballot voting. However, the convention replaced a provision of the Constitution of 1863 permitting the registration of voters, perhaps designed to discourage voting by secessionists, with language allowing a person to vote without registering.

The 1872 Constitution changed legislative meetings to biennial sessions of forty-five days, but a session could be extended by two-thirds vote of the membership, and the governor could call extraordinary legislative sessions for special purposes. Delegates were given two-year terms and senators were given four-year terms, with one-half of the Senate being elected every two years. Members stood for election in districts composed of one or several counties. Initially, the constitution disallowed legislators from dual office holding and holding a position as a "salaried officer of any railroad company." Following the Jacksonian trend to control legislative power, the constitution contained more elaborate restrictions on special legislation for specific interests than previous Virginia constitutions. As in the 1863 Constitution, there was a section requiring laws to address a single topic. It also required that state contracts be let to the lowest responsible bidder, and it required the legislature to meet in Charleston unless a law designated another meeting place. Following a provision in the 1863 Constitution, the 1872 Constitution authorized the legislature to prohibit liquor sales. It was also authorized to adopt married women's property acts and to establish proportional representation for the Senate.

The executive branch consisted of the same five elected offices established in the 1863 Constitution: a governor serving a four-year term ineligible for an immediate second term, a state superintendent of free schools, a treasurer, an auditor, and an attorney general. The secretary of state was a gubernatorial appointee. The most important change from Virginia practice and the 1863 Constitution was the creation of the gubernatorial veto and the line-item veto for appropriation bills. The governor was also authorized to fill vacancies in the other elected executive offices, and those officeholders were required to provide the governor with a semiannual report of their receipts and disbursements.

The 1872 Constitution expanded the Supreme Court of Appeals to four members and defined in more detail the jurisdiction of the circuit courts. It also provided for justices of the peace, to be elected for four-year terms in districts within a county, and limited the justices' power to seize and sell property for actions related to the prosection of the Civil War. The 1872 Constitution replaced township government with county courts composed of a president elected to a four-year term and at least two justices of the peace. The county courts performed police, fiscal, and selected judicial functions in probate and the appellate review of a single justice's decisions at bimonthly meetings. Also, county voters selected a sheriff for a single term, a surveyor, a prosecuting attorney, assessors, and constables. The county court selected the coroner, overseer of the poor, and surveyors of roads.

The Constitution of 1872 signaled a return to the institutional forms of the

1851 Constitution of Virginia and its Jacksonian roots. Jacksonian ideas of states' rights, the election of a plural executive, judges, and local officials, limited legislative sessions and other limitations on official authority and taxation, and limitations on state investments all appear in the 1872 West Virginia Constitution. Less noteworthy constitutional sections on topics like married women's property acts, judicial divorce, general incorporation acts, banking provisions, and railroads reflect the anti-patriarchal ideas and the hostility to special privileges that surfaced among some Jacksonian factions. Overall, the Constitution of 1872 signaled a distrust of government and a fear that without proper institutional restraints the people's voice would be excluded from state policymaking.

CONSTITUTIONAL AMENDMENTS AND REFORM CAMPAIGNS

Since 1872 the legislature has proposed 112 amendments to the West Virginia Constitution. By 1996, 64 of these amendments had been ratified by the voters. Some of them are listed at the end of the constitution, but unlike the U.S. Constitution, most have been incorporated into its text. In 1960 the voters approved an amendment containing a preamble to the constitution. Other proposed amendments fall into one of seven general categories: the protection of personal rights and political representation, legislative operations, executive organization and operations, judicial operations, county and local governance, state finance, public education, and the claims of special interests. The majority of the amendments were designed to improve government management and reflect the influence of the Progressive movement and the economic and political changes of the early twentieth century on political ideas in the state.[12] However, although the amendments have improved state government management, the state constitution still retains many provisions reflecting the Jacksonian political values of the 1872 document.

Personal Rights and Political Representation

West Virginia voters have approved several amendments to the state's Bill of Rights, but these have not radically diminished the state's historical commitment to personal rights. The section on jury trial was amended in 1880 to allow for six-member jury trials in civil cases of more than $20 in value before a justice of the peace; in 1974 an amendment replaced the language on justices of the peace with "courts of limited jurisdiction"; and in 1956 women became eligible for jury service. In 1986 the voters ratified a right to bear arms for "defense of self, family, home, and state, and for lawful hunting and recreational use." The article on elections and officers was amended twice: in 1884 to change the date of the fall election from October to the Tuesday after the first Monday in November and in 1902 to require the legislature to adopt voter registration laws, a Progressive-era change designed to control corrupt party machines and, in some states, to prevent blacks from voting. In 1934 the voters rejected conditioning the right to vote on the payment of a capitation tax, a tax often associated with denying blacks the right to vote. An amendment requiring a period of private contemplation, meditation, or prayer in the public schools was approved in 1984, but a federal district court quickly held that it was an unconstitutional violation of the federal Constitution's First Amendment.[13]

Legislative Operations

The voters have approved several amendments to increase the legislature's capacity to make policy. In 1953 biennial legislative sessions were replaced with annual sessions, and in 1970 the Legislative Improvement Amendment excluded state employees and other governmental officers from legislative service, permitted salaried railroad company officers to run for the legislature, and set the start of the annual session on the second Wednesday in January.[14] The 1970 amendment also fixed the date for the governor's submission of a budget to the legislature, established a sixty-calendar-day legislative session that the legislature could extend by two-thirds vote, and created a legislative compensation commission to submit resolutions on legislative compensation and expenses for legislative approval. In 1936 the voters ratified an amendment to eliminate the immunity of county and local governments and officers from garnishment and attachment actions to collect debts. The voters amended the section on lotteries in 1980 to provide counties an option to legalize bingo games and raffles for charitable purposes and in 1984 to provide for a state lottery. An amendment adopted in 1912 prohibited the manufacture or sale of liquor, but it was repealed in 1934 in favor of state regulation of liquor sales and consumption.

The Executive Branch

Amendments to the executive department article, ratified in 1902, 1958, and 1970, incrementally changed the election and eligibility requirements for several executive offices. The 1902 amendment provided for the election of a secretary of state, the 1958 amendment allowed the governor to appoint the state superintendent of free schools instead of having that office filled by an election, and the 1970 amendment permitted the governor to hold two successive terms and adjusted the list of offices for which the governor could fill a vacancy. Various amendments to unify the executive branch under the governor, modeled after the federal presidency, failed to win voter approval in 1930, 1940, 1946, and 1989.

The Judicial Branch

In 1880 an amendment rewrote the entire text of Article VIII on the Judicial Power, making minor changes in sections on the Supreme Court of Appeals, circuit court jurisdiction, the number of circuit court sessions per year, circuit court district boundaries, and the duties of court clerks. It also removed the justices of the peace from the county court. The county court became a body of three elected commissioners with no judicial duties except in probate, family law, and election disputes. The civil small-claims jurisdiction of the justices of the peace was also adjusted.

The Judicial Amendment of 1902 increased the size of the Supreme Court of Appeals to five members. However, other attempts to change the judiciary's organization failed in 1888 (to change jury trial provisions), 1910 (to change the number of Supreme Court of Appeals justices), 1930 (to provide probate commissioners and to redistrict the circuit courts), 1940 (to provide summary courts in each county), and 1966 (to change circuit judge assignments and authorize different duties for courts established by the legislature).

In 1974 the voters approved the Judicial Reorganization Amendment, which completely replaced Article VIII. It redefined the jurisdiction of the Supreme Court of Appeals and the circuit courts, left circuit court redistricting to the legislature, gave the Supreme Court of Appeals extensive supervisory power over the administration of the courts and the bar, abolished specialized courts established by the legislature, established systems for judicial discipline, retirement, and removal, phased out the county court's judicial duties, and, most importantly, replaced the justices of the peace with magistrate courts for each county. With the exception of the retention of an elected judiciary, the amendment made judicial organization parallel the professional pattern emerging in other state constitutions.[15] Heavily promoted by professional legal groups, it was the most significant change in the constitution designed to improve government management.

Local Governance

There have been relatively few efforts to amend the state constitution in order to strengthen the capacity of local governments to make public policy. The Judicial Reorganization Amendment of 1974, for example, stripped county commissioners of most of their judicial duties. The 1932 Tax Limitation Amendment limited property tax rates on both personal and real property and, in the process, severely restrained local governments' capacity to raise revenue. In 1936 the voters did ratify an amendment giving home rule to municipalities with more than two thousand residents, but as discussed in chapter 10, the provision is essentially meaningless. Amendments to increase commissioners' salaries (1908, 1916), to repeal or alter the sheriff's succession amendment (1982, 1986, 1994), and to permit the reorganization of county government, to merge or reorganize county and municipal government with voter approval, and to expand county legislative powers (1989) were rejected by the voters. They did approve an amendment in 1973 to allow sheriffs to serve two consecutive terms.

State Finance

Most of the amendments affecting the state's finances were designed to improve fiscal management, not to increase state revenue. Prior to 1918 there was no state budget. In 1918 the Budget Amendment created the Board of Public Works, composed of the (then) seven elected state executive officers, which was to submit annual budgets to the legislature for the two forthcoming fiscal years.[16] A 1954 amendment provided for an annual legislative session, which in even-numbered years was to meet for thirty days to consider the budget. Voters rejected other amendments to the budget and appropriations process in 1926, 1940, and 1962, but in 1968 they approved the Modern Budget Amendment. It required the governor to submit a detailed executive budget, with itemized information on proposed expenditures, to the legislature for its consideration. The governor was also required to submit to the legislature a budget bill containing proposed appropriations for its consideration. Today, the legislature can amend this bill as long as it does not create a deficit, change official salaries in midterm, decrease the judiciary's budget, or increase estimated revenues. If the legislature fails to act on the bill, the governor can extend the legislative session for its enactment. Once the legislature approves the bill, the governor can approve the bill, veto the entire bill, or item-veto parts of it. Budget lines subjected to a line-item veto can be overridden by a two-thirds vote of both houses. Supplementary appropriations can be made later if taxes are not increased.

Although West Virginia has moved to centralized budgeting, constitutional amendments have severely restricted state and local governments' ability to raise revenue. An amendment to limit tax rates was rejected in 1926, but as mentioned previously, the 1932 Tax Limitation Amendment limited tax rates on both personal and real property. Efforts to increase taxes beyond these limits require a special levy vote that must be approved by 60 percent of the voters within counties or municipalities and, as amended in 1982, 50 percent for school districts. However, the same amendment permitted a state income tax. Other amendments have imposed additional constraints on revenue generation and spending by the state and, especially, local governments. For example, the Homestead Exemption Amendment of 1982 exempts the first $20,000 in value of owner-occupied homes from the property tax if the owner is at least sixty-five years old or is disabled. Also, some amendments channel state revenue to specific ends, such as a 1942 amendment on taxation for highway construction and a 1946 amendment on the use of a severance tax on harvested trees. Many of these amendments were designed to improve financial management, but as a group, they have not removed the constitution's Jacksonian values about the necessity for direct, popular control over public spending.

Public Education

Proposals to amend the constitution's education article have focused on school finance. In 1902 the constitution was amended to require more revenue to be placed in an "irreducible" school fund, with the fund's interest to be spent on schools. Amendments in 1950 and 1958 expanded the ability of school districts to float bonds to raise funds with voter approval, and a 1982 amendment changed the required voter approval from 60 percent to a simple majority. An amendment permitting a bond issue for school construction and renovation was approved in 1972. Efforts to provide more money for schools through bond issues in 1966, 1978, and 1986 failed to win voter approval. To improve school administration, a 1958 amendment established a state board of education appointed by the governor, with Senate approval, to supervise state schools and select a state superintendent of schools. In 1986 an amendment provided for nonpartisan election of county school board members and geographic diversion of representation within the county served by the school boards. Efforts to amend the constitution to provide for more uniformity in school funding (1988) and to place educational administration under legislative discretion (1989) were rejected by the voters.

Claims of Special Interests

A few constitutional amendments provide benefits to special interests. The provision on bank corporations was amended in 1938 to eliminate the liability of bank stockholders to creditors and to provide for a general incorporation law for banks. A 1958 amendment allowed corporations to issue more varieties of stock, including nonvoting shares. Together, these two amendments adjusted West Virginia law toward uniformity with the corporate law of other states. Special constitutional amendments adopted in 1920, 1928, 1948, 1964, 1968, and 1973 permitted the state to float bonds to pay for highway construction, but voters rejected similar amendments in 1981, 1984, 1986, and 1988. An amendment to float bonds for water and sewer projects passed in 1994. Other amendments authorized the sale of bonds for bonuses to veterans of World Wars I and II, the Korean War, the Vietnam War, the Persian Gulf War, and the conflicts in Grenada, Lebanon, and Panama and for veterans' housing. The electorate also approved a few miscellaneous changes in the constitution. For example, an amendment was adopted in 1960 that allowed the legislature to provide for succession to office and continuity of government in times of "enemy attack."

FEDERAL CONSTITUTIONAL LAW AND THE
WEST VIRGINIA CONSTITUTION

Federal constitutional amendments and judicial decisions interpreting the federal Constitution have resulted in the de facto amendment of some state constitutional provisions. For example, the denial of implied powers and the states' rights emphasis contained in the West Virginia Constitution have been rendered essentially meaningless by several decisions of the U.S. Supreme Court. Also, unlike the federal Constitution, the state's Constitution of 1872 lacked an equal protection clause, contained language prohibiting women from voting, and required racial segregation of the schools. The prohibition against women's suffrage and the racial segregation of the schools were rendered null and void by federal court decisions. The voters formally repealed the school segregation section in 1994.[17]

Constitutional amendments and the decisions of the U.S. Supreme Court about legislative apportionment and voting rights have also resulted in de facto amendment of the West Virginia Constitution. The Twenty-Sixth Amendment to the federal Constitution (1971), the right to vote at age eighteen, clarified the exclusion of "minors" from the vote in West Virginia. Federal judicial interpretations of residency requirements for voting imply that the one-year residency requirement to qualify for voting and the ban on voting by members of the military stationed in the state have no force.[18] Although an amendment to rewrite constitutional apportionment provisions was rejected in 1962, federal intervention secured fairer apportionment. In 1964 the apportionment procedures for House of Delegates and Senate districts to ensure equal representation came under regular federal judicial scrutiny after the federal Supreme Court decision in *Reynolds v. Sims*.[19] Finally, because state judges recognized the supremacy of federal judicial constructions of rights, federal judicial interpretation of federal constitutional rights has normally guided the West Virginia judiciary in its interpretation of similar rights, especially personal liberties of speech and press and criminal justice rights.

Unlike many other states that have adopted significant constitutional changes during the twentieth century, West Virginia has made largely incremental changes to its 1872 document. For example, West Virginians have not followed the lead of many other states that have centralized their executive branch operations in the governor's office, and they have refused to establish a full-time, professional legislature. On the other hand, West Virginians have also avoided nationally popular anti-legislative measures like initiative and referendum, recall, and term-limitation amendments. The amendments that the voters ratified ensured a less chaotic and more centrally directed budget process, made county and local government focus more on services than adjudication, and rationalized judicial operations. These changes were designed to improve state management, especially in judicial administration and budget preparation, but the Jacksonian principles of limited government and popular electoral control remain embedded in the West Virginia Constitution. Thus, the state constitution reflects a traditional political design based on nineteenth-century political culture, but it is overlaid with and exists in tension with twentieth-century provisions designed to provide state officials with greater policymaking authority.

CHAPTER SIX

The State Legislature

Over the past thirty years many states have developed their legislatures into mini-Congresses, with increased staff and salary and nearly year-round sessions.[1] West Virginia's legislature, however, reflects Jacksonian political thought, which holds that elected officials should be "average" citizens who are closely in touch with the public's needs. Although a full-time governor and bureaucracy can be necessary to cope with the complex nature of modern government operations, the legislature is thought to be best guided by bright people from a wide range of professional experiences who come to the capitol for a few weeks out of the year "to bring some common sense to the government."

THE CITIZEN'S LEGISLATURE

West Virginia's legislature is marked by short legislative sessions, low legislative salaries, low levels of legislative staff, limited legislative facilities, and high turnover among members. The maximum length of the annual regular legislative session is only sixty calendar days. Although this is more than the alternating sixty- and thirty-day annual sessions held before 1973 and the biennial sixty-day sessions held before 1955, it means that legislating is a long way from being a full-time occupation for legislators. The legislature convenes on the second Wednesday in January[2] and works at an increasingly hectic pace until the second week in March. The session can be extended for successive three-day periods by gubernatorial order, but the sixty-day limit is close to the actual length of almost all sessions. The two most important impacts of having limited sessions is that the legislators spend most of their time back in their home districts and therefore are less likely than other state lawmakers to become deeply indoctrinated into the "capital culture," and that they are probably less knowledgeable about the policies they debate than they would be if they had longer sessions.

Legislative salaries in West Virginia, at $15,000 per year, plus reimbursement for some expenses, are relatively low. Although this salary is considerably better than the $6,500 per year they made before 1995, or the $500 per year they made before 1955, it is far less than the income most legislators could make in their chosen professions. The assumption behind having low salaries is that legislators should have another job to support themselves. In this way, they will have regular and close contact with people other than their fellow legislators, giving them insight into the problems that ordinary citizens face. The need to earn additional money, however, also diminishes their ability to legislate thoroughly and impartially because their "regular" job often takes their attention away from their legislative duties. There may even be subtle conflicts of interest as, for example, when an insurance agent–legislator has to vote on a bill regulating the insurance industry. Further, the types of jobs and professions that allow a person to take off work for two months every winter are limited and not representative of the entire job market. For example, it is much easier for an attorney to rearrange his or her schedule to serve in the legislature than a coal miner working for an hourly wage.

The legislature provides itself with relatively few full-time staff, another indication of its citizen legislature status. It relies mainly on temporary staff hired for the sixty-day session. In this way, the legislature does not become dominated by a professional staff that may have a political agenda of its own, a concern raised both in Congress and in some other state legislatures. The lack of staff, however, also makes for less informed decision making.

The legislature's facilities in the capitol building have improved greatly over the years but are still limited. Until the 1950s members had only their desks on the chamber floor to call their own. Today, senators have small private offices, and delegates either have a private office, if they hold a committee chair or are a party leader, or share an office with up to three other delegates. The lack of extensive private facilities keeps legislators from feeling too much "at home" in the capitol, but it also impinges on their ability to organize their files and meet privately with colleagues, constituents, and lobbyists.

Finally, the legislature's nonprofessional nature is reflected in the high rate of turnover in its membership. Typically, about one-third of the House and one-quarter of the Senate seats up for election change hands following each election. Although some turnover results from members losing an election, most of it is voluntary. Few see the legislature as a career opportunity. This is likely true, at least in part, because of the financial and personal hardship involved with campaigning and serving. Although high turnover allows a variety of citizens the opportunity to serve in the legislature, it also reduces the experience and institutional memory that can be brought to bear on the state's public problems.

REPRESENTATION

Because individual state legislators represent far fewer citizens than the governor and other state elected officials, they are in a good position to assess and reflect their constituents' opinions. The quality of that representation, however, is difficult to measure. It can be evaluated along two dimensions: how well the legislature reflects the public's social and economic characteristics, and the number of constituents each representative serves.

Social and Economic Characteristics

West Virginia legislators, like other elected officials in the United States, are far more likely than the average citizen to be male and white and to make their living as a lawyer or as a businessperson. In 1995 only 14.9 percent of the legislators were women (20 of 134). The national figure was 20.0 percent. Also, despite the fact that African Americans constitute 2.9 percent of the state population, only 2.2 percent of the legislators were African Americans (3 of 134). The representation of African Americans, however, compares favorably to other states. Nationally, African Americans hold 6.9 percent of state legislative seats while accounting for slightly more than 12 percent of the population. Consequently, although the legislature underrepresents women and African Americans, women are better represented today than in the past (in 1967–68, for example, only 5.2 percent of the legislators were women), and the representation of African Americans, as a percentage of the state's population, is higher than in most other states.

Most state legislatures, including West Virginia's, have a higher percentage of lawyers and business owners than in the population generally.[3] This disparity is understandable given the time and money required to run for and to serve in the legislature. Lawyers and business owners often have more flexible schedules and better financial resources to accommodate these demands. Also, legislative service can be advantageous to the careers of lawyers and certain types of businesspersons, encouraging them to seek legislative seats.[4]

Constituency Size

Unlike most other states, West Virginia uses many multimember legislative districts. In the House of Delegates, districts are represented by one to seven delegates, with an average of 1.8 per district. Most of the multimember districts are located in the state's more heavily populated areas, such as Wood, Kanawha, and Cabell Counties.

If representation entails knowing the district's needs and preferences and reflecting them accurately in the legislature, then large-population multimember districts are more difficult to represent than smaller single-member districts. As the number of constituents increases, there are more opinions to represent. More importantly, the more populous a district is, the more likely it is that it will be heterogeneous in politically relevant ways. For example, under the apportionment plan enacted in 1992, the Fifth House of Delegates district in Wetzel County has approximately 18,000 citizens, most of whom are white, Democratic, and longtime rural and small-town residents. The Thirtieth House district in Kanawha County, in contrast, has approximately 121,000 citizens, with a much more diverse set of interests and needs. The rural poor, coal miners, chemical workers, city dwellers, government workers, and others all compete for the ear of the seven Kanawha delegates. This makes representation more difficult for the Kanawha delegates because they must work to understand these often conflicting interests and points of view and then must choose among them. This also makes it more likely that certain citizens' interests might not be understood or acted upon.

Multi-member districts also disrupt the link between citizen and legislator because the effort required to cast a thoughtful vote in a state legislative election is multiplied by the number of candidates on the ballot. For example, a Wetzel County voter typically needs to evaluate only two major party candidates for the House of Delegates in the general election, whereas a Kanawha County resident must evaluate more than a dozen candidates. Given the limited amount of time available to assess the candidates, Wetzel County residents are likely to be better informed about their candidates' views than Kanawha County residents. Poorly informed voting leads to poor representation, increasing the likelihood that those entering office will not reflect their constituents' opinions and values.

Only four other state senates and ten other state houses currently have multimember districts, and almost none of these states use them to the extent found in West Virginia. The legislature persists in using multimember districts for two reasons. First, the state constitution mandates that all Senate districts be bounded by county lines and be equal in population. With population differences between counties, these requirements mean that some counties, or groups of counties in a single senatorial district, will need to elect more than one senator. Although the House of Delegates is under no explicit requirement to be apportioned along county lines, counties have been used as the starting point for the districting of that chamber as well. Second, as a practical matter, it is easier to carve the state into fewer districts that are proportional in population than two or three times as many districts that are equal in population.[5]

PROCEDURES

The two most important aspects of the legislature's day-to-day operations are the strength of the leadership and the use of the committee system. The leadership is especially powerful because of the legislature's nonprofessional nature.

Party Leadership

The president of the Senate and the Speaker of the House of Delegates are by far the most important players in the legislative process, with the possible exception of the governor. As one longtime participant in the legislative process confided, "if they [the Speaker and president] decide to paint the chambers polky dot, then they will likely be painted polky dot." This is a typical pattern in citizen legislatures because most members are too busy with their full-time jobs to spend the time necessary to understand the entire context of legislative action.[6] The leaders, however, are compensated an extra $100 per legislative day plus another $100 per day for up to eighty days for working when the legislature is not in session. The extra compensation is intended to allow the leaders to focus their time and effort on the legislature. Also, the short legislative session means that a strong authority is required to keep members on track if anything is going to get done.[7] Sixty days pass quickly when there is much work to do, and a well-defined agenda is needed so that legislators can have some direction to their activities.

How Leaders Are Selected. The House Speaker and Senate president are elected by a majority vote in the relevant chamber at the beginning of each new session. Practically speaking, however, the election takes place in the majority party caucus. Candidates woo their colleagues with promises of committee seats or chairs and other perks, and there is much discussion of each candidate's policy preferences and his or her proposed "leadership team" (the members who will be influential if that candidate succeeds).

Once a candidate gains the support of a majority of his or her party caucus, the selection is then ratified on the floor of the chamber with all majority party members voting for the consensus candidate, whether or not they supported that candidate in caucus. Tradition holds that the Speaker or president, once elected, serves as long as he or she holds a legislative seat and wishes to serve as a leader. This means that the longer the leader serves, the more independent he or she is of the caucus, as the deals made initially to gain the position lose their force as time passes, membership turnover occurs, and the Speaker or president garners obligations by distributing benefits while serving as leader. For example, Robert "Chuck" Chambers (D-Cabell County) served longer as House Speaker than any recent leader (1987–96) and, consequently, was a very strong leader.

Leadership Power. The Speaker and president's powers fall into two general categories: procedural controls and colleague benefits. Both leaders, but especially the Speaker, control the flow of legislation through their procedural powers. Each controls floor debate as his or her chamber's presiding officer and as chair of the chamber's Rules Committee, which decides when legislation will be taken up on the floor for final debate and which bills are given special rules that allow them to jump ahead of other bills on the regular calendar. Special rules are important because there is never enough time for the full chamber to take up all the bills reported out of the substantive committees. The Rules Committee is therefore a powerful checkpoint in the legislative process. The Speaker and president not only chair their respective chamber's Rules Committee but also appoint all of its members, giving them great control over its actions.

Both leaders also garner a great deal of strength from the benefits they distribute to their colleagues. For example, they both appoint all committee memberships and chairs in their respective chambers. Because members care strongly about these assignments, leaders can trade them for future favors. The leaders can also craft the chambers' committees to reflect their policy preferences by putting like-minded individuals in key chairs and on key committees.

Legislative Committees

There are three distinct types of committees: standing committees, conference committees, and interim committees. *Standing committees* exist from one legislative session to another. They are divided along substantive policy lines, except for the Rules Committee, and do the bulk of the legislative processing. There are currently thirteen standing committees in the House and seventeen in the Senate, each made up of between seven and twenty-five members. Each bill is referred by the chamber leader to at least one standing committee for review.

The job of each standing committee is to investigate the bills referred to it, amend them as members see fit, and make recommendations about the bills to the full chamber. However, because of the large volume of bills that are introduced each session, most bills die quietly without any debate. It is largely up to the committee chair to determine which bills are discussed. The chair has great authority in setting the committee's agenda, and although the other committee members may overrule the chair's decision not to consider a bill, it is rarely done. When deciding which bills to bring before the full committee, the chair considers the quality of the legislation, the bill's "passability" (since they do not want to waste precious time on a sure loser), the leadership's wishes, and his or her own political and policy concerns.

Public hearings are typically held for only the most important bills, and most consist of testimony from only the bill's sponsor and the executive official responsible for implementing the bill. The latter's opinion often carries decisive weight, given their expertise and the lack of legislative staff to provide alternative information. Testimony by interest-group representatives and the public is, of course, taken seriously by committee members, but the vast majority of legislation creates little interest outside of the capitol building.

Conference committees are formed to reconcile the inevitable discrepancies between bills passed by each chamber. A bill must pass both chambers in identical form before it can be sent to the governor for final approval and passage into law. Once a bill is passed in each chamber, the Speaker and president appoint members of their respective chambers to serve on the bill's conference committee. These members are usually the chairs and key members of the standing committees that had initial jurisdiction over the bill, plus other interested or important members, perhaps including the bill's sponsor.

Conference committee members try to keep the final bill as close to their home chamber's version as possible, but their ultimate goal is to achieve a compromise that will pass both chambers and be signed by the governor. Once the committee reaches an agreement, the final bill is sent to each chamber, where it must be considered on a yes-or-no vote, with no amendments.

The fact that bills reported out of conference committees routinely pass on the chamber floor is an indication of both the conference's importance and the quality of the conferees' negotiating skills.

Interim committees are joint committees used by the legislature as a way to get around its limited session. Beginning in the 1940s as an ad hoc way to study issues away from the legislative session's hectic environment, interim committees are now an integral part of the legislative process. They meet for a few days each month between regular legislative sessions and are staffed by the Legislative Services Office, which houses most of the legislature's few full-time, year-round staff. Interim committee members are appointed by the chamber leadership, but unlike the standing committees, not all legislators gain seats on them. Appointment to an interim committee is prestigious and an indication that the leadership views that legislator as a hardworking, important, and loyal member.

LEGISLATIVE CAPACITY

The legislature's capacity to represent public demands affects the quality of state governance and the quality of life for its citizens. Measuring legislative capacity is difficult because it is a multidimensional concept. Some scholars have measured it as the level of resources the legislature has at its disposal.[8] The more resources, the argument goes, the better the legislature. This is often translated into a few easily measured characteristics that are based primarily on a state's ability and willingness to spend money on its legislature, such as legislative pay, legislative staffing, and the legislature's total annual budget. Although these kinds of measures identify the legislature's capacity to attract capable personnel, inform them about policy alternatives, and retain experienced legislators, focusing exclusively on them is misleading. Money-based scales are biased against poorer, rural states, such as West Virginia. It therefore should be no surprise that states like West Virginia, Wyoming, North Dakota, and Arkansas consistently rank at the bottom of these scales, while wealthy, urban states like California, New York, Massachusetts, and Pennsylvania rank at the top.

Although money and the things a legislature can purchase with it, such as a year-round, professional staff, are undeniably important, legislatures have other attributes that cost no tax dollars and can be used to improve their legislative capacity. For example, a legislature can improve its policymaking capacity by creating a committee system that facilitates decision making, by establishing rules and procedures that expedite bill processing, and by empowering its executive oversight committees.

The Committee System

State legislatures vary dramatically in the number of standing committees they employ, from seventy-three in the Missouri legislature to only ten in Maine. Legislatures have traditionally shown no disinclination to form committees; in fact, the principal problem reformers of the 1960s and 1970s saw in this regard was that legislatures formed too many committees.[9] When there are too many committees, the legislature is a confusing place, with competition for members' time and attention taking energy away from legislating. West Virginia's legislature reduced the number of committees in both chambers between 1955 and 1969 from fifty-four to twenty-eight and has since kept the total number of committees at about that level.[10] Currently, West Virginia's thirty legislative committees compare favorably to the U.S. median of thirty-five.[11]

Another important feature of the committee system is the number of legislative committee assignments. The fewer committee assignments, the more the legislator can focus his or her attention on specific pieces of legislation. This may be as simple as being able to attend all of a committee's hearings, rather than being forced to choose between two or three hearings scheduled at the same time by different committees. A committee cannot fulfill its information gathering and deliberative functions if its members do not attend its meetings. This is a problem in the Senate, where senators average 5.7 committee assignments.[12] This is much higher than the national average of 3.2 assignments for state senators.[13] Delegates have a greater opportunity to specialize in their committee work because they average only 2.9 committees each, which is nearly equal to the national average of 3.0 committee assignments per house member. Although senators are expected to be somewhat less specialized in their legislative activities than delegates and to take a broader view of policy corresponding to their larger districts, this almost doubling of the average amount of committee work for West Virginia's senators is extreme and works against the purpose of dividing up labor into committees in the first place. Moreover, the legislature has evolved an informal practice that works against the even distribution of work among its committees. In both the House and Senate there is a tacit designation of primary and secondary substantive committees. The primary committees, Finance, Education, Judiciary, and Government Organization, receive most of the important legislation. In this sense, each chamber has four important substantive committees instead of seventeen (Senate) or thirteen (House) of equal status. This may expedite the consideration of key legislation, but it does not take full advantage of the potential efficiency that a fuller division of labor into committees could provide.

Two aspects of this primary-secondary committee arrangement likely mitigate against any significant loss of efficiency, however. First, each member is traditionally appointed to at least one primary committee, giving the member an opportunity to get involved in important legislation. Also, legislators traditionally serve on no more than one primary committee in the House and no more than two in the Senate, which prevents any member from becoming overburdened by these chores. The second mitigating factor is the regular use of subcommittees in the important committees to divide up the workload. Subcommittees allow members to specialize on their subcommittee work, as is done in the U.S. Congress. The use of subcommittees is an important, positive aspect of the West Virginia legislative committee system, one that is seen in only twenty-two other state senates and twenty-nine other state houses.[14]

The amount of experience committee members and chairs have on their committees is an important legislative resource. Although the legislature's high turnover rate does not bode well for its committee stability, there is a tradition of members staying on the same committees throughout their careers, with less committee hopping than is found in most other legislatures.[15] This suggests that although a significant number of new committee members come on board with each new legislature, there is usually a block of experienced members to provide continuity and expertise.

Finally, the level of committee autonomy also affects legislative capacity. Highly autonomous committees have a firm control over their own agendas and a large degree of input concerning the laws the legislature produces in their policy areas. This gives committee members and other actors interested in that policy area an incentive to work within the committee structure, where the decisions are made by legislative specialists. In the U.S. Congress, where committees are extremely autonomous, the chamber leadership's role is largely one of traffic control. State legislatures, on the other hand, have traditionally been dominated by their chamber leaders.[16] As mentioned previously, West Virginia's committees are dominated by the leadership. This is not necessarily bad, however, because a strong leader can coordinate the legislature's activities and outputs, resulting in more efficient legislating.

The Legislative Process

Legislatures can improve their policymaking capacity by establishing rules and mechanisms that expedite and streamline bill processing. The Council of State Governments has identified seven such mechanisms: establishing deadlines for bill introduction, for committee action on bills, and for action on bills in both chambers; allowing for the prefiling of bills and for companion bills; allowing the use of committee bills; and allowing bills to carry over from the first to the second session.[17] These mechanisms make bill processing more efficient by reducing duplication of effort, regularizing the process, and decreasing end-of-session logjams.[18]

The House of Delegates uses all seven of these mechanisms. Senate rules allow for three: the prefiling of bills, deadlines for bill introduction, and the use of companion bills. Nationally, the median state legislature uses 7.5 of these mechanisms; West Virginia's use of ten ranks it tied for sixth highest in the nation. As a result, although the legislature does not take full advantage of its committee system, it does rank among the best legislatures in the country in the processing of bills.

Along these same lines, the quantity of legislation introduced in state legislatures has increased dramatically since the 1960s. Some state legislatures have responded to this increased workload by essentially abandoning their deliberative role and passing legislation into law at a high rate. For example, the Virginia, South Dakota, North Dakota, Nevada, and Montana legislatures pass into law over 60 percent of the legislation introduced in them. The passage rate in Arkansas is an astonishing 78 percent. Clearly these legislatures have become "legislative assembly lines" where relatively little consideration is given to each of the laws they pass.[19] West Virginia is different. During the 1993 legislative session, the legislature considered 1,616 bills and resolutions, close to the national average, but adopted only 18.6 percent of them, much lower than the national average of 27.3 percent.[20] If it is assumed that the quality of the bills introduced is reasonably constant across the states, this indicates that the West Virginia legislature takes its deliberative role as seriously as any legislature in the country, working hard to protect the state from poorly crafted or ill-considered proposals.

Another measure of the level of scrutiny each bill receives in the legislature is the number of bills passed per legislative workday. The more bills that are passed each day, the less consideration each is likely to receive. Although the length of the deliberation does not necessarily equate with the quality of the deliberation, these are likely to be highly correlated. During the 1993 regular legislative session, the median U.S. legislature produced 5.2 laws per day. West Virginia's production rate of 2.4 bills per day was far lower than average, again boding well for the level of legislative deliberation.

Oversight of the Executive Bureaucracy

The legislature maintains partial control of policy outcomes through its oversight of the executive branch. Although this duty was only "dimly perceived and spasmodically practiced" by most state legislatures until the 1970s, many now attempt to oversee the bureaucracy more seriously because they have come to realize its great influence and discretion in implementing state public policy.[21] Assessing legislative oversight is difficult because it is not routinely practiced and rarely documented; however, comparative data exist concerning the powers available to those committees that have the responsibility to review administrative rules, the existence of "sunset legislation" regarding executive agencies, and certain aspects of the legislature's oversight role in the budget process.

The Council of State Governments has identified five powers that legislative committees charged with overseeing administrative rules can have, including whether it can review existing and/or proposed rules and whether it can suspend a rule with or without the full legislature's agreement. The West Virginia joint Legislative Rulemaking Review Committee, a statutorily defined interim committee that has the primary responsibility for legislative oversight, has only two of these five powers (the ability to review proposed rules and the requirement of explicitly approving each rule). This is the median level of control of oversight committees for all state legislatures.

Sunset laws require a thorough, periodic reevaluation of an agency (typically every five to ten years), with an explicit legislative reauthorization if the agency is to continue. Sunset legislation was designed to force legislatures to oversee agencies more closely (if only periodically) and to cause agencies to be more aware of their accountability to the legislature.[22] Although the impact of these reviews has been less than the promise, the legislation still provides an incentive for legislative oversight. West Virginia is one of twenty-three states that has regularized sunset legislation.[23] Nine states have comprehensive sunset legislation; West Virginia's legislation applies only to selective agencies. This places the legislature in the median category nationally.

In almost every state legislature, consideration of the governor's proposed state budget is the session's single most important activity.[24] The budget is one of the best tools the legislature has to control the governor and the bureaucracy. West Virginia's legislature gives as much attention to the budget as is possible in its limited session. One indicator of this is the level of legislative experience of those serving on the House and Senate Finance Committees, which are given principal responsibility for the budget bill. These committees are made up of legislators with more experience in the legislature and on these key committees than is the norm for their chambers.[25] The average number of years of legislative service was 3.8 for all members of the 1991–92 House of Delegates, whereas those serving on the Finance Committee averaged 5.1 years. In the Senate the numbers were 7.7 and 8.9 years, respectively. Perhaps even more telling is the fact that only three of twenty-five members of the 1991–92 House Finance Committee had no state legislative experience at all. This means that only 12 percent of this committee were rookies, as compared to 31 percent of the full House. In the Senate only one first-year senator was appointed to the Finance Committee, giving that committee 6 percent freshmen versus 15 percent in the full chamber.

The Finance Committees' members also have a higher level of on-committee experience than almost any other legislative committee. During the 1991 legislative session, they averaged 2.4 years on the House Finance committee, compared to 1.6 years for all other standing committees. Senate Finance Committee members averaged 4.8 years of committee experience, compared to 2.6 years for other standing committees. The greater committee and legislative experience for the members of both Finance Committees indicates that these committees have greater than average legislative resources to draw upon in conducting their important business.

The Finance Committees are also extremely powerful because of their influence on the drafting of the *Digest of the Enrolled Budget Bill*,[26] which formally defines, in more explicit detail than the budget bill, how the legislature intends for agencies to spend their funds. Although the Supreme Court of Appeals has held that this document does not have the force of law, there is a powerful incentive for bureaucrats to give careful consideration to its directives.[27] This process is controversial because of the power it gives to a small group of legislators, but it is undoubtedly a potent way for the Finance Committees to control the bureaucracy's activities.

Legislative oversight of the executive branch is difficult to document in ways that allow for cross-state comparisons. However, the evidence indicates that the West Virginia legislature understands its oversight responsibilities and pursues them in a moderately rigorous way. Despite its below-average legislative resources, it appears to oversee the bureaucracy at a level comparable to the average state legislature.

Overall, West Virginia's legislature is not significantly different than most other legislatures, especially those in other rural states. Given the state's economic difficulties, this "average" ranking is quite an accomplishment. The one area where the legislature lags far behind others is legislative resources. With little money to spend, the state ranks low on staff and overall expenditures used to maintain a capable membership with access to a variety of sources of policy information and technical expertise. Also, the use of multimember districts makes it more difficult for the legislature to understand and accurately represent their constituents' values and opinions.

CHAPTER SEVEN

The Governor and Executive Branch

The governor, regardless of partisan affiliation or margin of victory, is the central figure in West Virginia's political system. The governor is, among other things, expected to establish the state's legislative agenda through the preparation of the executive budget request, actively participate in the legislature's deliberations both on budgetary matters and state policy initiatives, promote and direct the state's economic development efforts, champion the state's interests against encroachments by the federal government, lead his or her political party, and provide both moral and policy guidance for both the state legislature and the general public. Moreover, state executive departments expect the governor to establish and enforce the state's administrative goals and implementation strategies.

The relatively high expectations placed on the governor put him or her in a unique and somewhat precarious political situation. The governor is often praised or blamed for what occurs within the state's borders, regardless of his or her role in determining the outcome of those events. Often, these events are influenced by forces far beyond the governor's control, such as national economic trends and natural disasters, which can have a significant impact on the state government's fiscal capacity to provide public services. Moreover, the governor operates within a federal system increasingly dominated by federal policymakers. The state's budget priorities are often determined, at least in part, by the availability of federal grants-in-aid or by federal mandates. Federal grants currently account for over one-quarter of West Virginia's state budget. In addition, federal conditions attached to these grants often shape the state's implementation strategies and administrative procedures.[1]

The governor's authority is also limited because he or she both shares and competes for political power with the state legislature and the state judiciary. Although the governor has a number of institutional and political weapons at his or her disposal to influence the legislature's behavior, such as the line-item veto and the ability to award or refuse to award coveted administrative appointments to individuals recommended by state legislators, the governor does not possess the authority to enact a bill. He or she is forced to work with the legislature to achieve policy objectives. Although West Virginia's governor and legislative leaders are usually Democrats, making disagreements over policy objectives and strategies a matter of degree rather than of kind, the legislature rarely "rolls over and plays dead." Bargains must be struck and compromises consummated, sometimes in favor of the legislature, sometimes in favor of the governor. Moreover, although the courts typically stay out of the day-to-day politics in Charleston, they occasionally play a large role in redefining state policy. In 1982, for example, Judge Arthur Recht ruled in the now-famous Lincoln County School Case, *Pauley v. Bailey*, that the then-existing system of financing the public schools was unconstitutional because its reliance on property taxes rendered it discriminatory against children in poorer counties. This decision forced the state to revamp its funding policies for schools and to reform its property tax system.

The governor also shares and competes for power with independently elected heads of the state's major executive departments, including the secretary of state, attorney general, state treasurer, state auditor, and commissioner of agriculture. In many instances these officeholders do not share the governor's views on public policy, are not necessarily members of the governor's political party, and might even have gubernatorial ambitions of their own. For example, in 1992 two of the state's elected executives ran against Governor Gaston Caperton. The state's attorney general, Mario Palumbo, was defeated by Caperton in the Democratic primary. The state's commissioner of agriculture, Cleve Benedict, a Republican, then attempted to unseat Caperton in the general election. Caperton survived the challenge, but the attempts to unseat him clearly signal that the governor cannot count on the heads of the state's executive departments to always follow his lead.

Given these constraints, it is appropriate to ask if the governor has the institutional powers necessary to alter the course of state government. It is also appropriate to ask if the governor's office is a reliable and responsive mechanism for West Virginia's citizens to have their views on public policy translated into government action.

THE HISTORICAL CONTEXT

Prior to the 1960s it was commonplace for journalists, political scientists, historians, and others familiar with the workings of state government to ridicule the performance of state government officials and, especially, the performance of governors. Among the terms used to describe many of the American governors who served during the first half of this century were "flowery old courthouse politicians," "political machine dupes," "political pipsqueaks," and "good-time Charlies."[2] Of course, not all governors who served at that time were described in such acerbic terms. For example, six of the ten governors named to the mythical Twentieth Century Statehouse Hall of Fame in 1982 served before 1950.[3] For the most part, however, it is generally accepted by state government scholars that most of the approximately one thousand governors who served during the first half of the 1900s were second-rate politicians. They did not generate much notice outside of their own state, and once their tenure in office was completed, they were not long remembered even within their state.

Although there have been and continue to be notable exceptions to the general rule, it is now accepted by most gubernatorial scholars that contemporary governors are, on the whole, more capable, creative, hard-working, forward-looking, and experienced than their predecessors.[4] This turnabout is partly a reflection of the increased responsibilities that states have assumed since the federal government launched its War on Poverty during the 1960s. Individuals interested in altering social and economic conditions in American society recognized that state governments had become viable mechanisms to achieve those goals, which elevated the stature of state government service as a career. Moreover, at the same time state governments became more important and state government service became more attractive, reformers in many states were transforming the governor's office from that of a symbolic figurehead to a powerful chief executive whose powers rivaled and, in some instances, surpassed the powers of the state legislature. Gubernatorial terms were lengthened, veto powers were expanded, the short ballot (electing the governor and lieutenant governor as a team rather than on separate ballots and restricting the number of executive officials that are elected) was imposed, appointment and removal powers were strengthened, control over the budget was centralized, and reorganization powers expanded.[5] Moreover, between 1965 and 1975, twenty states restructured their executive branches and another twenty-four states reorganized at least one executive agency or department in an attempt to strengthen the governor's capacity to act in a decisive manner.[6]

West Virginia also strengthened its governor's powers during this period. In 1968 West Virginians approved a state constitutional amendment that substantially increased the governor's budgetary powers. The Modern Budget

Amendment shifted the power to prepare the state budget proposal from the Board of Public Works, which consisted of the governor, secretary of state, auditor, attorney general, treasurer, commissioner of agriculture, and super-intendent of schools, to the governor alone. It also empowered the governor to determine the state government's projected revenues for the ensuing fiscal year and prohibited the legislature from appropriating funds in excess of that amount without the governor's approval.

In 1970 West Virginians approved the Governor's Succession Amendment, increasing the governor's political power by permitting the governor to serve two consecutive four-year terms.[7] This reduced the likelihood of West Virginia's governor being perceived by members of the state legislature and by other political organizations as a "lame duck" during the third and fourth years of his or her first term in office. This, in turn, strengthened the governor's bargaining power with both the legislature and other political organizations interested in influencing the direction of state government policies.

As gubernatorial powers grew throughout the nation, many men and women who would have otherwise not considered it worthwhile to expose themselves to the physical and emotional trials and tribulations that accompany a modern campaign for the governor's office decided that it was a prize worth pursuing. One indication of the governorship's increased value is the escalating cost of gubernatorial campaigns. The typical gubernatorial candidate now spends between $1 million and $5 million to make a serious bid to become a governor. In high population states, such as California, Texas, and New York, it is not unusual for gubernatorial candidates to spend more than $10 million during the primary and general election campaigns.[8] Although West Virginia is a relatively small state in both population and size, its gubernatorial campaigns have featured some of the highest expenditures per voter in the nation. Republican Arch Moore and Democrat Clyde See, for example, spent a combined total of $9.7 million running for the governor's office in 1984. Four years later, Democrat Gaston Caperton spent $4.6 million, much of it his own money, in his successful bid to unseat Moore. Moore spent $2.4 million that year.[9]

THE PLURAL EXECUTIVE

West Virginia's constitution, like most others, mandates a plural executive consisting of the governor, secretary of state, attorney general, state trea-surer, state auditor, and commissioner of agriculture. Each is elected in presidential election years to a four-year term, and with the exception of the governor, each can serve an unlimited number of terms in succession. Unlike most other states, West Virginia does not have a lieutenant governor. If the governor is unable to perform his or her duties, the president of the Senate is designated as next in line of succession, followed by the Speaker of the House of Delegates.

The secretary of state's main duties are to supervise elections and voter registration, maintain the state's records and documents, file state agency rules and regulations, register charitable organizations and corporations, and publish the state government's administrative rules and regulations. The office is considered a potential steppingstone to the governorship primarily because it enhances the occupant's name recognition. Moreover, although the secretary of state's duties are primarily custodial, not political, in nature, the secretary of state sometimes becomes directly involved in major political controversies. For example, in 1994 Secretary of State Ken Hechler set off a firestorm of controversy by attacking the state tax department's method of assessing the value of natural resources (primarily coal) for property taxation. He claimed that the department's appraisal methods undervalued natural resources at the expense of homeowners. Governor Caperton defended the tax department's methods, but disclosures concerning errors in the department's tax books forced the governor to order a comprehensive reassessment of the tax department's appraisal methods.

The attorney general's primary duties are to provide legal advice, when asked, to state government agencies, county prosecuting attorneys, and the state legislature, to interpret state statutes and regulations, to serve as legal counsel for the state, to administer consumer protection programs, and to adjust or prosecute consumer complaints. The attorney general's office is also considered a prime steppingstone to the governorship. Interpreting state statutes and regulations and representing the state on legal matters provide the attorney general an opportunity to comment on and influence the direction of state legislation. This, in turn, attracts newspaper and television coverage, which can be used by the attorney general to increase his or her name recognition and to create an image as an important policymaker who can handle the responsibilities of the governor's office.

The state treasurer is responsible for receiving and depositing the state's revenue in financial institutions, maintaining a record of all appropriations made by the legislature, endorsing state checks, and investing any of the state's available funds in financial institutions. Although the treasurer's duties are custodial in nature, the importance of this office became evident when the state's Consolidated Investment Fund, headed by the treasurer, lost $279 million in investments in "junk bonds" and speculative trading options between 1987 and 1989. The state treasurer at that time, A. James Manchin, was subsequently impeached by the House of Delegates on 29 March 1989 by a vote of 65–34. He resigned on 9 July 1989, before the Senate voted on whether he should be removed from office.[10]

The state auditor, the state government's official bookkeeper, determines if claims presented to the state for payment are valid and, along with the state treasurer, endorses state checks, administers Social Security payments and a savings bond program for state employees, receives state tax revenues that are collected by sheriffs, and collects and distributes public utility taxes for the state and counties.

The commissioner of agriculture administers the Department of Agriculture and is also responsible for inspecting agricultural products, regulating pesticides, disseminating statistical data on soils, climate, natural resources, and market opportunities in the state, and publishing and distributing reports on all phases of agriculture and forestry.

A state constitutional amendment that would have eliminated the elected status of the secretary of state, commissioner of agriculture, and treasurer was soundly rejected by the state's voters in 1989 (28,634 voted for it and 220,700 voted against it). Respondents to a statewide survey taken shortly after the vote indicated that the amendment failed because the voters were convinced that it would give the then-incumbent governor (Gaston Caperton) too much power.[11] As a result, although West Virginia's constitution declares that the chief executive power shall be vested in the governor and requires the governor to take care that the state laws be faithfully executed, the governor, like most other governors, shares this authority with others and must rely on his or her reputation, popularity, knowledge of what should be done, and ability to communicate effectively, especially with the state's electorate, to influence the actions of others in the executive branch.

THE GOVERNOR'S INFORMAL POWERS

Recent studies have suggested that as a group, governors who have served during the latter half of the twentieth century exhibited stronger interpersonal skills than their predecessors and have been more adept at influencing the actions of others in state government. Moreover, the governors' leadership abilities are reflected in their career paths once their tenure in office has expired. The recent governors are now more likely than their predecessors to move on to other important political jobs, particularly the U.S. Senate and the presidency. Nationally, former governors are also more likely than before to be appointed to federal government cabinet positions and major ambassadorships, as well as federal and state government judgeships.[12]

Unfortunately, it can be argued that this trend toward more thoroughly trained, better regarded, and more capable governors has not held in West Virginia. On the positive side, all of West Virginia's eight governors who have served in office since 1950 were, arguably, well trained for the job. All had earned a college or university undergraduate degree, three also had a law degree (William Marland, William Barron, and Arch Moore Jr.), one had earned a graduate degree (Cecil Underwood), and another had additional graduate education (John "Jay" Rockefeller IV) prior to becoming governor. In addition, each had distinguished himself as a successful businessman (Okey Patteson, Hulett Smith, and Caperton), as an attorney (Marland, Barron, and Moore), or as an educator (Underwood and Rockefeller) prior to being elected governor. Moreover, four had served in the West Virginia House of Delegates (Underwood, Barron, Moore, and Rockefeller), and Moore had served seven terms in the U.S. House of Representatives prior to his election to the governor's office.[13]

On the other hand, two of these governors, Barron and Moore, were indicted, convicted, and sentenced to prison for criminal acts committed while in office. In 1971, six years after leaving the governor's office, Barron was sentenced by a federal court judge to twenty-five years in prison. Previously he had been found not guilty of bribery and conspiracy charges concerning his role in rigging state purchasing contracts while governor. However, he received the federal sentence after the jury foreman revealed that Barron's wife, under her husband's direction, delivered $25,000 in cash to him in a brown paper bag to ensure that the jury's verdict would be not guilty. Barron's sentence was subsequently reduced to twelve years in prison plus a $50,000 fine. He was later released after serving about four years in prison.[14] Moore received a sentence of five years and ten months plus a $170,000 fine in 1990 for extortion, mail fraud, tax fraud, and obstruction of justice. The charges stemmed from Moore's filing false campaign statements during his 1984 gubernatorial campaign, receiving a $573,000 kickback in 1985 from a coal company in exchange for a $2.3 million refund from the state's black lung disease fund, failing to report on his federal income tax form the $573,000 as income as well as another $70,000 he received from lobbyists in 1984 and 1985, and asking his campaign manager and the representative of the coal company providing the kickback to lie to federal investigators about his campaign contributions and spending.[15]

Barron and Moore's convictions make it difficult to argue that West Virginia's recent governors have lived up to the enhanced reputations governors have earned in other states. However, even if those two governorships are dismissed as aberrations, the career paths of the state's most recent governors do not compare particularly well with governors in other states. Only Rockefeller was subsequently elected to another public office (the U.S. Senate); none were appointed to a federal office or commission; only two (Smith and Underwood) were subsequently appointed to a state commission; and one former governor (Marland), recovering from alcoholism, attracted nationwide attention in 1965 after he was discovered by reporters driving a taxicab in Chicago.[16] The scandals that have rocked the governor's office, coupled with the indictments and convictions of several executive branch administrators and state legislators during the 1980s, have shaken West Virginians' confidence in their state's political leadership.

THE GOVERNOR'S MANAGEMENT RESOURCES

Governors have three types of management resources available to them when they interact with others in state government: personal, enabling, and institutional. Personal resources consist of the governor's general intellectual, political, and verbal skills, including charm, charisma, and sense of humor. These resources reflect the governor's ability to persuade others to take actions that the governor believes must be taken. Many knowledgeable observers of West Virginia politics, for example, would argue that former Republican governor Arch Moore Jr. was the most charismatic governor in West Virginia's modern history. Not only did he battle gladly with the Democratic legislature, vetoing twenty-six bills in his first term alone, but he even went so far as to personally argue a case before the West Virginia Supreme Court, the only governor ever to do so. Many considered Moore's speaking ability to be second to none, and his speeches always generated loud and enthusiastic applause.[17]

Personal resources vary from governor to governor, with some being more charismatic than others, some being more assertive than others, and, unfortunately, some being less honest than others. Although the governor's personal resources are crucial in determining the governor's "style" and his or her ability to influence the outcome of state policy, these resources are, for the most part, qualities that cannot be changed by the deliberate action of state government. West Virginia's gubernatorial enabling and institutional resources, on the other hand, are directly affected by state government policy.

Enabling resources include staff assistance, funding for the governor's office, access to information, and time. They reflect the governor's ability to process information in a way that enables him or her to reach decisions independently from other organizations that compete for power, such as interest groups and the state legislature. West Virginia's gubernatorial enabling resources have been improved in recent years. The governor's staff size has increased steadily since the 1960s, reaching forty-eight members in 1993. The governor's staff not only helps the governor to keep track of legislative and administrative details; they have also become an important source of ideas about legislation, budgetary matters, and administrative strategies. Also, the governor now has ready access to a state automobile, helicopter, and airplane to assist him or her in attending meetings. Although much of this traveling is done for political purposes, such as dedicating a new bridge or speaking before the local rotary or chamber of commerce, the ability to travel the state allows the governor to "keep in touch" with the people who live outside of the Charleston area. West Virginia also adopted a sweeping executive branch reform initiative in 1989 that expanded the governor's control over state agencies.[18] Instead of dealing directly with more than one hundred departments, commissions, and boards, the governor now appoints seven "super-secretaries," heading the Departments of Administration, Commerce, Education and the Arts, Health and Human Services, Public Safety, Tax and Revenue, and Transportation, to deal with the various agencies. The super-secretaries, who comprise the governor's cabinet, report directly to the governor and, along with the governor's personal staff, are an important source of ideas on policy alternatives, budgetary matters, legislative strategy, and implementation decisions.[19]

Another important enabling resource, often overlooked, is the proximity of the governor's mansion to the state capitol building. The stately brick mansion is located on the edge of the capitol grounds, within easy walking distance to the capitol building. Moreover, the governor is provided a suite of offices within the capitol itself, on the ground floor of the main unit. This makes it fairly easy for the governor to interact with members of the legislature on a face-to-face basis both at work and at home. Governor Caperton, for example, regularly convened a meeting of legislative leaders at the mansion prior to the start of each annual legislative session to discuss his policy priorities and budgetary decisions. He also held regular face-to-face meetings with legislative leaders in his capitol office once the legislative session was underway and often invited legislators over to the mansion for lunch or dinner. These engagements were sometimes just friendly get-togethers; at other times they provided an opportunity for the governor to have a frank and private discussion with a legislator about specific state policies and state politics.

Finally, institutional resources vary with the issue at hand and the audience the governor is addressing. They typically include knowledge of the issue being discussed, familiarity with the political environment surrounding the issue, and the authority to act, either from state statute or the state constitution. These resources reflect the governor's ability to force others to take actions that the governor believes must be taken.[20]

THE GOVERNOR'S INSTITUTIONAL POWERS

All U.S. governors have the authority to issue executive orders to declare emergencies or to create advisory commissions and task forces, to grant pardons and to commute sentences, either unilaterally or in conjunction with a state pardoning board, and to act as commander in chief of the state's National Guard. However, governors' other institutional powers vary widely from state to state.

In 1987 the National Governors' Association (NGA) created a scale to measure the extent of governors' institutional powers.[21] The scale consisted of six indices, including the governor's tenure potential, appointment powers, budget-making powers, veto powers, political strength in the state legislature, and the legislature's budget-changing authority. The first three indices measure the governor's power to influence the executive branch's actions. The last three indices measure the governor's power to influence the state legislature's actions.[22] The NGA indices revealed that between 1965 and 1985 governors' institutional powers had increased overall, from a cumulative average index score of 20.7 to 21.1. However, the growth in gubernatorial power was uneven, with increases in their power to influence the executive branch (tenure potential, appointive powers, and budget-making authority) and slight decreases in their power to influence the state legislature (veto powers, political strength in the legislature, and the legislature's budget-changing authority).

The NGA study revealed that the institutional powers of West Virginia's governors increased dramatically between 1965 and 1985, from a score of 18 in 1965 (tied with five other states for thirty-sixth place) to 26 in 1985 (tied with New York for third place).[23] This was the largest increase in institutional powers recorded by the study and can be attributed primarily to the adoption of the Modern Budget Amendment of 1968 and the Governors' Succession Amendment of 1970. The Modern Budget Amendment increased the governor's authority over the executive budget request, and the Governors' Succession Amendment increased the governor's tenure potential.

A slightly revised version of NGA's institutional powers scale was used to measure the institutional powers of each state's governor in 1995. It revealed that the institutional powers of the West Virginia governor are currently among the strongest in the nation. West Virginia scored 26 out of a possible 30 points, tied behind Tennessee with Hawaii, Maryland, Massachusetts, Rhode Island, and Utah for second place. The average score for all states was 22.

The revised institutional powers scale consisted of the following six indices: gubernatorial tenure potential, appointment powers, budget-making authority, control over budget cuts necessary to balance the state budget once the appropriations bill has been enacted, veto powers, and party control over the legislature. Each of these indices of gubernatorial power were rated from 1 (very weak) to 5 (very strong).

West Virginia's governor's office received a 4 (strong) for tenure potential. Although the governor can serve an unlimited number of four-year terms (which would have generated a score of 5), he or she is prohibited from serving more than two of those terms in succession. The governor's office received a 3 (average) for executive appointment powers (based on the governor's control over the appointment of seven major administrative department heads), a 5 (very strong) for budget-making authority (the governor has total control over the creation of the state executive budget), a 4 (strong) for control over budget cuts necessary to balance the state budget once the appropriations bill has been enacted (the governor cannot reduce budget items at will but can make uniform, across-the-board reductions as long as special protection is provided for educational appropriations), and a 5 (very strong) for veto powers (the governor can use the package, item, and reduction vetoes). Finally, the governor's office received a 5 (very strong) for party control over the state legislature (more than 75 percent of the seats in both the House of Delegates and the Senate were held by members of the governor's party in 1995).

West Virginia's cumulative score of 26 on the gubernatorial institutional powers scale indicates that its governor enjoys relatively strong institutional powers when compared to those held by governors in other states. The institutional framework clearly exists for the governor to exercise a very strong influence on state government. If the governor is unable to alter the course of state government, he or she cannot blame this failure on the office's lack of institutional powers.

Gubernatorial Power and Policy

Just as beauty is in the eye of the beholder, there is no universally accepted definition of what constitutes a successful governor. Some of the factors that must be considered are the governor's ability to establish the state's political agenda, to focus public and legislative debate on selected policy alternatives, and, ultimately, to alter state policy outcomes. Of course, given the complexity of the policymaking process, it is difficult to measure the precise nature of any governor's impact on the state's political agenda or on specific policy outcomes. However, it is generally accepted that the governor's ability to set the agenda and alter state policy outcomes is strongly related to the governor's institutional powers. Although having strong institutional powers does not guarantee that the governor will be able to alter the course of state government, lacking them makes that task nearly impossible.

West Virginia's governors do not have this problem. Their institutional powers are among the strongest in the nation. However, having the power to get things accomplished does not necessarily mean that the governor will be successful. West Virginia's recent governors have had a mixed record of success. Each has had his share of accomplishments. Moore, for example, was instrumental in promoting highway construction, increasing welfare benefits, and increasing funding for teachers' salaries. Rockefeller eliminated the 3 percent sales tax on food and increased funding for secondary highways. Caperton resolved the state government's revenue problems during the early 1990s by raising taxes (including the return of the sales tax on food), increased teachers' salaries and funding for school construction, and shepherded through the legislature complex environmental legislation that regulated landfills and protected groundwater supplies. However, despite their accomplishments, West Virginia's recent governors have not always proven to be well regarded and admired by either the electorate or state legislative leaders. The criminal convictions of Governors Barron and Moore have had a particularly denigrating impact on the public's perception of both politicians in general and of elected state government officials in particular. Although the governor's relatively strong institutional powers have provided him or her with the tools and weapons necessary to alter the course of state government, past experience indicates that it is the governor's personal resources, especially his or her honesty, vision, and ability to inspire others to follow his or her lead, that will ultimately determine if a particular governor will be remembered as a success or as a failure.

CHAPTER EIGHT

The State Budget Process

West Virginia's political system cannot be understood without taking into account the state's budget process. All political decisions center around the budget. It determines precisely how state funds can be spent and, to a large extent, which policies can be pursued throughout the fiscal year.

THE IMPORTANCE OF REVENUE

The budget process is a battle about the scope and direction of public policy. The battle is both intensified and constrained by the scarcity of resources. As noted in chapter 5, the state constitution places constraints on state property taxation and deficit spending. Additionally, the out-migration of many productive citizens and the loss of high-paying mining jobs during the 1970s and 1980s created a fiscal crisis as state revenue could not keep pace with budgetary demands and inflation. In 1988, faced with the prospect of eliminating government services or raising taxes, the state raised the sales tax from 5 to 6 percent, extended it to all sales and nonprofessional service transactions, and eliminated all itemized deductions in the state's personal income tax. The tax increases resolved the state's cash flow problem and also moved its "tax effort" from forty-third to eighth among the states.[1] The size of the increase and the rise of anti-taxation sentiment since then has precluded any further efforts to raise taxes. Coupled with little change in federal assistance, the central strategy for all participants in the budgeting process has become the defense of previous allocations and a desperate search for a few extra dollars to meet new demands and to account for inflation.

A little over one-third of the state's $6.2 billion in revenue in 1996 ($2.2 billion) came from the state's general fund (collected from twenty-four revenue sources, including $761 million from the consumer sales tax and $739 million from the personal income tax), another third came from federal grants ($2.1 billion), about 16 percent came from special revenue accounts, such as college and university tuition ($986 million), and the remaining 13 percent came from the state road fund, including the state gasoline tax, privilege tax and license tax ($809 million).[2]

Most of this revenue is spent on health and welfare programs, mostly Medicaid and public assistance programs ($2.6 billion), education ($2 billion), highways ($861 million), other costs ($600 million), and debt service ($97 million).[3]

Surprisingly, although money is tight, the budget process is not marked by high levels of conflict. All participants recognize that there is little money to go around and have adopted strategies that allow them to predict what other participants will do, thus enabling the process to work smoothly. Although this "pax austeritus" reduces uncertainty, it causes at least two problems. First, the constant scrambling for small sources of revenue wears away at the fabric of government, raising officials' stress levels as rainy-day funds are routinely ferreted out and spent. Also, because agencies protect their previous budgets, and because much of the state's money comes from the federal government and is governed by their rules, it is very difficult to make major shifts in budgetary priorities.[4]

A BRIEF HISTORY OF THE STATE BUDGET PROCESS

The evolution of the state's budget process has two important attributes.[5] First, there was a steady, if slow, shifting of decision-making power away from the bureaucracy and toward the governor and the legislature. Second, many of the state's budgetary procedures are embedded in its constitution. Because the constitution is relatively difficult to amend, change in the budget process has come slowly.

Initially, budgeting under the Constitution of 1872 was very fragmented. "The budget" was really many budgets, as executive branch agencies prepared and submitted their expenditure requests individually to the appropriate legislative committees. The governor had no central coordinating role and no power to veto appropriations passed by the legislature. The legislature had no coordinating role, either. It voted on agencies' budgets piecemeal, with little thought given to overall state expenditures, either in terms of priorities or levels.

West Virginia's response to this state of affairs was the ratification of the

Budget Amendment of 1918, which created the Board of Public Works, consisting of the governor, the secretary of state, the auditor, the state superintendent of schools, the treasurer, the attorney general, and the commissioner of agriculture. The board's primary responsibility was to ascertain that the state did not spend more money than it received. To accomplish this, the board collected executive agency budget requests, modified them, and presented a comprehensive budget to the legislature. The legislature was prohibited from increasing the board's requests on any line item and was required to adhere to the board's revenue estimate for the coming fiscal year when passing a balanced comprehensive budget.

From 1918 to 1935 the governor had relatively little control over the budget. This began to change following the creation of the Office of Budget Director in 1935. The director was the state's first full-time budget officer. Although officially a staff officer of the Board of Public Works, the director was appointed by and served at the governor's pleasure. The director soon came to be seen as the governor's agent, giving the governor more leverage on the board than the other members. In 1953 the Office of the Legislative Auditor was established to provide the legislature with similar staff assistance in performing its budgetary duties. Then, in 1955 the state shifted from a system of biennial to annual budgeting with the implementation of a thirty-day legislative "budget session" in even-numbered years. This gave both the board and the legislature more control over agency spending because expenditure needs and revenue estimates were more accurately gauged, and agency performance came under more frequent scrutiny. In 1957 the Department of Finance and Administration was created to consolidate financial management in the executive branch, including budget preparation and administration. The commissioner of this department took over the budget director's role and was appointed by the governor for a six-year term. The commissioner reported to both the governor individually and the Board of Public Works as a group, further establishing the governor as the board's most influential member.

Although these developments increased the governor's role in the budget process, the ratification of the Modern Budget Amendment in 1968 took a giant step in this direction, resulting in the basic structure of today's budget process. The governor was given the sole authority to prepare the budget proposal for the legislature and to estimate future state revenue. The Department of Finance and Administration, now renamed the Department of Administration, was made a line agency directly responsible to the governor. The governor was also given the line-item and reduction vetoes and the power to amend his or her budget request and revenue estimate during the legislative session.

The Modern Budget Amendment also increased the legislature's role in the budget process so that it could increase, decrease, or even strike any line items it chose. However, it still could not raise the governor's revenue estimate or pass a budget with a projected deficit.

West Virginia's budget process is now similar to that used in most other states. What distinguishes it from others is how the participants use their powers and tools in the face of high service demands and low resources.

BUDGET PREPARATION

West Virginia, like thirty-one other states, has an annual budget cycle, running from 1 July to 30 June.[6] But to call this an "annual" budget cycle is misleading. The work on any fiscal year's budget takes place over the course of at least three calendar years. A cross-section of budget activity on any given day would reveal people planning next year's budget, others administering this year's budget, and still others assessing the administration of last year's budget. Each phase of the process is thoroughly linked to the phases that precede and follow it in time and to the budgets that have come before it and those that will follow it.

The budget process begins almost a year before the commencement of the fiscal year, with the preparation of the governor's budget proposal. The key participants in this phase are the governor, officials of executive branch agencies, and the Department of Administration. All have different goals and pursue different strategies to achieve them.

Executive agencies are viewed as "big spenders" because they believe deeply in the jobs they are doing for the state and have the natural political desire to become more powerful and to control more resources.[7] Their two primary goals are to increase their budget and to increase their discretion in spending this money. The Department of Administration, on the other hand, is the state's "Finance Ministry." Its primary goal is to match spending with revenue. As the governor's agents, the secretary of the Department of Administration and the director of the Budget Office (now a subordinate of the secretary) try meet the governor's goal of compiling a balanced budget that also reflects his or her spending priorities.

The potential for conflict between the agencies and the governor and his or her agents sets up the tension that characterizes this phase of the budget process. Since state revenue almost always falls short of agency requests, tight controls from above, rigid guidelines for requests, and a focus on maintaining current levels of spending are the rule. In fact, the revenue constraint has been so severe since the mid-1980s that agencies now rarely seek major funding increases. Instead, their goal is to protect their "base," typically their previous year's spending level.

Budget preparation begins formally in early July, a full year before the budget takes effect. At this time, all agencies are sent the Department of Administration's annual publication, "Appropriations Request Instructions," which lists the agencies' current budgets and requires them to submit a request for funding that is similar to that level, called the "current-level budget." Not only is incremental change mandated, but the size and direction of that incremental change are also usually specified. However, agencies are allowed to specify a small number of "Improvement Packages," or requests for an increase in funding for a specific project. These improvements must be justified individually in a brief accompanying narrative and identified clearly as either an ongoing or single-year project. Isolating requests for increased funding makes it easier for the Department of Administration to select those few increases that the state can afford and fit them into the governor's program.

All executive departments must submit their budget requests to the secretary of the Department of Administration by 1 September. The Budget Office compiles these requests, reviews and verifies the information contained therein, and checks to see that the budget preparation instructions were followed. By 1 October, the Budget Office reports its findings and the compiled budget requests to the secretary of the Department of Administration.

In most states, the central budget office conducts a critical review of the budget requests to assess whether they are in line with the governor's agenda and whether they meet any applicable professional, legislative, or gubernatorial criteria.[8] West Virginia's budget office, however, lacks the resources necessary to conduct a thorough analysis of the budget. For example, in 1993 it employed only three budget analysts, the lowest number in the nation and far below the national average of twenty-four analysts.[9]

The secretary of the Department of Administration and the director of the Budget Office sit down with each department's super-secretary and selected division heads in October and November to review their budget requests. These hearings provide yet another opportunity for the governor's agents to inject the governor's priorities into the budget. The super-secretaries then revise their budget requests and resubmit them to the Budget Office by 1 December. Budget Office analysts use these requests to draft the budget bill and the budget document by 15 December.

The budget bill is the actual legislation the governor submits to the legislature for its consideration. Most of the proposed expenditures are itemized at a broad level, with most agencies having their expenses divided into the following four categories: personal services, including salaries; annual increment, or small increases in personal services authorized in the "Appropriations Request Instructions"; employee benefits; and unclassified. The unclassified category is the bill's most critical category.[10] Both the governor and the legislature are reluctant to embed too many specific appropriations into the budget bill because once it is passed, it is a rigid legal mandate. The unclassified category provides the governor and the legislature some flexibility in the budget's administration. Agencies try to keep as much of their budget as possible in the unclassified line for the same reason. But legal rigidity is sometimes useful to the governor, such as when he or she wants to keep another participant, especially the agency involved, from having flexibility with an expenditure.

The budget document is typically over five hundred pages long. It includes a general budgetary statement by the governor to the legislature, the governor's summary report regarding the state's finances, and the Appropriations Request forms from each agency, which specify detailed information regarding proposed expenditures for the coming fiscal year.

The budget document does not have the force of law, even after the budget bill is enacted. It is largely a signal to the legislature and the agencies of the governor's intentions concerning how the state's money should be spent. But even without the force of law, it is taken seriously by all participants and has held a pivotal place in West Virginia's budget process for more than forty years. It provides the legislature with the detailed information it needs to consider the budget intelligently, especially in its comparison of proposed, current, and previous expenditures. It also provides the detailed budgetary information necessary for the agencies to develop their future budget requests. The budget document therefore facilitates an incremental approach to budgeting, which is appropriate for West Virginia. Because state revenues are not growing rapidly, the current year's expenditures are a good guide to what is possible in the new year.

The Budget Office drafts the budget bill and the budget document during the first fifteen days in December. Because the office has so few analysts and only fifteen days to complete their massive job, late nights, Saturday and Sunday duty, and cold pizza are the rule. The secretary of the Department of

Administration presents the drafts of the budget bill and the budget document to the governor on 15 December.

The governor has two weeks to review these drafts and put the finishing touches on them. Rarely are major changes made at this time because the governor's agents (the super-secretaries, the director of the Budget Office, and the secretary of the Department of Administration) have had a firm hand in shaping the draft requests. Most of the modifications involve setting the political stage for legislative consideration. For example, the governor may make small changes in the proposal either to enhance its potential political support or to provide bargaining chips for later negotiations.

During this two-week period, the governor's office finalizes its revenue estimate for the coming fiscal year. The Department of Tax and Revenue's Research Division assists the governor in the estimation process, taking into account the previous year's revenue, national trends, and economic and demographic factors in the state. The governor has the constitutional authority to make this estimate unilaterally, however, and no one has the legal authority to change his or her official estimate. The revenue estimate is crucial because it sets the upper limit for the budget bill's proposed expenditures. The legislature is prohibited by law from passing a budget in which the proposed expenditures exceed the governor's revenue estimate. Therefore, the governor may control legislative additions to the budget by underestimating revenue. This is a powerful device for the governor, one that only three other states give their chief executives.[11] Although a governor may or may not intentionally underestimate revenue for this purpose, many participants in the process believe that this is done, at least occasionally. Further, given the unpredictability of the future, it makes sense for the governor to underestimate revenue. It is much less of a political problem to have more revenue than expected during a fiscal year than it is to announce budget reductions and employee layoffs if revenues fall short of expectations.

The governor's office develops its strategy for presenting the budget to the legislature and the state during this two-week period, including deciding which aspects of the massive proposal to emphasize. Is this an "austerity budget for hard times" or "an education budget, with massive shifts in funding to our children?" The budget's theme, or even just those aspects the governor thinks are important and salable, are emphasized in press conferences, press releases, and especially in the State of the State address. Presented by the governor before a joint session of the legislature at the beginning of its session, the State of the State address is covered by all major state media and carried live statewide on West Virginia Public Television. The address allows the governor to set the agenda for the budget debate. Because of the legislature's lack of staff and the traditional deference accorded the governor, the governor's opinion of important aspects of the budget is usually respected. This speech, given on the second Wednesday of January,[12] and the official presentation of the budget bill and document to the legislature are the starting point for legislative budgetary debate and the next stage of the state budgetary process.

BUDGET ADOPTION

After the governor submits the budget proposal to the legislature at the beginning of the legislative session, the House and Senate Finance Committees immediately study it, with the goal of finding extra money. Any additional resources the committees can find or create allows them to add as much of the legislative agenda to the budget as possible. They examine the budget proposal in fine detail for about fifty days of the sixty-day legislative session, beginning with hearings with the department super-secretaries and selected division heads and then forming subcommittees to study the budget proposal in detail. The subcommittee chairs meet with the full Finance Committee chairs and the chamber's majority party leadership (the Speaker or the president) to discuss budget priorities. Each subcommittee chair then tries to instill the agreed-upon priorities into his or her piece of the budget. Individual subcommittee members are assigned specific agency accounts to search through for additional resources. Even with high legislative turnover, Finance Committee members usually serve on the same subcommittees for several years and often evaluate the same individual agency accounts during their entire subcommittee service. This leads to a better legislative "feel" for what goes on in each agency's accounts and compensates somewhat for the Finance Committees' lack of staff assistance.

As subcommittee members go over these accounts, they scramble for any spare funds, even in small amounts. One strategy is to cut vacant employee positions (which is why agencies are loath to leave positions open for long). Cutting empty bureaucratic positions is a time-honored tradition in state budgeting in tight times because there is little political heat for doing so.[13] Subcommittee members also look for "unusual" expenditures, typically meaning new items or significant increases over the previous year's appropriation. Also, agencies that spent less than expected in the previous year may be seen as having been overfunded. These items are all fair game for subcommittee cuts, and an agency's officials must justify the open positions and new expenses to the subcommittee member evaluating its account. It is often the persuasive power of this justification and the personal relationship between the subcommittee member and an agency official that determine whether an item is kept in the budget or "reclaimed" into the legislative discretionary pool.

A variety of accounting tricks are also used by the Finance subcommittees in their desperate search for extra funds. Salaries of employees may be shifted from general revenue to special funds (which are paid for by federal or earmarked tax money) when their jobs are related to the tasks these special funds cover. Charges and fees for government services may also be used to pay for programs without raising taxes. Since 1978 this has occurred with increasing frequency, with charges having increased from less than 10 percent of total state revenue to over 17 percent in 1996. Further, special revenue accounts can take in more money than expected in a given year, and these extra funds may be incorporated into the legislature's budget. The Finance Committees have been so desperate for extra funds in recent years that they have stripped the balances that are kept in many of these accounts in case of unexpected demands.

Once a subcommittee completes its work of eking out a few extra dollars from the budget proposal, it uses these funds to put the legislature's stamp on the budget. Some of the additions are policy changes that are on the leadership's agenda, but some are made to satisfy the policy or political demands of specific members. "Bringing members on board with the budget" in the state legislature is, as elsewhere in the United States, one part rational argument, one part bluster, and one part pure horse trading. Much of this negotiation occurs in closed sessions of the majority party caucus. There, out of the light of media scrutiny, legislators not on the Finance Committees push for their pet projects. These caucus sessions can be loud and long as noncommittee members have one of their few chances to influence the budget. The Speaker and president ride herd over their respective caucuses, trying to give in to parochial interests as little as necessary to gain sufficient support for passage.

Although the majority party leaders and governor have little official role in the adoption phase of the budget process, their informal role and influence through their surrogates make them the dominating forces behind the scenes. The Speaker and the president appoint the members of the Finance Committees, as well as the chairs of these committees and their subcommittees. Finance Committee positions are highly prized by legislators, and the appointment to one makes a legislator quite beholden to the leadership. Indeed, Finance Committee and subcommittee chairs are part of the "leadership team" in both chambers, working closely with the majority leader to pursue the leadership agenda. Constant informal negotiation and discussion occur between committee and subcommittee chairs and the Speaker or president throughout the legislative session to ensure that the approved budget meets the leadership's goals to the maximum extent possible.

Similarly, the governor exerts his or her influence throughout the adoption phase by closely monitoring the legislature and engaging in discussions where issues arise, either through surrogates, such as the secretary of the Department of Administration or gubernatorial staff, or personally. Often, the most important negotiations in this phase occur between the governor and the legislative leadership. Although they have little formal role in this phase (i.e., the veto, and scheduling the budget bill for floor consideration, respectively), the governor and legislative leaders dominate it through their informal and indirect influence.

Once the negotiations and modifications are complete, the Finance Committees compile their subcommittee reports and officially report their versions of the budget bill to their respective chambers. There is usually some debate on the chamber floor to clarify certain provisions of the bill and to give those who have lost out in the negotiations a chance to vent their frustration. But because all members know that more changes are still to be made in the budget bill, floor voting is usually pro forma, with few amendments being passed.

There are inevitably major discrepancies between the House and Senate versions of the budget bill. Since the budget, like any bill, must pass both chambers in precisely the same form, a conference committee is necessary to work out the differences. The Speaker and the president each appoint to this committee six key members of their respective Finance Committees, and the conference committee cochairs are traditionally the chairs of the Finance Committees. The conferees meet in public sessions to negotiate a budget bill upon which both chambers can agree. This occurs in the last few days of the legislative session, often after the constitutionally allotted session length has expired, requiring the governor to extend the session for consecutive three-day periods by executive order.

The floor vote on the conference budget report is usually the session's last legislative act, so there is pressure on the conference committee members to conclude their negotiations, yet each chamber's representatives try to hold out for a budget that resembles its chamber's bill as closely as possible. This balancing act leads to long, tough negotiating sessions as the conferees work through each account in turn, arriving at agreement and then closing that account.

Finally, after several days of negotiations, the conferees agree to a bill and report this compromise to each chamber. No amendments are allowed, and the bill is usually passed with no further difficulty on a roll call vote by a majority of the members elected, as required by statute.

The bill is then sent to the governor for approval. Although the governor's budgetary veto powers are strong, consisting of both the line-item and reduction vetoes, with two-thirds of the elected members of each chamber required to override a veto, they are rarely used because of the governor's involvement in the budgetary process and the legislature's limited changes to the governor's budget proposal. The use of the veto can vary, depending on the governor's relationship with the legislature. For example, during the 1970s and the 1980s Republican Arch Moore used the budgetary vetoes to a much greater extent than his Democratic successors.

Once the governor signs the budget bill, it becomes the state's official budget for the upcoming fiscal year. The legislature then develops the Digest of the Enrolled Budget Bill to present executive agencies with the "intent of the legislature" on some of the details of the coming year's budget, suggesting how the agencies should spend money, especially in the budget's unclassified lines. The *budget digest*, as it is known, is written after the legislative session by the staff of the Finance Committees and the Legislative Auditor's office, with the final approval coming from members of the budget conference committee. Until 1992, only the cochairs of the committee approved this document, but the Supreme Court of Appeals ruled that this is an unconstitutional abdication of legislative power, and required both conference committees to approve the budget digest in public session.[14]

The legislature uses the budget digest as an alternative to imbedding all legislative instruction into the budget bill because it is difficult to develop such detailed instructions before the session ends. The broad strokes painted in the budget bill, characterized by large amounts of money in unclassified line items, are difficult enough to compromise upon. The more detailed the instructions, the more controversy and the longer and more difficult the negotiations. Moreover, the budget digest adds a degree of flexibility to the budget. It can list specific levels of appropriation, but because it does not have the force of law, no new legislation has to be passed to modify it. However, executive agency officers consider the budget digest instructions seriously in their expenditure decisions, as the Finance Committees will have a say in their budgets for the following year.[15] In this way, the budget digest becomes a firm but flexible set of guidelines for executive discretionary spending of unclassified line items.

BUDGET IMPLEMENTATION AND ADMINISTRATION

The administration of the budget begins after the official budget for the coming fiscal year has been finalized. Although this phase of the budget process is less visible to the public than the adoption phase, decisions are often made during the administration of the budget that have an important impact on state policy.

After the budget digest is completed but prior to the start of the fiscal year on 1 July, the budget officer of each spending agency is required to submit to the Budget Office a quarterly allotment request for the coming fiscal year. Deviations from this request, especially requests for more money, need to be justified thoroughly. The Budget Office then prepares a monthly expenditure schedule for each agency and compares these schedules to the month-by-month estimate of revenue that the Budget Office prepares to see where potential gaps may arise during the upcoming year. These comparisons are made continuously throughout the fiscal year to keep the Budget Office and its director up to date regarding future balances of accounts.

It is the responsibility of the secretary of the Department of Administration to ensure that the state's accounts are balanced on a daily basis, so his or her agent, the director of the Budget Office, watches this carefully. As potential revenue shortfalls are identified throughout the year, agencies can be instructed to put off certain nonessential spending to a later date.

Spending agencies are also required to submit requests for quarterly budget allocations to the Budget Office thirty days before each quarter, which must be pursuant to their expenditure schedules. If the director of the Budget Office, the secretary of the Department of Administration, and the governor conclude that the revenues for a quarter will not cover allocations, the governor must rescind the rest of the year's allocations by equal rates for all agencies, with special consideration for education accounts. These cuts are made unilaterally, with no legislative approval, but the governor typically consults with legislative leaders before doing so. Since these cuts apply to all programs equally, this budget rescission power is useful in ensuring a balance of accounts rather than in affecting the state's policy priorities. A midyear budget rescission took place four times between 1989 and 1994, much to the consternation of the state's agencies and taxpayers.

To make an appropriation, an agency submits a requisition to the Budget

Office, where it is checked against the agency's expenditure schedule, the budget act, and the budget digest. Once the appropriation is approved, the auditor, acting as a controller, checks if the expenditure is congruent with the budget act and if there is sufficient money in the particular account before authorizing the treasurer to issue the check.

On 30 June the fiscal year comes to an end. No claims may be made on the state's budget that have not been incurred on or before this date. Payments are issued throughout July, but after 31 July all appropriations for the previous fiscal year are vacated, and no more claims may be submitted to the Budget Office. Any remaining claims for the fiscal year just ended must be brought before the Court of Claims, with payment, if approved, issued from the following year's budget. This great delay in paying late claims gives vendors, agencies, and other claimants strong incentive to submit their claims in a timely manner.

The budget cycle for a given fiscal year does not end until a series of post-audits is undertaken. These are primarily fiscal audits, designed to ensure propriety in the expenditure of the state's funds. The Legislative Auditor's office oversees these audits, usually contracting them out to private accounting firms since the Legislative Auditor's office employs only seventeen auditors.

The low level of staffing in the Legislative Auditor's Office helps to explain why so few performance audits have been undertaken in recent years. Performance audits examine not just the fiscal propriety of an expense but also whether the expenditure had the expected program results.[16] Many states regularly conduct performance audits to provide feedback on program effectiveness and budgetary efficiency. Recognizing the need for performance audits, the legislature established a ten-person legislative staff office called the Legislative Research and Performance Evaluation Division in 1993 to conduct performance audits and related policy implementation and evaluation analysis. Under a schedule established by the joint Committee on Government Operations, the new legislative office now conducts performance audits once every six years for about 120 agencies or agency divisions. Besides recommending changes in agency operations, it offers advice to the legislature on the termination of programs in conjunction with an agency's sunset law review.

West Virginia's budget process is a long and extremely complicated set of interactions among most of the state's major governmental participants. It is the fundamental rhythm of the state government. The recurrent themes of the state budget process arise from the overriding characteristics of the state's fiscal situation: a steadily increasing demand for services and a consistent lack of adequate fiscal resources to meet all of these demands. After years of working in an environment of fiscal austerity, West Virginia budgeteers have settled into a stable set of roles that allow everyone in the process to anticipate the actions of others and plan for the future. In this sense, the predictable nature of the fiscal environment produces less conflict than might be the case in a state with rapidly changing resources or needs. Although the budget process has evolved as a workable response to severe revenue constraints, it is not an optimal process. The lack of adequate analytic information, whether in the budget document or legislative and Budget Office staff resources, reduces the scope of the policy alternatives considered by state officials and their capability to evaluate their options. The incremental modification of budgets also limits the state's ability to respond adequately to changing public needs. Finally, the continual scrambling for small amounts of money, especially the chipping away at the numbers of state employees and the stripping of account balances by the legislature, puts increased stress on the governmental process. A decade or more of fiscal austerity has taken its toll by causing high levels of turnover in budgeteers in all phases of the process and by decreasing the margin of safety between cash on hand and incurred expenses.

CHAPTER NINE

The Judiciary

The just resolution of disputes is one of the most important services provided by government. Although legislative and executive branch officials resolve disputes, the judiciary resolves most two-party private disputes and some more complex public disputes. The judiciary's capacity to resolve disputes and other legal conflicts often plays a critical role in West Virginia's public policymaking.[1] This chapter examines the duties and responsibilities of the Supreme Court of Appeals, the circuit courts, the magistrate courts, and the family law masters.

THE STRUCTURE OF THE WEST VIRGINIA JUDICIARY

The Supreme Court of Appeals is the state's only appellate court. Its five justices review trial court decisions and certain other adjudications. All appellants must petition the justices to docket (list) the case for consideration. Thus, the Supreme Court, by majority vote, has complete discretion over its docket.

West Virginia's thirty-one circuit courts, with exclusive jurisdiction over all criminal, civil, and juvenile matters except torts (accidents and other personal injuries), small claims about contracts, and misdemeanors, serve as the state's comprehensive trial courts of general jurisdiction. The state's magistrate courts have countywide jurisdiction over criminal matters and small civil claims. The legislature specifies the magistrates' duties, salaries, and other requirements, and prohibits immediate family members from serving as magistrates in the same county. It also requires magistrates to complete a course of instruction after their election and to attend continuing education sessions or be subject to penalties imposed through the state's system of judicial discipline.

The Reorganization Amendment of 1974 allowed cities and towns to establish municipal courts with jurisdiction over municipal ordinances, especially local traffic ordinances. In 1986 the legislature created a unique family law master system to fulfill its responsibilities under the federal Child Support Enforcement Amendments of 1984. Child support issues have a critical effect on public welfare costs and on the deeply personal conflicts related to divorce and child custody. Family law masters are attorneys appointed for twenty-one regions of the state for four-year terms by the governor. Two masters serve in Kanawha County.

The Reorganization Amendment of 1974 kept the number of justices of the Supreme Court of Appeals at five but allowed the legislature to determine the number of circuits and circuit judges. The legislature has gradually increased the number of circuit judges from thirty to sixty-two and changed the number of circuits to thirty-one. Although court is held in every county, fourteen circuits include more than one county, and thirteen circuits have only one judge. There are currently 152 magistrates. Today, the constitution apportions at least two magistrates to each county and provides the more populous counties additional magistrates through an apportionment scheme. The Supreme Court of Appeals retains the authority to reassign judges and magistrates from one circuit or county to another on a temporary basis. Also, to reduce caseloads, it can assign senior circuit and Supreme Court of Appeals judges to try cases.

Several offices provide administrative support for the judiciary, the most important of which is the Administrative Office of the Supreme Court of Appeals. This office manages the money appropriated for all courts and determines judicial branch personnel policies, including compensation, job classification, and health and retirement policies.[2] Circuit courts receive most of their finances from the state, but bailiffs and security personnel, courtrooms, and office space are provided by county commissions. The clerk of courts, an elected county post, manages case filings and case records and collects court fees. Circuit judges can appoint commissioners in chancery and general receivers, official reporters, and jury commissioners. Official court reporters are employees of the Supreme Court of Appeals and are subject to its "regulation, control, and discipline."[3] Magistrate court clerks, assistants, and deputy clerks can be assigned to serve the magistrate court by the judge or chief judge of the circuit court for that county.

THE TRIAL JUDICIARY: THE CIRCUIT COURTS, MAGISTRATE COURTS, AND FAMILY LAW MASTERS

The Judicial Reorganization Amendment of 1974 retained the historical process of electing the judiciary by partisan ballot. Supreme Court justices serve staggered twelve-year terms and circuit judges serve eight-year terms, with all circuit judges being selected in the same election year. Supreme Court justices must be admitted to the practice of law for ten years prior to election, while circuit court judges must be admitted to legal practice for five years. A 1992 survey of the state's circuit judges revealed that they had a median of twenty-four years of legal practice, ranging from five to forty-three years.[4] The median years of service as a circuit judge was seven. Most of the judges (75.6 percent) were in private practice immediately before their election as judges.

Magistrates are not required to possess a law degree. In the 1992 survey only three magistrates (2.9 percent) reported that they possessed a law degree, while 22.9 percent had earned a college degree, 45.7 percent claimed some college level instruction, 24.8 percent held only a high school diploma, and 3.8 percent possessed a GED The majority of magistrates (52.4 percent) had a career in the private sector prior to their election, while 20.0 percent were civil servants and 12.4 percent held other elected office. The range of careers was diverse, from farmer to police officer to homemaker.

The survey also revealed that circuit judges and magistrates are politically active and aware. Nearly half (46.3 percent) of the circuit judges but only 16.2 percent of the magistrates said that they considered themselves to be politicians. However, nearly half of the magistrates reported they were either very involved or involved to some extent with their county party organization. Less than one-quarter of the circuit judges said that they were either very or somewhat involved with their county party organization. Magistrates also reported they spent more time campaigning for office (52.9 percent spent more than nine hours a week) than did the circuit judges (41.7 percent spent more than nine hours a week). Thus, it appears that many magistrates act like politicians even if they do not consider themselves to be politicians. Circuit judges and magistrates also reported that they pay a great deal of attention to the legislature's actions, communicate regularly with at least one member of the legislature, and discuss all sorts of political issues with legislators. They reported having few contacts with other public officials.

West Virginia's judiciary, like the judiciaries of other states, remains overwhelmingly white and male. Franklin Cleckley became the first black justice of the Supreme Court of Appeals when he was appointed to fill a vacancy in 1994. There are only three black circuit judges. Only one of the magistrates responding to the 1992 survey chose black as a racial identity, and no other judges or magistrates identified themselves as members of another racial group. Despite the election of a female justice to the Supreme Court of Appeals in 1988, in 1994 there was only one female circuit judge. However, 49 (31.4 percent) of the magistrates were female. Of the circuit judges responding to the 1992 survey, 82.9 percent had attended the West Virginia University College of Law, the state's only law school.

Like most other states, West Virginia has taken steps to train new judges. The Supreme Court of Appeals encourages and financially supports the training of circuit judges in various out-of-state programs, such as the American Academy of Judicial Education and the National Judicial College, which offer courses on court procedural and operational management. Also, circuit judges are required to attend two three-day state judicial conferences that feature presentations on changes in current state law, federal decisions affecting state court procedures, and other timely topics.[5] Magistrates must attend yearly conferences and scheduled training sessions run by firms under contract to the Supreme Court of Appeals or face disciplinary action.

The West Virginia Trial Judiciary at Work

The term *courtroom work group* is often used to describe the representatives of the various independent offices that interact to adjudicate or settle legal conflicts. What is striking about the majority of courtroom work groups in West Virginia is their small membership. According to the 1992 survey, most circuit judges (60.0 percent) work in a circuit with only one or two judges. This means that circuit judges generally handle a case throughout its adjudication, from pleading to remedy. Similarly, the vast majority of magistrates work in counties with two or three magistrates. In 1995 only eleven counties had more than three magistrates, thirteen counties had three magistrates, and thirty-one counties had only two magistrates. However, circuit judges and magistrates occasionally sit outside their circuit or county.

West Virginia has a small bar of about 3,100 active attorneys; 1,129 (36 percent) practice privately or work for the government in Kanawha County. Most attorneys graduated from the West Virginia University College of Law (approximately 75 percent) and work in small partnerships or as solo practitioners. The effect of a small bar is seen in the composition of courtroom work groups. In their most recent fifty civil cases, the magistrates reported the appearance of fewer than fifteen different attorneys as plaintiff attorneys 88.6 percent of the time and fewer than fifteen different attorneys appearing as defendant attorneys 87.6 percent of the time. Circuit judges reported contacts with more attorneys: 46.4 percent saw more than thirty different plaintiff attorneys and 29.3 percent saw more than thirty different defense attorneys in their most recent fifty civil cases. However, when compared to data from a national judicial survey, the number of lawyers appearing before each West Virginia court was low.[6] In criminal cases, the circuit judges and magistrates see the same county prosecuting attorney or assistant prosecuting attorney in case after case.

Currently, criminal defense counsel for indigent persons is provided either by one of thirty-two public defenders assigned to eleven of the thirty-one judicial circuits or by judicially appointed attorneys. The public defender system is a relatively new feature of the court system. Only three public defender offices operated prior to 1990, and the establishment of a branch of this system in all circuits remains incomplete. Data from the 1991 fiscal year indicate that public defenders appeared in only about four percent of nontraffic criminal cases heard by circuit and magistrate courts and only about fifteen percent of all cases where counsel was appointed for indigent persons. The public defender system is directed by a small state agency called Public Defender Services. Selection of appointed defense counsel and control of its services remain with the circuit judges. However, Public Defender Services compensates and audits the expenses of the judicially appointed defense counsel.[7]

Most of the cases on the dockets of circuit judges and magistrates do not go to trial and are settled out of court. For example, in FY 1995 approximately 2 percent of the sixty thousand cases filed in circuit courts were decided by a bench trial and another 2 percent were decided by jury trial. The figures are even smaller for the magistrate courts. Fewer than one hundred of their three hundred thousand filed cases were settled by a jury trial and less than 1 percent by bench trial.

The Family Law Masters

The legislature created the West Virginia family law master system in response to federal legislation designed to enforce child support orders and reduce federal welfare spending for children with absent fathers. The family law masters, acting as agents of the circuit court judges, serve as part-time officers to whom the judge of the local circuit court refers matters affecting the assignment of child custody and disputes about child custody, parental visitation rights, child support payments, and paternity. All masters are attorneys. They receive limited yearly training from a supervisor in the Administrative Office and are free to adopt local rules of practice and documentation within the confines of the law.[8]

Because family law master districts do not often correspond to the boundaries of circuit courts, the masters often serve under the jurisdiction of two or three chief circuit judges. Upon motion, circuit judges can revoke the referral of a case to a master. The family law masters are in frequent contact with Child Advocates, the children's support enforcement arm of the state's Department of Human Services. Child Advocates offer alternative mediation and counseling so parties can avoid taking post-divorce or other child support matters to the family law master, enforce and collect child support and medical support obligations, and establish the paternity of illegitimate children. These functions are performed both for welfare recipients to offset the cost of child welfare payments under what is called the "IV-D" program and, in a more limited fashion, for other parties.[9]

Judicial Performance, Ethics, and Discipline

Other than elections, there is no procedure for evaluating judicial performance. The Supreme Court of Appeals does, however, exert some control over circuit judge behavior through appellate review and through its power to hold circuit judges in contempt of court for actions counter to Supreme Court of Appeals orders.[10] It can also censure or temporarily suspend any justice, judge, or magistrate for violation of ethical rules and can retire judges when eligible by age or when physically or mentally incapacitated.

Recommendations for disciplinary action against justices, judges, and magistrates begin with complaints received by the state's Judicial Investigation Commission.[11] After consideration of the evidence about a complaint mustered by its counsel at one of about six meetings a year, the commission can choose, by majority vote, to file a complaint with the Judicial Hearing Board. The board considers the complaint and will hold a public hearing if the complaint cannot be resolved by prehearing action. If it finds an ethical violation, it can recommend the judge's admonishment, public or private reprimand, temporary suspension from duties for up to a year, a fine of up to $5,000, or retirement if the judge is incapacitated. The Supreme Court of Appeals then decides whether to enforce the Judicial Hearing Board's recommendation. Magistrates can be removed after conviction of a felony, a misdemeanor involving moral turpitude, or a willful violation of statutory duties or court rules established by the Supreme Court of Appeals.

Community Relations

Judges and magistrates are significant public figures in any community, and because they are elected officials, they might desire to maintain their prestige as a resource for use in a reelection bid. However, when surveyed about external scrutiny of their activities, only 51.3 percent of the responding circuit judges and only 42.7 percent of the responding magistrates reported hotly contested judicial elections in which their actions might be challenged. Only 58.5 percent of respondent judges and 43.8 percent of the magistrates reported extensive newspaper coverage of their court. Because of their office's prestige and their desire to meet voters, circuit judges and magistrates must spend some time associating with the public. The judicial survey indicated that most of the judges and magistrates spend between one and eight hours per month on community relations activities. Also, judges have the opportunity to devote time to professional bar associations. However, 46.3 percent of the judges reported they devoted no time to organized bar activities, and 39.0 percent devoted only one or two hours a month to such activities. As attorneys, judges must be members of the West Virginia State Bar; however, only six claimed membership in the American Bar Association.

The Disposition of Cases

The ultimate measure of the quality of any political organization is its policy product. Most frequently, the judicial policy product is the settlement of personal disputes and the penalization of criminal law offenders. As with courts nationally, in the period between 1978 and 1991 both the circuit and the magistrate courts in West Virginia saw an increase in case dispositions. The increase in cases was most noticeable in the number of criminal cases, especially because statutes redefined some traffic offenses involving alcohol use as crimes. However, most of these cases ended with a disposition arranged by the parties, including 96.3 percent of the cases filed in circuit courts and 89.9 percent of the cases filed with magistrates. Most of the criminal cases were bargained to a guilty plea by prosecutors, and most civil cases were settled by negotiations between the parties, were not pursued by parties, or were dismissed by judges. Thus, the attrition of cases is enormous. Consequently, magistrates and circuit judges have relatively limited opportunity to enforce, adjust, or innovate local legal policy; they primarily manage the routine disposition of disputes.

THE SUPREME COURT OF APPEALS

The Supreme Court of Appeals is the court of last resort for disputes arising under the laws of West Virginia. It is the state's only appellate court, with the power to review and possibly correct the decisions of the state's circuit courts and some administrative agency decisions. With only one exception, all of the justices elected to the Supreme Court during the past twenty years have been Democrats, and most were active in partisan politics prior to their election. Since 1970 only five Republican justices have served briefly on the court, all initially appointed by Republican governor Arch Moore to fill vacancies. With one exception, they lost their seats in the next general election. The elected Republican resigned to accept a federal judgeship.

Because a decided majority of the registered voters in West Virginia are Democrats, the most important electoral contests for seats on the court in recent memory have occurred in the Democratic primary. The 1988 Democratic primary earned a dubious place in the folklore of the state's legal community. In contrast to previous elections, the court's policy role was a prominent campaign issue. The candidates' sizable campaign expenditures also made the election unique. The three challenger candidates (Fred Fox, John Hey, and Margaret Workman) labeled the two incumbent candidates (Darrell McGraw and Thomas Miller) as activists who made decisions that went beyond proper limits of judicial power. The incumbents were accused of using the court to make policies that aided special interests such as labor unions, personal injury claimants, workers' compensation claimants, and criminal defendants. The Democratic challengers all promised to act in a more restrained manner if they were elected to the court. The candidates spent a total of $749,000 during the primary, forcing many of them to seek financial and other assistance from various interest groups.[12]

The 1988 primary election suggests that West Virginia's judicial elections are not always low-key political events. When organized and well-financed interests perceive that they have been damaged by a justice, they will move to oust the justice. In this regard, the 1988 Supreme Court of Appeals primary was not unusual when compared to the costly nonpartisan Supreme Court elections in Ohio or Supreme Court judicial retention elections in California. Nevertheless, the cost of running for office concerns the justices of the court and the members of the state bar.[13] For example, one justice indicated in an interview with the authors that "I don't like the idea of having to raise the kind of money we have to raise." Despite their recognition that the cost of campaigns can create potential conflicts of interest, they indicated that elections have a positive side. As one former justice noted, "In general, elected judges tend to be slightly more populist than appointed judges. In general, elected judges tend to be more substantially accommodating to the people who appear in their court because they're also their constituents."[14]

Appellate Review Procedures

The five members of the Supreme Court of Appeals determine the scope and pace of their work. As amended in 1974, the West Virginia Constitution gives the Supreme Court jurisdiction in cases in which appellants petition for appeal, petition the justices for relief by seeking legal documents called writs of certiorari, habeas corpus, mandamus, or prohibition that affects state executive branch operations or the enforcement of the law, and when parties request certification of a legal question from a case under consideration by a circuit court. The justices decide by majority vote whether to grant these petitions or other documents necessary for the initiation of review. Thus, they have complete discretion to fix their docket or the list of cases that they review.

A court's role in public policymaking depends on the kinds of disputes it confronts. In recent years there has been an increasing demand on American courts for the resolution of all sorts of public and private disputes, and the Supreme Court of Appeals has not been immune to this trend. Applications for review filed with the Supreme Court of Appeals rose from 1,159 in 1983 to 3,180 in 1991. Much of the increased demand for review came from parties seeking review of workers' compensation cases. In 1991, 61.2 percent of appeals to the court involved workers' compensation cases. The remaining appeals involved civil cases (16.5 percent), criminal cases (5.7 percent), habeas corpus cases (4.7 percent), and other cases (11.9 percent). During the 1980s, the court also heard more cases, increasing both the number of petitions for review granted from 397 in 1980 to 973 in 1991 and the number of cases docketed for decision from 66 in 1969 to 588 in 1989.[15] As the press of business has increased, the justices have moved from the constitutionally mandated two sessions a year to nearly continuous sessions. In 1989 the increased caseload resulted in the disposition of 281 cases by a signed opinion, reflecting a detailed response to the cases by the court.

Despite the increasing caseload, the Supreme Court of Appeals has not moved to reduce the number of cases it reviews by being more selective when screening cases for review. Data collected by the National Center for State Courts indicate that the Supreme Court of Appeals is more likely than any other court of last resort in the nation to grant discretionary petitions for review. Given the court has no mandatory jurisdiction and that the total appellate filings per capita are only slightly above the national mean, these figures suggest that the justices are creating greater opportunities for the court to affect a wide range of law and policy matters. Indeed, they sometimes even accept *pro se* petitions for review from unrepresented litigants dissatisfied with a circuit court ruling.[16] They have deliberately chosen to be readily accessible to litigant demands.

The Supreme Court's procedural rules deserve special attention because they determine if and how final policy disputes are considered. For the most part, applications for review reach the court from one of four arenas: from the circuit courts, from the Workers' Compensation Appeal Board, from the Judicial Hearing Board, or from the Hearing Panel of the West Virginia State Bar. A very few cases are remanded (returned for further consideration) to the court by federal appeals courts or are certified to the court by federal courts seeking a definitive interpretation of West Virginia law. In 1991 roughly 38 percent of applications for review made to the Supreme Court of Appeals asked for reconsideration of circuit court decisions. West Virginia is among a small number of states that permit an applicant for workers' compensation to appeal an adverse administrative determination directly to the court of last resort rather than to a trial or intermediate appellate court. As mentioned previously, applications for review of workers' compensation decisions account for more than 61 percent of the applications for review filed with the court. Less than 1 percent of cases filed for review deal with the review of decisions about judicial or attorney conduct.

To take a case to the court, litigants must first file copies of a petition for the appropriate form of relief with the clerk of the court. Those seeking a writ must also offer any exhibits or affidavits that support their need for a writ, a memorandum on the legal authority for the writ, and a list of the persons on whom the writ is to be served within four months of the circuit court decision or other action in the case. All respondent parties or their attorneys must then be served with copies of all documents filed by the petitioner. The respondents can then file a response of up to fifty pages in length with the clerk or move to dismiss the appeal. Respondents requesting writs might enter into a procedure called *discovery* to specify the dispute's material facts for the court.

Petitions for review are evaluated not just on the basis of initial briefs or written summaries of their claim but, at the appellants' request, at a "motion" or petition hearing before the justices. Petitioners must schedule the hearing on the court's motion docket within thirty days of the filing of a petition. These hearings are mostly scheduled early in one of the court's two yearly terms, which begin in September and January, or during the special summer term common in recent years. At the hearing the justices inquire into the reasons why the appellant's counsel thinks that the docketing of the case is necessary. Over thirty motions are heard on a typical day when the motion docket is scheduled, and some motions are also heard on days when oral arguments are heard or when a petitioner seeks an extraordinary session. Because many issues are relatively simple, the motion hearing is often less than the court-imposed limit of ten minutes. Despite the rapidity of the hearings, they give attorneys an opportunity to emphasize the merits of their petition directly with the justices or to show cause why they need to have the court issue a writ. Rarely, *pro se* petitioners (those without an attorney) will present the merits of their petition. The justices report that they find the motion hearing to be of great value when determining their vote for review, and some indicated that they rely on it far more than the written briefs when evaluating the merits of a case.[17] This procedure is not used in federal appellate courts. Workers' compensation cases are selected for review without oral presentations.

The court's staff play an important role in processing cases. For example, five staff attorneys, known as writ clerks, prepare summaries or "bench memoranda" on petitions for review that are not presented on the motions docket. The writ clerks also summarize the workers' compensation appeal petitions in memoranda, as they are a special group of cases excluded from the motion docket. Recently, because of the press of court business, the justices' personal and per curiam clerks (whose duties are explained below) have assisted in this task. The memoranda are presented by the writ clerks to the justices. At scheduled conferences, the writ clerks report to the justices' conference room, stand at the end of the conference table opposite the chief justice, and address questions about the petitions for review and memoranda. To facilitate this process, workers' compensation cases do not normally receive oral presentations from a writ clerk unless initial briefs disclose a novel issue.

After the motion hearing or the writ clerk's presentation on the petition and brief, the justices decide by majority vote whether to grant the docketing of a petition for appeal, certification, or a special writ. Two votes for review will suffice when a justice is recused or is incapable of participation because of illness or special circumstances. The vote occurs at the justices' weekly conference in reverse order of seniority on the court. Once the court grants a petition for review, information on transcripts of previous adjudications must be filed by the petitioner with the clerk of the court. Transcripts must be made available to the court after a petition is granted. Petitioners, now called appellants, must also file a brief, a summary of the legal arguments in favor of their claims of error in the lower court or agency, with the clerk of the court and the respondent party. Respondents, now called appellees, have fifteen days to file a brief in response. Parties who do not file a brief in the required time can be sanctioned by the court. The court also allows parties not involved in the litigation to file briefs, called amicus curiae (friend of the court) briefs, to enlighten the justices about the ramifications of the case. State officials and agencies do not need the court's permission to file an amicus brief. Normally those filing an amicus curiae brief do not participate in oral argument.

Some less significant and routine cases feature per curiam opinions, or brief opinions signed "by the Court" after the consideration of briefs but without oral argument. One of the justices assumes the task of sorting out cases for per curiam disposition. Normally these cases raise no novel issues of law and demand no clarification of existing law. The drafting of the seventy to eighty per curiam opinions or orders per year is then assigned in rotation to one of the five per curiam clerks, staff attorneys of the court who are assigned one to each justice.

When the court is in session, it hears motions for review and considers oral arguments on docketed cases, called the "Argument Docket," on Tuesdays and Wednesdays. The amount of time dedicated to hearings and oral arguments decreases during the course of a term as more time is spent on the preparation of opinions. Oral arguments in cases granted review are heard in the courtroom in the East Wing of the state capitol. At oral argument, counsel speak from a podium for periods of up to twenty minutes supervised by the chief justice, but unlike the U.S. Supreme Court, the chief allows occasional latitude in presentation time. Appellants are also allocated up to ten minutes rebuttal time. Appellees have no rebuttal time. The justices typically intervene in counsel's presentation with numerous questions about a case, so much so that counsel often try to state the key themes of their argument in simple declarative sentences at the opening of their presentation.

Thursdays are reserved for the conference, at which the justices, after ruling on petitions for review, consider the cases argued that week. The discussion of cases opens with the justice assigned a particular case and then proceeds with the comments of the other justices in reverse seniority and additional colloquy that the justices describe as both open and frank. Once the discussion of a case is concluded, a vote is taken in reverse order of seniority. A justice in the majority then writes the Opinion of the Court for the case. The assignment of opinion-writing duties rotates sequentially so that each justice writes in every fifth case in which she or he is in the majority. Justices will occasionally trade their assignments, primarily to allow them to write on topics in which they have expertise. They can also write dissenting opinions, and, in a rarely exercised option, can write concurring opinions that support the majority's decision for different legal reasons. The court's opinions are similar in form and length to those of other state supreme courts.

Each justice has one or two personal law clerks to assist with petitions and the accompanying briefs and the drafting and documentation of opinions. These personal clerks, usually recent law school graduates, normally serve for a year. When a justice has a draft Opinion of the Court ready, it is circulated to the other justices, who usually discuss their opinions personally with each other before releasing the final opinion. Almost all cases are disposed of either during the term they are filed or within six months of the initial filing of the case with the clerk. Such rapidity led one justice to remark, "This is probably the fastest court of appeals in the world."[18]

Although many state courts of last resort rotate the chief justiceship, West Virginia's Supreme Court of Appeals is the only one that does so yearly on the basis of seniority of service.[19] Because the chief justice lacks the internal control of opinion assignment held by the Chief Justice of the U.S. Supreme Court and because the court is such a small body, the West Virginia chief justice's primary duties are administrative. The chief manages the conduct of oral argument and the conference, keeping track of votes and case assignments. Importantly, the chief justice assumes the supervision and oversees the agenda of special projects for the Administrative Office for the year.

Building Support for the Supreme Court

The justices engage in several activities to ensure the court's independence and the preservation of its duties. The concern for reelection encourages the justices to keep in touch with the public. For example, unlike the members of the U.S. Supreme Court, the justices, for the most part, are willing to speak with members of the media and are also more likely to make presentations at public events. They also maintain an informal liaison with the state legislature and regularly communicate with the president of the Senate, the Speaker of the House, and the chairs of the House and Senate Finance Committees about the judicial branch budget and legislation affecting the courts. They also report occasional informal contact with the governor's staff and, more rarely, with federal judges and the judiciary of other states. Supreme Court justices frequently interact with circuit court judges at judicial conferences, bar meetings, and social events and when the judges come to the capitol to attend to business with the Administrative Office. In West Virginia, judicial independence does not appear to be threatened by the court's partisan election or by its contacts with other officeholders. However, the partisan electoral system does produce justices with an acute awareness of the political nature of their actions and with an openness to the public.

A second important maintenance function of the Supreme Court of Appeals is the development of policies about the management of the state judiciary and state bar, including policies in situations of procedural rule making, fiscal and staff management, and oversight of the ethics of the bench and bar. The justices' decisions on court management seemingly affect only the internal work of courts but have an important but rarely visible effect on West Virginians' ability to find relief for their grievances in court. The Judicial Reorganization Amendment of 1974 gave the Supreme Court of Appeals broad authority to determine policy on a wide range of the procedural aspects of judicial administration. The court was empowered to "promulgate rules" and to exercise "general supervisory control" over all state courts. The supervisory power permitted the creation of what is commonly called a "unified court system" in which administrative authority for the judiciary is vested in a single court or individual. Using this power, which also made the chief justice the administrative head of all courts, the Supreme Court of Appeals has substantially altered the conduct of judicial business in the state. The court has used its capacity to promulgate procedural rules to define public access to the courts, court operations, court costs, and the evidence that a party might present in arguing its case.

The 1974 amendment also gave the Supreme Court of Appeals control over its personnel and some authority to establish policies governing many of the state courts' nonjudicial employees. The head of the Administrative Office, the administrative director, manages the court's personnel and finances and handles minor inquiries about the court. The director also prepares with the justices the budget for all courts, discusses the budget with legislative leaders, and prepares new and modified court rules.

The Supreme Court of Appeals was granted responsibility in a 1945 state statute for the regulation of legal practice and the creation of an "administrative agency of the supreme court of appeals . . . known as 'the West Virginia state bar.' "[20] Consequently, the court can establish policies affecting the nature and availability of legal services in the state. The Board of Law Examiners, an arm of the Supreme Court of Appeals, supervises lawyers, who must join, pay dues to, and submit to the regulations of the West Virginia State Bar, a quasi-governmental body. The state bar's tasks include the supervision of legal ethics, its "highest priority," the management of programs for the mandatory twenty-four hours of continuing legal education required yearly for all bar members, the management of a program that provides funds for free civil legal assistance in the state, the pro bono (free) legal assistance referral project, and the pursuit of proposals for legal or judicial reform suggested by its many committees.[21] Also, to fulfill the court's supervisory responsibility, the chief justice meets quarterly with the leadership of the state bar. The administrative director of the court and the executive director of the state bar also hold monthly meetings to address matters deemed to be of concern.[22] This informal supervision and consultation with the state bar appears to be similar to or more intensive than that in the other integrated bar states. The Supreme Court of Appeals also has the responsibility to police the state bar. It established Rules for the Admission to the Practice of Law in 1973 and Rules of Professional Conduct. State bar findings and recommendations about lawyer's ethical problems are sent to the Supreme Court of Appeals, which affords the lawyer in question a hearing and an opportunity to raise objections to the findings. Then, the court can order a reprimand, suspension, or removal of the lawyer's license to practice law in the state.[23] In this way, the justices can maintain the reputation of the state's legal profession.

The Supreme Court of Appeals and Public Policy

The Supreme Court of Appeals has emerged as a significant entity in state policymaking on a number of important issues.[24] Its decisions since the Reorganization Amendment went into effect in 1976 can be categorized as being either innovative (creating a new doctrine), incremental (expanding or contracting an existing doctrine), reinforcing (reiterating an existing doctrine, known as stare decisis), or involutional (compounding the complexity of the law). Examples of each of these forms of policy choice are presented to provide evidence of the court's role in public policymaking.

Most of the Supreme Court's decisions fall into the reinforcing and involutional categories. For example, the justices have chosen to reinforce interpretations in the meaning of the law concerning sales and related transactions in the state.[25] Also, the court has tended to elaborate on the dictates of the federal Constitution and the standards set by the U.S. Supreme Court. This is especially true for cases involving the federal Fourteenth Amendment's privileges and immunities clause, its exclusionary rule standards, and federal *Miranda* rules.[26] For example, in rejecting "palimony" cases, the court refused to develop new doctrine fashioned by other courts when the doctrine contravened West Virginia common law and statutes.[27] Finally, as with its support of most aspects of the legislature's preparation of the budget digest, it can choose to avoid policy pronouncements about important legislative practices. Most of the court's decisions thus either reinforce established policies about adjudication or elaborate on the approved models of procedure and evidentiary analysis.

The court occasionally makes decisions that fall into the incremental category, especially when it interprets or clarifies statutory language, adjusts common-law doctrines, or elaborates on legal standards set by the U.S. Supreme Court or other federal courts. For example, the Supreme Court of Appeals clarified state statutes on the assignment of real property and financial contributions for child support and complemented child custody law by adopting the primary caretaker rule. The rule effectively met legislative guidelines eliminating gender-based presumptions in awarding custody, but because mothers usually are the primary caregivers, it complemented the statute by introducing an additional policy guideline often favorable to maternal custody.[28] The justices also complemented child support statutes by permitting circuit judges extensive contempt powers to enforce child support orders.[29] The justices read custody law so the fathers of illegitimate children could have standing to seek visitation rights.[30] The justices have also made incremental changes in some federal rulings. Examples include the court's development of two tests to determine if state tax law contravened the federal commerce clause as interpreted by the U.S. Supreme Court and the elaboration of the federal and state right to petition and protest the behavior of a firm to the government without fear of defamation suits.[31] It has also provided more liberal readings of rights than the federal Supreme Court did when construing the U.S. Constitution.[32] These incremental adjustments of federal rulings include the court's recognition of a right to the equal funding of education in all public schools, a right to proportionality in the sentencing of habitual offenders, a right to media access to pretrial hearings, and a due process protection against punishment for addiction to alcohol.[33]

Occasionally, the court has made decisions that fall into the innovative category, especially with cases involving personal injury law. For example, the justices directly adopted a modified comparative negligence doctrine for the remedy of personal injury claims that greatly affected the ability of injured parties to recover money damages in auto accidents.[34] This doctrine rejected the former doctrine of contributory negligence that prohibited injured parties from any recovery for an accident if they incidentally or partially caused the accident. The new doctrine allowed a more generous proportional recovery for parties contributing to an accident if their damages were less than 50 percent of the total accident losses.

The court also revolutionized products liability law by adopting a rule of strict liability that made the manufacturer responsible for harms caused by all types of products, not the narrow range of products called "inherently" dangerous by the old common law of torts.[35] Additionally, the court adopted the "crashworthiness doctrine," which is more liberal to plaintiffs in automobile products liability cases.[36] Through changes like these, the justices have steered West Virginia's law to favor victims of harms more than in the past. The justices have also significantly liberalized the ability of workers to recover for injuries by narrowing the immunity of employers from suits by injured workers. The court has held that workers can sue for injuries caused by intentional employer negligence or wanton, willful, and reckless misconduct in addition to the compensation achieved through workers' compensation.[37]

The Supreme Court of Appeals has also engaged in innovation in cases dealing with education finance. In *Pauley v. Kelly,* it ruled in favor of parents in Lincoln County who filed a class action lawsuit against the state treasurer, contending that the state education funding system denied their children their Fourteenth Amendment right to the equal protection of the laws and contravened state constitutional provisions on education finance. The court, relying on a provision in Article XII Section I of the state constitution requiring a "thorough and efficient system of free schools," concluded that the constitutional provision demonstrated that education is a fundamental constitutional right in the state. Any discrimination or classification with regard to the exercise of the right can stand only if there is a compelling state interest to justify the unequal classification. Turning to the pattern of state financing and the Lincoln County system, the court ordered the circuit court that had tried the case to examine inequities in state financial assistance formulas that governed the distribution of state aid to local districts, in supplemental state aid for local districts, property tax appraisal, allocation of funds from the state school-building fund, and the roles of state and local officials in affecting the efficiency of the school's operations.[38] Later, the court also interpreted the state constitution to require the state to provide a preliminary factual justification before reducing appropriated funding for public schools.[39] These decisions forced the issues of state and local school finance, taxation for education, and education operations onto the state's political agenda. However, the court has recently displayed more caution in education policy disputes. For example, during a state teacher strike in 1990, it refused to become involved in the dispute and limited the power of circuit judges to provide injunctive relief beyond the boundaries of their circuit.[40]

The Supreme Court and the Limits of Judicial Power

Not all government officials think or act alike, yet officials temper their conflicts out of concern for the future of the regime; they are not interested in its destruction. However, sometimes within the federal structure of American government and the separated powers system of West Virginia government, conflicts arise that restrict or revoke the policy choices made by the Supreme Court of Appeals. Despite the court's ability to engage in a variety of forms of policymaking, it sometimes finds that its policy choices meet rejection.

Both the legislature, through constitutional amendments submitted for voter ratification, and the U.S. Supreme Court have overturned some decisions of the Supreme Court of Appeals. For example, the federal Court invalidated a Supreme Court of Appeals decision in 1987 that upheld the decision by the Webster County commissioners, sitting in their capacity as the county's Board of Equalization, to assess a recently purchased coal property at full market value even though other properties in the county were assessed at only a fraction of their full value. Instead, the coal company was told that it could seek to have the other properties in the county reassessed at full market value.[41] Oneida Coal and other firms appealed the court's decision to the U.S. Supreme Court, which unanimously held that the disparities in the assessment of the properties did not satisfy the state's requirement of a uniform tax rate. Additionally, the intentional lack of uniformity created by the county commissioners, as the Board of Equalization, violated the equal protection clause by selecting out some individuals for discriminatory treatment.[42] The U.S. Supreme Court's decision not only chastened the Supreme

Court of Appeals, but it also returned property assessment practices onto West Virginia's political agenda.

Consequently, the Supreme Court of Appeals recognizes that its choices can be rejected or restricted when it chooses policy stasis, as in the case of Oneida Coal, as well as when it chooses policy innovation. Also, the circuit judges and magistrates know that their choices can be rejected or modified by the Supreme Court of Appeals. Although hard data on the frequency of the rejection of any West Virginia judicial choices are hard to come by, the knowledge of the cost of rejection likely limits what policy choices seem feasible to a judge or magistrate. The perception of the costs of rejection promotes policy stasis or involution and a degree of stability in the law. Moreover, like most American judiciaries, the West Virginia courts depend on the parties to a suit to bring policy issues before them. Consequently, the courts can act on major policy problems only when people, firms, or interest groups see a potential advantage in judicial action. Further, courts can provide only limited remedies for people's problems. They work best in acting on interpersonal problems, such as disputes about debts, divorce arrangements, and auto accidents, where a simple order or allocation of monetary damages can resolve the dispute, or in deciding criminal cases. As a result, the judiciary has concentrated its efforts on the efficient processing of ordinary conflicts in ways that do not work innovations into civil or criminal legal law or policy. It sometimes breaks new doctrinal ground or resets the political agenda, as it did for educational finance, but this is the exception, not the rule.

CHAPTER TEN

Local Government

There are 707 local governments in West Virginia, including 55 counties, 55 school districts, 231 municipalities, and 366 special districts. Each is subject to the West Virginia Constitution, which places rather severe limits on their autonomy, saddles them with institutional rules and organizational structures that make it difficult for them to be innovative and creative, and imposes upon them relatively severe fiscal restraints that cause them to be heavily dependent on state assistance. Thus, despite the existence since 1936 of a home rule provision for municipalities with populations of two thousand and more, West Virginia's local governments continue to have a classic unitary relationship with their state government.

COUNTY GOVERNMENTS

The current structure of county government was put into place by a state constitutional amendment, adopted in 1880, clearly establishing that counties were administrative arms of the state government, not autonomous political entities. Their main constitutional duties were to record deeds and other papers presented for record within their geographic boundaries, conduct elections for county and district officers, serve as judges when the outcome of county or district elections were contested or when the qualifications of those running for county or district office were challenged, and assist the state government in the administration of justice by enforcing state laws within the county's boundaries and by providing and maintaining a county jail. They were also allowed to construct and maintain county roads, bridges, public landings, ferries, and mills and to set levy rates on property located within their boundaries to pay for these services.

Although the state government has historically been reluctant to expand county responsibilities, counties have been granted additional authority in several areas over the years. Counties were authorized to fund public libraries in 1915, and beginning in 1929 they were allowed to construct, lease, own, and operate airports. In 1949 they were authorized to construct waterworks, sewer systems, and wastewater treatment plants and to improve streets, alleys, and sidewalks that are not in the state road system. As of 1951 counties were allowed to maintain and operate fire stations and fire prevention units and to establish park and recreation commissions. In 1955 they were given permission to provide garbage disposal services in areas outside of municipalities and operate landfills. In 1959 they were allowed to create county planning and zoning commissions. In 1968 counties were allowed to establish building and housing codes. Since then, counties have been authorized to construct flood walls and make navigation improvements to protect their citizens from floods (1975), provide emergency ambulance services (1975), and fund hospitals and long-term care facilities (1989). They are also allowed to perform several other services related to the maintenance of law and order and the protection and enhancement of public health and welfare.[1]

Although counties have been granted additional responsibilities over the years, the state constitution continues to deny them home rule. The constitution, and subsequent court rulings, have established that counties possess only those powers that are expressly granted to them by the state constitution or by state statute.

County Offices

When West Virginia amended its constitution in 1880, it not only denied counties home rule but also separated county government powers among seven independently elected offices: the county commission, county clerk, circuit clerk (discussed in chapter 9 because their primary duties are with the court system), county sheriff, county assessor, county prosecuting attorney, and county surveyor of lands. The amendment reflected the Jacksonian belief that governments with many elected officers exercising separate powers are less likely to violate the public trust than governments with few elected officials and unified powers. However, plural government offices also make it more difficult for government to respond to citizen demands for services because there is no centralized mechanism to coordinate the various functions performed by the independently elected offices.

The state constitution allows county voters to elect three commissioners on a countywide partisan ballot (Jefferson County is allowed to elect five commissioners). The commissioners act as the county's legislative body and serve six-year terms, staggered so that one commissioner is elected every two years. No two commissioners can reside in the same magisterial district. Commissioners must meet at least four times a year at the county court-house. At the first meeting each year, they elect a president from among themselves to preside over meetings. The president is authorized to call a special session, with the concurrence of at least one other commissioner, whenever he or she believes that the public interest requires it. Most of the county commissions in counties with fewer than ten thousand people meet once or twice a month, most of the county commissions in counties with populations between ten and fifty thousand people meet once a week, and most of the commissions in counties with populations exceeding fifty thousand people meet twice a week. It takes two commissioners to constitute a quorum.

The county commission's primary duties are to determine the annual county budget, submit a balanced budget to the state tax commissioner for approval, set the county's levy rates on property in order to pay for the provision of county services, and serve as the board of equalization of review, which hears appeals concerning the appraisal and assessment of real and personal property in the county. Commissioners also appoint members to numerous advisory boards and commissions and are often involved in economic development projects. They also serve as members of the county court, but the court's jurisdiction was severely curtailed by the Judiciary Amendment of 1880. The commissioners retain jurisdiction only over probate, the appointment and qualification of personal representatives, guardians, and curators, and the settlement of accounts. State statutes require all county commissioners, clerks, assessors, and sheriffs to attend annual in-service training programs sponsored by the state tax commissioner.

County commissioners are considered part-time employees, but the actual time spent on their duties varies widely from commissioner to commissioner. Some commissioners just attend the county commission's meetings and are otherwise rarely seen in the county courthouse, whereas others devote more than forty hours a week to their duties, have an office in the county courthouse, and keep fairly regular office hours. The differences are primarily attributed to the commissioner's individual preferences and are not related to county population or to the size of the county budget.[2] The county commissions in the counties with mid to large populations typically appoint a county coordinator or administrator to handle the day-to-day operations of county governance. Most county coordinators or administrators make personnel decisions (subject to the consent of the county commission), assist in the preparation of the county budget, and make recommendations on policy issues before the commission. County commissioners are currently paid an annual salary that is determined by the total amount of assessed valuation of property in the county. In 1997 commissioners' salaries ranged from $15,000 in class X counties (where the assessed value of property is less than $200 million) to $28,000 in class I counties (with the assessed value exceeding 2 billion).

The county clerk is also elected on a countywide partisan ballot to a six-year term. The clerk serves as the custodian of all county records—including birth and death certificates, probated wills, transfers of property titles, lists of fiduciaries, deeds of convenience, and deeds of trust—and also is responsible for the issuance of licenses required by state government, including business and marriage licenses, and for the general management of elections, including registration of voters and the maintenance of voting machines. County clerks in class I counties are required to be full-time employees. However, most county clerks devote at least forty hours a week to their duties. Their salaries range from $32,000 in class X counties to $42,000 in class I counties.

The county sheriff is elected to a four-year term on a countywide partisan ballot. The sheriff is the only county elected officer who is subject to term limitations. Primarily because of corruption and mismanagement in the past, the state constitution formerly prohibited sheriffs from succeeding themselves in office. Moreover, they were not allowed to serve as a deputy or hold any other public office for at least one year after their term had expired. In 1973 a constitutional amendment relaxed these restrictions somewhat, allowing sheriffs to serve two consecutive terms. Another amendment that would have allowed sheriffs to serve an unlimited number of terms was soundly defeated at the polls in 1982 and again in 1994.

The sheriff's primary duties are to enforce the law and maintain order in the county. However, there are other responsibilities that have been associated with the office since colonial times. For example, the sheriff is the ex officio county treasurer for both the county government and the local school district. As county treasurer, the sheriff receives, collects, and disburses all moneys due to the county and the local school district and is required to keep an accurate account of all receipts and disbursements. Also, as an officer of the circuit court, county court, and any other court of record in the county, the sheriff is responsible for executing process (serving papers for the court), summoning and impaneling juries, and typically attends most, if not all, of the circuit court's sessions. The sheriff is also the county jailer and has custody of all prisoners in the county jail. The sheriff usually appoints, with the consent of the county commission, a deputy sheriff to run the county jail and keep it in "a clean, sanitary, and healthful condition" as required by state statute. The sheriff also auctions off delinquent lands, serves as ex officio county sealer of weights and measures in the absence of a regularly appointed county sealer, and appoints a deputy to serve as the county humane officer. The humane officer is responsible for investigating all complaints concerning the cruel or inhuman treatment of animals within the county.

Sheriffs in class I, II, and III counties are required to be full-time employees, as are all sheriffs with more than four deputies. Also, they are subject to strict guidelines concerning other employment to ensure that they are not subject to a conflict of interest when performing their duties. Their base salaries range from $29,000 in class X counties to $34,000 in class I counties. According to the West Virginia Sheriff's Association, all fifty-five county sheriffs are currently employed on a full-time basis. Sheriffs are also eligible for an annual salary supplement of up to $15,000 if, in their capacity as the county tax collector, they collect more than a predetermined amount established by the county commission.

The county assessor is elected to a four-year term on a countywide partisan ballot. The assessor's primary duties are to appraise at full market value real estate and personal properties owned in the county as of 1 July, keep an accurate account of all appraisals in the county cadaster (record book), and defend these appraisals when they are appealed to the county commission sitting as the county board of equalization and review. The county assessor is also responsible for assessing and collecting a "head" tax on all dogs in the county. Assessors can appoint, with the consent of the county commission, deputy assessors to assist them in their duties.

County assessors currently receive the same base salary as sheriffs, ranging from $29,000 in class X counties to $34,000 in class I counties. As an incentive to collect taxes, they also receive a 10 percent commission from all proceeds from the dog tax and a 10 percent salary increment for conducting the farm census for West Virginia's Department of Agriculture, and are eligible for an additional duties compensation amount (currently $15,000 annually in class I–V counties, $10,000 in class VI–VII counties, $9,000 in class VIII–IX counties, and $6,500 in class X counties) if they meet certain criteria established in state statutes and certified by the state department of Tax and Revenue. State statutes require only county assessors in class I–IX counties to be full-time. However, state statutes also require the county assessor's office to remain open throughout the year. This latter requirement, coupled with the responsibilities of the office, has caused all fifty-five county assessors in West Virginia to devote at least forty hours a week to their duties.[3]

The county prosecuting attorney is elected to a four-year term on a countywide partisan ballot. This is the only county elected officer not required to reside in the county he or she serves. Although the state constitution and enabling legislation do not specifically require the county prosecuting attorneys to be attorneys, the state's courts have ruled that the wording of state statutes imply that they must be attorneys licensed to practice in the state.[4] The county prosecuting attorneys' primary duty is to prosecute violators of the state's criminal laws. They also provide legal advice to the county commission and county school district and represent the county in all civil actions. With the permission of either the county commission, governor, or circuit court, prosecuting attorneys can offer rewards for the apprehension of people charged with crimes. Also, with the permission of the county commission, they can appoint full-time and part-time investigators to supplement the efforts of the county sheriff and other investigative agencies. Prosecuting attorneys are also required by state statute to assist the state attorney general in performing any legal duties that are not inconsistent with their duties as the legal representative of their particular county.

County prosecuting attorneys are the highest-paid county elected officials, with salaries ranging from $35,000 in class X counties to $76,000 in class I counties. Prosecuting attorneys in class I–VII counties are required by state statute to be full-time employees, and they often employ assistant prosecuting attorneys to help manage their caseloads. Prosecuting attorneys in counties with smaller populations can become full-time employees (and be compensated at a higher class level) with the consent of their county commission. There are currently twenty-three full-time prosecuting attorneys in West Virginia.[5] Most prosecutors in the state's smaller counties serve on a part-time basis.

The county surveyor of lands is also elected to a four-year term on a countywide partisan ballot. Although the county commission can hire any state-licensed surveyor to conduct its work, the county surveyor typically conducts most of the county's land surveys, usually involving right-of-ways and alignments of roads and the sale or purchase of county or school district land. The surveyor is also available to resolve disputes over boundary lines, keep all records, except for those that are in the deed books (including road maps, plats, and tracings), compile tax maps for the use of the county assessor and board of equalization and review, and perform any other duties that the county commission deems necessary.[6] Unlike for other county elected officials, the state does not mandate the county surveyor's compensation or indicate whether this must be either a full-time or part-time position. Currently, all county surveyors work on a part-time, on-call basis. After performing a requested service, they charge the county or school district a fee. As a result, their compensation varies from year to year according to the amount of work that they do in each county and the willingness of the county commission to pay what the surveyor requests.

Policy Activity

West Virginia's fifty-five counties spent about $225 million in 1996.[7] The extent of county services varies significantly from county to county, depending primarily on its population. West Virginia's ten counties with less than ten thousand people (Calhoun, Clay, Doddridge, Gilmer, Pendleton, Pleasants, Pocahontas, Tucker, Tyler, and Wirt Counties), for example, spent on average only $1.3 million each in 1996. Nearly all of that money was spent on salaries, supplies, and office expenses for the county's elected officials and the maintenance of the county courthouse and jail. Most of these counties have fewer than twenty employees and provide few services beyond those mandated by state law. West Virginia's thirty-five counties with populations between ten and fifty thousand spent on average $3.3 million each in 1996. Most of that money (75 percent) was spent on salaries, supplies, and office expenses for the county's elected officials and their staff and on the maintenance of the county courthouse and jail. They did, however, provide a greater variety of services than counties with populations below ten thousand. They were more likely than the counties with a smaller population to fund physical and mental health services, ambulance services, fire protection services, industrial parks, libraries, and visitor bureaus.

West Virginia's ten counties with populations exceeding fifty thousand (Berkeley, Cabell, Harrison, Kanawha, Marion, Mercer, Monongalia, Ohio, Raleigh, and Wood Counties) spent on average about $10 million each in 1996. Kanawha County, the state's most populous county with 207,619 residents, spent $25 million and had approximately 360 full-time county employees in 1996. Cabell County, the state's second most populous county with 96,827 residents, spent $10 million and had approximately 270 full-time county employees in 1996. Excluding Kanawha County, the remaining nine high-population counties spent on average about $8 million each.[8]

The state's ten counties with the largest populations offer a much broader range of services than the state's other counties. Seven provide fire protection services, eight sponsor industrial parks, eight offer library services, nine fund visitors' bureaus, seven subsidize the local magistrate courts, eight subsidize the local circuit court, five rent government buildings besides the courthouse and jail, nine finance physical health services, nine provide mental health care, and five sponsor ambulance services. However, salaries, supplies, and office expenses for the counties' elected officials and their staff and maintenance of the county courthouse and jail still account for nearly 60 percent of their total expenditures.

West Virginia's counties do not provide a particularly wide range of services when compared to counties in most other states. Over thirty years ago, a scholar studying West Virginia's county government concluded that county government was not important in West Virginia and that its functions were so few that they were top-heavy with elected officials and clerks.[9] Although counties provide many valuable services for their residents, and some of the state's counties with larger populations now offer many more services than in the past, this description still applies to many of the state's counties, especially those located in the state's most rural areas.

The lack of county services is explained, at least in part, by the large number of sparsely populated counties in the state. However, the state government has also played a key role in limiting the extent of county services. It has imposed a plural government structure on counties that inhibits their ability to respond efficiently to citizen demands for services. It has also placed severe restraints on the capacity of counties to raise revenues and, by denying them home rule, has forced them to seek permission from the state government before they can offer new services.

Revenues and Policy Activity

The West Virginia Constitution places relatively severe fiscal restraints on the state's counties. As in most other states, West Virginia counties are required to have a balanced operating budget. To account for unforeseen circumstances, counties are allowed to incur a "casual deficit," not to exceed its state-approved levy estimate by more than three percent, provided that the deficit is satisfied in the succeeding year. Counties also must follow strict state guidelines when incurring a deficit for capital expenses. For example, the West Virginia Constitution limits all local governments' individual aggregate outstanding bonded indebtedness to five percent of the local government's total assessed value of taxable property. Also, all local government debts must be retired within thirty-four years.

Besides these typical restraints on county revenues, the state government also prohibits counties, and all other local governments, from imposing either an income or sales tax. Moreover, the Tax Limitation Amendment of 1932 placed relatively severe limits on the ability of counties, and all other local governments, to raise revenue through the property tax. The amendment divided real and personal property into four classes and established maximum property tax levy rates for each class, ranging from 50 cents per $100 of assessed value for personal property used in farming to $2 per $100 of assessed value for commercial properties located within municipalities. These property tax levy rates are far below the national average.

The Tax Limitation Amendment of 1932 also established maximum property tax levy rates for each type of local government within the overall limits. For example, the state constitution established a maximum property tax levy rate of $1 per $100 of value for class II properties, which include farm real estate and owner-occupied homes. Counties are allowed to impose a property tax levy rate of up to $0.286 per $100 valuation on class II properties, school districts up to $0.459, municipalities up to $0.25, and the state up to $0.005. Approximately 21.3 percent of property tax revenue in West Virginia goes to counties, 71.5 percent to school districts, 7 percent to municipalities, and 0.3 percent to the state government. The amount sent to each government type and the percentages vary somewhat from year to year depending on changes in the value of properties within each class.

The only way to exceed the maximum property tax levy rates set by the Tax Limitation Amendment of 1932 is through voter-approved excess levies. Counties and municipalities can exceed their maximum property tax levy rates by up to 50 percent for a period of up to three years if 60 percent or more of the county's or municipality's voters approve the excess levy. Several of the state's municipalities and counties with larger populations rely on excess levies to fund public libraries, ambulance services, and their 911 emergency telephone number. School districts can exceed their maximum property tax levy rates by up to 100 percent for a period of up to five years if a majority of the district's voters approve the excess levy. Thirty-nine of West Virginia's fifty-five school districts currently have excess levies, generating over $220 million in additional property tax revenue for schools.

The Property Tax and Homestead Exemption Amendment of 1982 further limits local governments' property tax revenue by exempting the first $20,000 of assessed value of any residence owned by a citizen of the state who is at least sixty-five years old or who is permanently and totally disabled. This reduced property tax collections by approximately $38 million in 1996.[10]

Counties rely heavily on the property tax for most of their revenue. In 1996 property tax revenue accounted for approximately 62 percent of all county revenue ($140 million). The coal severance tax was the next largest revenue source ($17 million).[11]

Policy Outcomes and the Capacity of County Government

State officials have placed restraints on county governments for a number of reasons, including some that defy objective analysis, such as a desire to maximize their own personal power, control, and prestige as well as a desire to maintain access to and influence over the awarding of government patronage jobs. However, by having a long history of political corruption and mismanagement, county elected officials have made it relatively easy for state officials to justify their dominance of state/local government relations on the grounds that county government officials cannot be trusted with power. For example, the U.S. Attorney for West Virginia's Southern District successfully prosecuted over seventy locally elected officials between 1981 and 1992. Many of those convicted were county elected officials, including one county sheriff who paid $100,000 to his predecessor to ensure his election and who was later caught covering for a local drug dealer.[12] Also, between 1986 and 1991 the state Board of Risk and Insurance Management paid more than $1 million in claims against local government officials, most of them county elected officials, for firing employees for political reasons. The U.S. Supreme Court ruled in 1976 that government employees fired for political reasons can sue for damages.[13] Examples include five deputies fired by the Clay County sheriff, nine deputies fired by the Lincoln County sheriff, and five Mingo County courthouse employees all fired for political reasons.[14]

The public's concern about the integrity of its county officials is reinforced by the relatively common practice of county elected officials' hiring their relatives to work in their offices. Although this practice is legal, and perhaps even somewhat understandable given the difficult employment market in many communities, when West Virginians go to the county courthouse and see the sons, daughters, nephews, nieces, or cousins of county elected officials behind the counter, they cannot help but be reminded of the old style of politics of the "county courthouse gang."

Despite county government's limited fiscal capacity and the widespread concern about the integrity of county officials, there is evidence to suggest that county governance is improving. Many county elected officials are hard-working, public-spirited citizens committed to ending the stereotype of the politically motivated and corrupt courthouse gangs of the past. Their statewide organizations, especially the West Virginia Association of Counties and the County Commissioners' Association of West Virginia, have undertaken a number of education and training efforts to improve the capacity of county elected officials to make more informed decisions. For example, the County Commissioners' Association and the Institute for Public Affairs at West Virginia University initiated an education and training series in 1993. Over 70 percent of the state's county commissioners attended the initial two meetings in this series of workshops and presentations by practitioners and scholars, and attendance since then has continued to increase. Also, nearly all county commissioners attend an annual training seminar on property taxation that is sponsored by the state Department of Tax and Revenue. Obviously, West Virginia has many dedicated public servants in its county courthouses who are interested in improving their skills as policymakers and administrators. However, when confronted with a problem or a demand for additional county services, they are often prevented from acting because they either lack the authority or the financial resources to respond.

SCHOOL DISTRICTS

Funding, or more precisely the lack of funding, is the perennial issue facing West Virginia's fifty-five school districts. Organized along county lines, West Virginia's school districts are responsible for providing public education services, primarily to children. They currently spend about $1.6 billion annually. West Virginia ranks forty-third in the nation on spending for elementary and secondary education on a per capita basis. This relatively low ranking, however, does not result from a lack of commitment to education. West Virginia ranks ninth in the nation in spending for elementary and secondary education as a percentage of personal income. The financial difficulty faced by school districts, once again, results from the state's relatively anemic fiscal condition, which makes it difficult for the state to fund programs (even programs with widespread bipartisan support, such as elementary and secondary education) at levels found in most other states, and from the fiscal constraints placed on local governments by the state constitution.

School districts in most other states receive most of their revenue from local taxes. This is not true in West Virginia, where school districts receive two-thirds of their revenue from state government ($1.3 billion in 1995) and only one-quarter from property taxes ($390 million in 1995). The remainder is derived from federal grants ($130 million) and other taxes and fees ($70 million). Their relatively heavy reliance on state grants can be explained by the previously mentioned restrictions on property taxation and by state court decisions that mandate state government action to equalize school district revenues throughout the state. This requirement, first articulated in *Pauley v. Kelly* (1979) and refined in *State ex rel. Board of Education v. Rockefeller* (1981) and *Pauley v. Bailey* (1982), is based on the state constitutional requirement that the legislature provide "a thorough and efficient system of free schools." Altogether, state money and state law give the state government an important role in defining school districts' policy agendas.

Procedures

Each school district is run by a five-member county board of education, with the members individually elected on a countywide nonpartisan basis to four-year terms and with the terms staggered so that no more than two members of the board are elected during a single election. No more than two members can be from the same magisterial district. At their first meeting following an election, the school board members select a president from their membership to preside at their meetings until the next biennial election. A quorum consists of three or more members, and all decisions are reached by majority vote.

Most school boards meet twice a month, and all board members are considered part-time employees. The state has set their compensation at not more than $80 per meeting attended, with a limit of fifty-two meetings per year. The state also permits school board members to be reimbursed for travel, provided the member submits an itemized sworn statement indicating that the travel was conducted on official business. Each school board is given the authority to engage in nineteen specific activities, including the control and management of all existing schools in the county; deciding, subject to the approval of the West Virginia Board of Education, whether to open new schools or to close or consolidate existing schools (a contentious issue in rural counties); providing transportation services to its schools; and employing administrators, teachers, and teacher aides.

The county superintendent of schools handles the school district's day-to-day operations and is appointed by the county school board. State statutes require that the superintendent be hired for a term of at least one year, but not more than four years. There is no limit on the number of terms. State statutes require that all superintendents must hold a valid West Virginia teacher's certificate, an approved master's degree, at least twelve semester hours in school administration and supervision, and at least five years experience in public school teaching and/or supervision. The superintendent's salary is set annually by the school board and varies from school district to school district. In the state's more populous counties, annual compensation currently ranges from approximately $70,000 to $90,000.

Policymaking Capacity

State statutes provide county school superintendents with ten specific duties, including nominating all personnel to be employed; assigning, transferring, suspending, or promoting teachers and all other school district employees; closing schools when conditions are detrimental to the pupils' health, safety, or welfare; certifying all expenditures; and attending all school board meetings. The state government also establishes guidelines for nearly all aspects of public education, either through the adoption of state statutes (such as maximum teacher-pupil ratios, school-entry ages, the length of the school year, etc.) or through the actions of the West Virginia Board of Education.

The West Virginia Board of Education has twelve members, including the state superintendent of schools, the chancellor of the board of regents of the University of West Virginia system (West Virginia and Marshall Universities, their branches, and the medical schools), and the chancellor of the board of directors of the four-year college system, who sit on the board as ex officio members and are not allowed to vote. The remaining nine members are appointed by the governor, with the advice and consent of the Senate, for staggered nine-year terms. To ensure partisan and geographic balance, not more than five of the nine voting members can belong to the same political party and each congressional district is to be represented by three members.

School districts are, by far, the most regulated and controlled local government in West Virginia. Their relationship with the state government is a nearly perfect example of a classic unitary relationship in the organization of local governance. The state Board of Education's takeover of the Logan County school district in 1992, discussed in chapter 4, is a perfect example of the extent of the state government's control over public education in the state.

MUNICIPALITIES

West Virginia does not have any large metropolitan cities. The population of the state's largest city, Charleston, is only 57,083. Moreover, only 15 of the

231 cities in the state have a population over ten thousand. As a result, city politics in West Virginia is far different than city politics in most other states. It is essentially small-town politics, where the great issues facing America's major cities—drugs, the homeless, crime, pollution, urban decay, and race relations—are generally not issues of great concern. Although these problems exist, the scale is much smaller and less severe than in America's larger cities. As a result, city politics in many of West Virginia's cities is much more provincial than in other states. For example, elections in many of the state's smaller cities (especially those with populations under ten thousand) are often decided on the basis of the contestants' personalities and name recognition rather than on their positions on issues. This is not surprising given the relatively limited powers and resources available to city officials and the absence of earth-shattering issues to excite the electorate.

The one problem that West Virginia's municipalities share with America's larger cities is their relatively weak fiscal condition. Unlike many other cities across the county, West Virginia's cities are not allowed to impose a local sales or income tax. Moreover, their ability to generate revenue from property taxes is restrained by the provisions of the Tax Limitation Amendment of 1932 and the Property Tax and Homestead Exemption Amendment of 1982. However, unlike other local governments in the state, cities are allowed to impose a business and occupation tax (B&O tax) on the gross income of businesses operating within their city limits. State statutes require that the municipality's B&O tax rate cannot exceed the state's B&O tax rate. Despite this restriction, the B&O tax is the largest source of municipal revenues in West Virginia, generating nearly $100 million in 1996, or 40 percent of total municipal revenue (approximately $250 million). Fees collected for refuse collection, fire protection, municipal ice skating, police protection, parks, and other municipal services generated about $45 million, or 18 percent of the total. Property taxes were the third largest source of municipal revenue, accounting for nearly $40 million, or 16 percent of the total. Other important sources of revenue included the utilities tax, wine and liquor tax, coal severance tax, and the hotel occupancy tax.

Structure

Prior to the Home Rule Amendment of 1936, each time a municipality was formed and each time a municipality wanted to revise or amend its charter, it had to convince the state legislature to approve the action through the adoption of a state statute.[15] The Home Rule Amendment abolished this practice for municipalities with populations over two thousand, which are now allowed to create, revise, and amend their charters without state government approval. However, they are still required to meet specific requirements and follow detailed procedures established by state law. For example, state statutes dictate that municipalities can no longer be formed in areas that contain fewer than one hundred inhabitants (if less than one square mile in size) or five hundred inhabitants per square mile (if larger than one square mile in size). Also, municipalities cannot be formed in areas that are currently part of an existing municipality. Municipalities granted charters prior to the adoption of the Home Rule Amendment of 1936 were exempted from these requirements. Currently, 61 of the 231 municipalities in West Virginia have fewer than five hundred residents and could not meet the population requirements.

State statutes also specify how charters are to be created, revised, or amended. Residents interested in creating a municipality must petition their county commission to hold a special election to determine if the area should incorporate as a municipality. The petition must be signed by at least 30 percent of the residents in the area to be incorporated. If a majority of qualified voters within the area vote in favor of incorporation, the county commission is authorized by the state government to declare that area a municipal corporation. If the newly incorporated area has a population exceeding fifty thousand, it is classified as a class I city. If its population is between ten and fifty thousand, it is classified as a class II city. Class III cities contain between two and ten thousand residents, and class IV towns or villages have fewer than two thousand people. West Virginia currently has 2 class I cities (Charleston and Huntington), 13 class II cities, 50 class III cities, and 166 class IV towns and villages.[16] Transition from one class to another occurs automatically, depending on a city's population as determined by the U.S. Bureau of the Census or by a special census authorized by the state legislature or municipality.

Following the election for incorporation, voters elect a charter board to draft the municipality's charter, which determines the city's government structure and operating procedures. The state allows the charter board to choose from among five structures: the mayor-council plan, the strong-mayor plan, commission government, the city manager plan, and the city manager–mayor plan. Class IV towns and villages incorporated after the adoption of the Home Rule Amendment of 1936 operate under the state's general law, without individual charters. State statutes require them to use the mayor-council form of government.

After the charter board has completed its draft, the charter is submitted to the state attorney general, who verifies whether it meets state guidelines. If

approved by the attorney general, a public hearing is held at which residents
in the affected area have an opportunity to comment on the charter. Following the public hearing and any revisions, a special election is held on the
charter. If the charter is approved by a majority vote of the qualified voters in
the newly incorporated municipality, the charter takes effect the following 1
July. Subsequent revisions and amendments to the charter follow a similar
procedure.

Procedures

Nearly all of the municipalities in West Virginia use the mayor-council plan
of government (209 out of 231). It is used by 165 of the 166 class IV towns
and villages, 41 of the 50 class III cities, and 3 of the 13 class II cities. It features a city council, elected at large, by wards, or a combination of both, a
recorder elected at large, a mayor elected at large, and any other elected officials specified in the charter.

Under the mayor-council plan, the mayor is a member of the city council,
typically does not have the authority to veto city ordinances adopted by the
city council, has relatively little authority over the preparation of the city
budget, cannot hire or fire subordinates in the city's administration, and has
no real power to direct the city's day-to-day operations. The only organizational advantage the mayor has over other council members is that the mayor
is often the only city council member elected on an at-large basis, presides
over meetings, and represents the city at public ceremonies. Mayors in
mayor-council cities and towns do, from time to time, provide policy and administrative leadership in their community. However, their ability to do so
rests upon their individual political skills. The organizational powers of the
mayor's office in mayor-council systems are virtually nonexistent. As a result, communities with mayor-council systems generally lack strong leadership and are most appropriate in small towns where government services
are relatively few.

The strong-mayor plan is used in Charleston, Huntington, Parkersburg,
and South Charleston. It features a city council, elected at large, by wards,
or a combination of both, and a mayor elected at large. The city council
serves as the legislative body, and the mayor serves as the city's chief administrator. The mayor is not a member of the city council, typically has the authority to veto city ordinances adopted by the city council, prepares the city
budget for the city council's consideration, can hire or fire subordinates in
the city's administration, usually without the city council's approval, and di-
rects the city's day-to-day operations. The strong-mayor plan provides the

mayor with the organizational capacity to provide policy and administrative leadership. It is more appropriate than the mayor-council plan for larger cities that offer a relatively broad range of government services.

Ronceverte, population 1,754, is the only municipality in West Virginia that currently uses the commission form of government. Although the commission form enjoyed a brief period of popularity across the United States during the early 1900s, less than three percent of municipal governments in the country now use the system.[17] In West Virginia, cities have the option of selecting either a three-person or a five-person commission, elected at large, to run the city. In the three-person alternative (used by Ronceverte), one of the commissioners serves as the commissioner of finance, another serves as the commissioner of public works, and the third serves as the commissioner of public safety. They each enjoy full autonomy over their departments and elect a mayor from among themselves to preside over commission meetings. In the five-person alternative (available as an option for only class I and class II cities), there is also a commissioner of streets and a commissioner of public works.

Although the commission plan was hailed by reformers at the turn of the century as the "best and most professional" way to govern a city, it fell into disfavor primarily because no single person has the authority either to direct or to coordinate the city's day-to-day operations. In practice, political logrolling among the commissioners often led to levels of expenditures that threatened the city's fiscal stability. As a result, most of the larger American cities using the commission form of government have switched to the strong-mayor form, and most of the smaller cities have switched to the city manager form of government.

The city manager plan is used by nine of fifty class III cities and by eight of its thirteen class II cities (Bluefield, Clarksburg, Fairmont, Martinsburg, Morgantown, Moundsville, Weirton, and Wheeling). It features a city council of not fewer than five nor more than eleven members elected at large, from districts, or a combination of both, a mayor elected by the city council from among its members, and a city manager who is appointed by the city council. The mayor presides over city council meetings and represents the city at public ceremonies. Like mayors in the mayor-council system, the mayor in the city manager system lacks any major organizational advantages over other city council members. The city manager administers the city's day-to-day affairs under the supervision of the city council, prepares the city's budget for the city council's consideration, and provides the city council with policy recommendations. The city manager is supposed to provide the city council with nonpartisan, professional advice. However, it is often difficult for city managers to avoid political battles, and few stay in one city their entire career because the city council can fire or dismiss the city manager at any time, for any reason, by a majority vote. Huntington used the manager-mayor plan until it switched to the strong-mayor plan in 1985. The strong-mayor plan is identical to the city manager plan except that the mayor is elected on an at-large basis instead of from among the membership of the city council.

Besides detailing which government forms are available to municipalities, state statutes also regulate the length of municipal officials' terms of office. All municipal officials in class I, II, and III cities incorporated after the adoption of the Home Rule Amendment of 1936 must have four-year terms. Class IV towns and villages have the option of selecting either two- or four-year terms for their elected officials. However, because terms of office established prior to the adoption of the Home Rule Amendment of 1936 were exempted from these requirements, term lengths vary widely, with four-year terms prevailing in larger cities and two-year terms prevailing in smaller cities. There are no limitations on the number of terms an elected municipal officer can serve.

The number of city council members also varies widely, ranging from three in Bayard and Keyser to twenty-six in Charleston. Nearly all of the 166 city councils in class IV municipalities have five members, most class III cities have either five, six, or seven members, most class II cities have either seven, nine, or twelve members, Huntington's city council has eleven members, and Charleston's city council has twenty-six members. All but 27 of the 231 municipalities have opted to elect their officials on a nonpartisan basis.

Policymaking Capacity

Like counties, West Virginia's 231 municipalities have been granted additional responsibilities and powers over the years by the state government. They spend approximately $250 million annually to enforce city laws and maintain domestic order, provide fire protection, build, repair, and clean city roads, supply and purify water, offer park and recreational services, and provide a wide assortment of other services, including building inspections and libraries. Their largest expenditures are for police protection, fire protection, streets and highways, general administration, sanitation, city hall, park and recreation services, landfills, and libraries.[18]

The extent of municipal services varies widely. In 1996 the typical class

IV town or village spent less than $250,000, with most of the money going to running city hall, street maintenance, and one or two police officers. The typical class III city spent between $700,000 and $1.1 million. They offered a broader range of services than the typical class IV municipality but still spent most of their money on basic municipal services, such as police protection, fire protection, and street repairs. Expenditures among class II cities ranged from $2.7 million to $17 million, with most spending between $6 million and $12 million. They offered a broader range of services than class III cities. Besides providing basic municipal services, such as police and fire protection, most also funded housing programs, building inspectors, health programs, libraries, and a visitor center.

West Virginia's two class I cities, Huntington and Charleston, have significantly larger budgets than other cities in the state. Huntington spent $25 million and Charleston $36 million in 1996. They also offered a much broader range of services than other cities, including funding for civic centers, ambulance services, dog wardens, planning and zoning, and landfills. They also spent significantly more than other cities on libraries.

SPECIAL DISTRICTS

Special districts are independent governments that are usually established to perform a specific service, but they are occasionally established to perform several types of related services. They are often formed to take advantage of economies of scale, with governments banding together to provide a service to their residents that they cannot afford to provide by themselves. Nationally, the number of special districts has increased steadily since the 1950s. In 1957 there were 14,424 special districts. By 1972 that number had increased to 15,781. Today, there are 33,131 special districts in the United States. Most (30,457) provide a single, specific service, such as protection of natural resources (6,564), fire protection (5,354), housing (3,663), water (3,442), and sewer services (1,850).[19]

Structure and Policy Activities

The number of special districts in West Virginia has increased dramatically in the past four decades. In 1957 there were only 32 special districts; in 1987 there were 290. Today, there are 366. Most (336) provide a single, specific service.[20]

Most of the special districts in West Virginia are public service districts created by county commissions, with the advice and consent of the state's Public Service Commission, to provide water services (155), wastewater collection and treatment services (63), or both (27). West Virginia also has 50 solid-waste-management districts that are responsible for disposing of solid wastes; 36 housing authorities that buy and clear slums and blighted areas and oversee the provision of low-cost housing or other community facilities on the land; and 14 soil conservation districts that institute land-use regulations and construct terraces, dams, channel improvements, ponds, and other facilities to prevent soil erosion; and 6 airport districts.[21]

The increased number of special districts in West Virginia is partly a result of the state's dispersed, rural population. Many of the state's smaller municipalities individually lack the resources and revenues to provide capital-intensive public services at an economical cost to a small populace, such as the construction of water supply systems, wastewater treatment plants, and flood control projects. The increased number is also partly due to the state's decision to impose relatively severe restrictions on the ability of local governments to raise revenue. Moreover, the increased number, at least in part, is also a response to the state's decision to impose on counties a government structure that weakens their organizational capacity to respond effectively to citizen demands.

Unlike West Virginia's state institutions, which have benefited from constitutional changes and statutory reforms enabling them to respond more effectively to citizen demands, its local governments have neither the power nor the fiscal resources to provide more than the most basic level of services. Planning, for example, is virtually nonexistent in most of the state's county and municipal governments because there is no money available to hire planners. Moreover, rising costs and unfunded federal and state policy mandates threaten their capacity to maintain even basic services, such as police and fire protection, street maintenance, and snow removal. Despite these fiscal woes, state policymakers remain steadfastly opposed to the imposition of local sales and income taxes and to any proposal that would ease the restrictions of the Tax Limitation Amendment of 1932 or of the Property Tax and Homestead Exemption Amendment of 1982. As a result, the state's local governments continue to play a secondary role in West Virginia's political system and remain highly dependent on state grants and excess levies to provide many local government services that are taken for granted in other states.

CHAPTER ELEVEN

Policy Controversies and the Capacity of the State Government

As West Virginia prepares for a new century, its politics and government are at a critical stage. Although the state is gradually escaping the legacies of its economic dependence on natural resource extraction and the management-labor conflicts that marked its politics from the 1880s into the 1950s, it has not completely escaped the political and economic effects of nearly a century of limited public investment in the state's infrastructure and education systems. This limited funding continues to shape policy options for the state.

CONCLUSIONS CONCERNING THE DISTINCTIVENESS OF WEST VIRGINIA POLITICS

West Virginia's politics and policymaking processes are not exceptionally different from the politics and processes in most other states. Most of the differences that do exist are primarily related to the state's economic conditions. For example, like most Americans, most West Virginians do not participate in politics frequently, do not have a detailed knowledge of politics, and exhibit some distrust of government. This is not a backcountry cultural construction of politics. Although the Democratic party is stronger in West Virginia than in most other states, this is to be expected given the Democratic party's appeal to lower-income groups. West Virginia's per capita income is among the lowest in the nation. Moreover, many of the intraparty divisions among liberals and conservatives that occur nationally also appear in West Virginia's two parties. Also, the number of interest groups has increased. The bipolar politics of coal industry–UMWA conflict, which once played a dominate role in the state's politics, has decreased in significance. Both in numbers and tactics, West Virginia interest-group politics resembles the pluralism of group activity occurring in many other states. Finally, as in other states, funded and unfunded federal mandates have an important and growing influence on the state's policies. The only difference in this regard is that federal money and unfunded federal mandates affect West Virginia to a greater extent than most other states because the state lacks the fiscal resources available in other states.

The capacity of West Virginia's political institutions is not exceptionally different from many other states. The governor has exceptional agenda-setting power, including control over the state budget and the line-item and reduction vetoes. Although the plural executive can create some opposition to the governor's policies, the independent executive officers have relatively limited power over policy creation and implementation. The legislators, like legislators in many states with a small population, serve on a part-time basis, remaining close to the public they represent. These part-time legislators lack access to the professional staff expertise seen in most other states and are forced to perform their legislative duties in a limited time period. Nevertheless, the legislature's organizational structure and procedures have been modernized and are now fairly typical of the structures and procedures found in most other states. In most respects, the judiciary's organizational structure, processes, and policy role are also fairly typical.

Yet, there are some significant differences between the political capacity of governments in West Virginia and in other states. One difference is the state's economy. Although there has been some improvement in recent years, West Virginia is still saddled with a poorly educated work force that is ill-prepared for the national movement toward technologically sophisticated white-collar jobs. Moreover, the exodus of young, productive workers during the late 1980s left the state with one of the oldest and most government-dependent populations in the nation. This, coupled with the bond investment scandal during the late 1980s, forced state policymakers to increase taxes significantly to avoid massive service reductions. Given the state's economic difficulties, it has not been able to make public investments in the two basic building blocks of economic growth, infrastructure and education, at anywhere near the levels found in most other states. Moreover, West Virginia's financial institutions, most of which are locally operated, lack the capital to promote new, large-scale enterprises. Consequently, most West Virginians have never enjoyed the benefits of the economic boom times in post–World War II America. West Virginia's economy continues to lag far behind national averages on most economic indexes, such as per capita income and employment levels.[1]

West Virginia's longstanding economic difficulties probably will continue to pose problems for its state government. Although the state has recently increased its investment in both transportation and environmental infrastructure, that infrastructure is in relatively poor condition. Both transportation facilities, such as roads, bridges, and locks and dams, and environmental infrastructure, such as landfills, water treatment facilities, and sewer lines, are inadequate and in far worse condition than in surrounding states.[2] Despite increased funding for elementary and secondary education, West Virginians' education achievement levels continue to be among the lowest in the nation.[3] And although there has been some improvement in funding for higher education, the job skills of the state's residents are outmoded. West Virginia has primarily a high school–trained, blue-collar work force in an era of jobs requiring college-trained, white-collar workers. In addition to all of these difficulties, the state's rugged topography increases the cost of development and providing services. The rugged terrain, for example, bars easy access to West Virginia's ski slopes. The relatively low population density further reduces the state's desirability as a location for many larger companies. Finally, West Virginia lacks both a major airport and a major seaport facility, which reduces the state's attractiveness to businesses requiring ready access to other markets. In this situation, rapid increases in state revenue are unlikely, even when the national economy is flourishing.

As indicated in the discussion of the state's budget process, the state government has fully employed its taxation capacity and is still forced to practice budget austerity. Austerity works against state government efforts to provide what investors demand—technically educated workers, a sound and well maintained infrastructure, lucrative tax incentives, and ready access to large markets. Consequently, the state's continuing economic problems are due primarily to its historical dependence on natural resource extraction and other factors largely beyond the control of policymakers, such as the state's rugged topography, its lack of sunny beaches and a tropical climate, and its lack of ready access to the ocean. Although the political activities of out-of-state interests, such as efforts to fight environmental laws considered detrimental to their businesses and to keep business taxes as low as possible, have not always been in the best interests of all West Virginians, it cannot be said that they are the primary cause of West Virginia's problems.

Another difference between West Virginia and some other states is the state's political heritage. Despite strains of moralistic and individualistic cultural values introduced into the state by emigration, religion, and the UMWA, the state constitution reflects a traditionalist antebellum Virginia model and Jacksonian ideas about direct election of a large number of public offices, limitations on legislative sessions, restrictions on debt and borrowing, and popular electoral control of local taxation. Thus, West Virginia has an institutional legacy that opposes strong central management of public policy and policy creativity. Constitutional changes in the twentieth century have reduced these restrictions, providing the governor, for example, greater authority to coordinate state expenditures and to affect policy. Yet, local government authority remains tied to traditional concepts that make it a housekeeper, keeping public records, keeping the peace, keeping schools open, rather than a policy innovator. Additionally, all forms of local government face severe restrictions on their ability to generate revenue. Even in housekeeping tasks, like replacing decaying roads and sewers, paying teachers, and maintaining school buildings and jails, local governments are forced to rely heavily on state funds.

This situation has two important political effects. First, key policy choices have become centered in the hands of the governor and legislature. Their decisions, some of which are affected by the courts, provide revenue and place boundaries on what local governments do. Thus, the state government makes the decisions concerning school construction, teacher salaries, jail improvements, sewage plants, and waste disposal. In contrast, in neighboring states like Maryland, Ohio, or Pennsylvania, these are matters for both state and local government officials. Second, with key policy decision making located at the state level, interest groups seeking a more aggressive and activist style of policymaking—especially unions, individualist, growth-oriented businesses, and moralistic-minded reformers such as those in the environmental movement—focus their efforts on the legislature because they know that local governments typically lack the fiscal capacity and the legal authority to act.

POLITICAL CAPACITY: CONTEMPORARY POLITICS IN WEST VIRGINIA

The state government's dominance in state-local relations, the federal government's increasingly important role in policymaking, and the state's difficulty in finding the resources necessary to respond to citizen demands are borne out by contemporary political events. As indicated in chapter 2, West Virginians consider jobs and economic development to be the state's most pressing issue. The quality of the state's public education system and the cost and availability of health care also concern them. Have West Virginia's state and local government institutions addressed these issues? Also, has the nature of the state's political institutions affected the state's policy product? What does this product portend for the future?

Economic Development Policy

Subjected to a long economic recession and limited growth, West Virginia's policymakers have been keenly interested in economic development strategies, especially ones designed to diversify the state's economy. However, a combination of three structural economic factors proved to be especially damaging to the state's economy during the 1980s and solidified the importance of economic development strategies in West Virginia's political agenda. First, the national and international economies underwent a fundamental restructuring toward an economy whose growth was no longer determined primarily by goods-producing industries, such as mining and manufacturing. Instead, service and government sectors moved to the forefront of economic activity. As a result, the state's heavy reliance on metals and chemical manufacturing and on coal mining caused the state's economy to fall precipitously. Second, faced with competition from other energy sources and with depressed coal prices, the state's coal-mining industry made substantial investments in long-wall mining machines and draglines to increase productivity and to remain competitive. As a result, although coal output increased during the 1980s, coal mining employment fell dramatically, from 59,700 in 1980 to 24,200 in 1995. Third, stricter federal environmental laws adopted during the 1980s, capped by the Clean Air Act of 1990, adversely affected the market for the state's high-sulfur-content coal and increased costs in the chemical and steel industries.[4]

As the economy faltered during the 1980s, many people left the state in search of work. West Virginia was one of only two states to lose population during the 1980s, falling from 1.9 million people in 1980 to 1.7 million people in 1990. Much of the decline was due to the out-migration of young adults between the ages of twenty and thirty-four.[5] Faced with one of the worst and most rapid economic declines in modern history, West Virginia's policymakers, under the leadership of Republican Governor Arch Moore, enacted a number of tax credit programs during the 1980s to convince existing businesses to stay and to encourage out-of-state businesses to locate in the state. The programs were copied from policies developed in other states and currently reduce state tax collections by over $120 million annually. The largest tax credit program, the Business Investment and Jobs Expansion Tax Credit, called the "super tax credit," allows employers that create at least fifty new jobs to deduct a portion of their capital investment costs (ranging from 50 percent to 90 percent, depending on the number of new jobs created) against their state tax liability over a ten-year period. Used primarily by coal companies, the credit reduced the state's tax revenue by $90 million in 1993.[6] State policymakers also established or increased the financing for a number of low-interest loan programs to attract new businesses to the state.

Many policymakers now question the effectiveness of the state's tax credit programs. In 1992, each new job generated by the super tax credit program cost the state treasury approximately $106,000 in revenue. As a percentage of total tax collections, tax credits currently cost the state more than twice as much as in any other state.[7] Furthermore, some companies have earned their super tax credits in questionable ways. For example, a coal company received a $5 million tax credit for reopening a coal mine near Moundsville and hiring 300 nonunion coal miners. At the same time, it closed another mine nearby, laying off approximately 250 UMWA coal miners. Union leaders at the closed mine argued that their members were fired in exchange for the tax credits.[8]

Some state legislators have argued that all of the state's tax credit programs should be eliminated and the additional revenue used to reduce the state's corporate income tax rates. This would enable companies that do not qualify for the tax credits to compete on an even basis with companies that do qualify.[9] Another option would be to eliminate the tax credits and use the funds to improve the state's physical infrastructure. The debate over tax credits is symptomatic of the lack of consensus about the state's economic development policy. Some legislators argue for a supply-side economic solution featuring reduced taxes. Other legislators argue for a demand-side economic solution featuring government spending. Still others argue for a greater emphasis on government programs that focus on developing the state's transportation and environmental infrastructure.

The debate over economic development policy illustrates how state politics operates. Clearly, economic development was on the political agenda for a long time prior to the adoption of tax credits. Action on the issue, however, awaited an extreme crisis, and the state's response was to copy programs already operating in other states, rather than designing policies to meet West Virginia's unique problems. Since then, the state has focused its efforts on education and infrastructure development, again primarily in response to efforts in surrounding states. Thus, West Virginia is constantly trying to keep up with the other states, copying their programs and hoping for success.

The case of economic development policy suggests that West Virginia leaders will "act for" an economically desperate population. But, the action is restricted by the state's limited capacity. West Virginia copies programs because it lacks the funds to hire the professional expertise necessary to design its own programs. Although the West Virginia Development Office works hard to generate economic development policies, it suffers, like most other state agencies, from high turnover due to low wages and the lack of staff. Also, the state's anemic economy precludes spending the large sums necessary to compete successfully with states like Ohio, Pennsylvania, Maryland, and Virginia in the construction of industrial sites and infrastructure, in the provision of direct loans and grants to business, or in efforts to improve worker skills.

Education Policy

West Virginia's public education system is troubled, but improving. The state has markedly improved its expenditures per pupil in elementary and secondary education, moving from fortieth among the states in 1982–83 to nineteenth in 1992–93. Its high school graduation rate is currently about 80 percent, sixteenth best in the nation, and in 1994 the standardized test scores of its third, sixth, ninth, and eleventh graders had improved to just slightly below the national average. West Virginia's college-bound seniors also tested only slightly below the national average on the American College Test, the most commonly used achievement test for state students considering college. However, only 43 percent of West Virginia's high school students enter college, compared to 53 percent in other southern states. West Virginia also has the fewest college graduates per capita in the nation.[10]

The state government made a series of incremental changes in its education policy in the early 1990s that affected the funding, facilities, and operations of the state's schools. The impetus for these policy changes, which affected all elementary and secondary grade levels and higher education, came from several sources outside of government. In March 1990 the West Virginia Education Association (WVEA) staged an illegal six-day statewide strike over salaries.[11] At that time, teacher's salaries were ranked forty-ninth in the nation, at an average of $22,842. As the schools closed, Governor Caperton called a special legislative session. Recognizing that school districts lacked the fiscal resources necessary to pay teachers at anywhere near national averages, the state government adopted a three-year, state-funded program to increase teachers' salaries by $5,000. As part of the "deal," the legislation included provisions to reduce the teaching work force as student populations declined. By 1993–94 teachers' average salary had risen to $30,547, thirty-third in the nation. Also, the state expanded computer education in primary schools, established a computerized state library network, and, as an incentive for students to stay in school, withheld drivers' licenses from high school dropouts under age eighteen.[12] The state also initiated a school construction program to replace dilapidated school buildings and those having no special facilities to accommodate the needs of the disabled.

The state also reexamined public higher education. About 93 percent of the college and university students in West Virginia attend state institutions. In 1967–68 the state devoted 13.9 percent of its general revenue budget to higher education, but the allocation had dropped to 11.3 percent in 1989–90, the lowest rate in the southern United States. Moreover, public higher education faculty and staff compensation was far below both national and southern averages.[13] This resulted in high faculty-student ratios, insufficient libraries, computer systems, and laboratories, and the loss of faculty to other states.

Faced with another shortfall in state revenues, the governor recognized that the state could not afford to address the funding problems of both higher education and elementary and secondary education simultaneously. In fact, higher education's spending was cut by three percent to help finance teachers' pay raises. This frustrated higher education officials and employees, but they lacked the political clout to change the situation. Then, with the financial support of a civic trust, experts from the Carnegie Foundation for Higher Education conducted a study of higher education in the state.[14] The governor and legislature heartily adopted most of the experts' recommendations, primarily because most of them did not require large sums of money.[15] Legislation split higher education into two administrative units, each with a separate board of trustees, chancellor, and administrative staff in Charleston. The University System of West Virginia, designed to manage the state's research institutions, consists of West Virginia University, its two branch campuses at Parkersburg and the Potomac State College, Marshall University, and the College of Graduate Studies at Institute. The former teachers' colleges and four-year institutions come under a separate State College System. As yet, no complete analysis has been undertaken of the effects of the implementation of the dual organizational systems.[16]

In 1992 the governor established a Higher Education Action Team (HEAT) to hold hearings around the state in order to study the problems of higher education. Most of the HEAT report's recommendations were subsequently adopted in 1993. The most noticeable result was a three-year $5,000 pay raise for faculty and staff and a state mandate to bring faculty salaries closer to the South's regional averages for peer institutions. Like the teachers' raise, part of the "deal" was a requirement that state institutions of higher education have a 10 percent greater student-faculty ratio than similar schools in the South to "increase productivity," and that the institutions be more frequently subjected to assessments.[17]

The changes made at all levels of public education in the state illustrate the governor's and legislature's strong hand in education policy. Although the education agenda was set in part by the WVEA, and the state's financial difficulties prevented more than incremental changes in policy, the governor and the legislature were able to respond to the public's demand for a stronger educational system.

Health-Care Policy

West Virginia does not have an especially healthy population, and the great economic costs associated with delivering health services in thinly populated rural areas continues to beset the state. Although it does not have extreme alcohol abuse or AIDS problems and the state's infant mortality rate continues to decline, the rates for cancer, heart disease, pulmonary disease, and accidents are above the national average. As of 1992 West Virginia had the fourth highest percentage of obese residents and the highest rate of smokeless tobacco use in the nation. The state ranked tenth highest in tobacco smoking, seventh in sedentary lifestyle, and third in high blood pressure.[18]

Since 1989 the state government has confronted two major public health issues: the funding of health care for welfare and other poor clients through the federal Medicaid program and the design of a rural health-care delivery system. Medicaid was established as a joint federal-state program in 1965 to provide medical assistance to the poor.[19] For each state dollar spent on a list of eligible health services for the poor, the federal government contributes roughly three dollars. Although Congress has modified the program significantly over the years, the state government determines whether a person is eligible for the program, whether "optional" services beyond the base package are offered, whether reimbursements are paid to health-service providers retrospectively or prospectively and at "reasonable," "customary," or "allowable" charges, and how the administrative system, with related overhead costs, is structured.

Since 1989 the state has often failed to reimburse the state's Medicaid health-care providers in a timely fashion. In June 1989, for example, the state was $68 million in arrears. Initially, the legislature responded by appropriating additional money, but it also extended the number of days of hospital stay for which it reimbursed to prevent hospitals from losing income.[20] This increased costs and helped to perpetuate the state's difficulty in funding its share of the program's cost. In 1991 the legislature resolved Medicaid's funding problem, at least in the short run, by taxing doctors, hospitals, and other health providers who treat Medicaid patients. In effect, the tax was counted as a cost and was used to attract federal matching funds. The added income was then returned to health-care providers by increasing reimbursement rates and expanding optional coverage for recipients. In 1995 more than three hundred thousand state residents qualified for Medicaid. As enrollments and reimbursement rates increased, so did Medicaid costs, rising from $483 million in FY 1991 to over $1.3 billion in FY 1995.

In 1992 the federal government issued new rules that restricted the use of taxes to generate Medicaid matching funds. In 1993 the legislature and the governor became locked in a dispute over how to respond to the new rules. Eventually, a special session reduced reimbursement rates to health-care providers and modified the state's provider tax to comply with the federal government's new rules.[21] Medicaid's budget now exceeds $1.3 billion, in a virtual dead heat with education spending as the largest single budgetary item in the state budget.

Medicaid illustrates the federal government's effect on the state's policy agenda. Although the state has always provided some resources to meet the health-care needs of the poor, the federal government used its generous three-to-one matching of funds to encourage the state to create a comprehensive assistance program. As the issue was considered, interest groups, especially those in the health-care industry, became critical players with an agenda that sought more spending. Caught in the web of federal, interest-group, revenue, and budgetary pressures, the governor and the legislature tried different options, including the formation of a special "blue ribbon" commission in 1995 to address the issue of Medicaid costs. Clearly, the Medicaid issue remains unresolved because the state does not have the financial capacity to finance the health-care needs of its residents without federal assistance, and the amount of federal assistance depends on the outcome of partisan contests in Washington.

Rural health care is a major problem in West Virginia. Medical schools produce relatively few doctors who are interested in general practice in rural regions because these areas generally provide physicians with less income than urban areas and lack the population density necessary to support physicians with medical specialties. Many graduates of the state's two largest medical schools, for example, often chose to practice outside the state. This led to an emotional debate over which of the state's two major medical schools, West Virginia University or Marshall University, did more for the state and deserved more state financial support. Also, the overhead costs of medical practice in rural areas and the operation of rural clinics are greater than in urban areas because the lack of population hinders the achievement of economies of scale. Although these problems with rural health care, compounded by the state's high poverty rates, have beset West Virginia for generations, the state's funding problems precluded major action until 1991. At that time, the state received a $6 million grant from the W. K. Kellogg Foundation to fund a rural health-care initiative run by the state's medical centers. The state matched the funds and used the money to fund eight rural clinics and to improve clinical education in general practice, obstetrics and gynecology, geriatrics, and pharmacy. The clinical education program was designed to encourage state medical and pharmacy school graduates to choose a rural practice.[22] The change initiated by this program has yet to receive a professional evaluation, but preliminary evidence suggests that both medical schools are now producing more graduates who are interested in staying within the state and that the health-care services provided in the state's more isolated areas are improving.

West Virginia's state and local governments have yet to offer comprehensive solutions to other public health problems. The state's death rate for auto accidents, second highest among all states in 1992, is being reduced through a mandatory seat belt law enacted in 1993, but dangerous and winding roads continue to service the homes and jobs of much of the population. Despite federal intervention, occupational safety remains a problem because of the concentration of workers in mining and logging. With the second oldest population in the nation, problems of long-term care, home care, nutrition, and health-related social services for an aging population continue to grow.[23] The absence of comprehensive health insurance and rural care programs hampers the remediation of these problems. Also, the state government has not taken aggressive preventative action, such as laws to discourage smoking. Only a few local anti-smoking ordinances are in place. Action on many of these problems, the availability of health insurance for the roughly 17 percent of the population without coverage, and the licensing of professionals was recommended by the state's Health Care Planning Commission in 1992.[24] In 1993 the governor proposed the establishment of a Health Care Authority to develop comprehensive measures to reform the state's health-care system, including billing practices, medical malpractice issues, data collection, loans to medical students, and numerous other items over a three-year period. The legislature has yet to act on this proposal.[25]

Other states have pursued public health issues more aggressively. Hawaii has established a state-managed universal health insurance system, and several states have experimented with their Medicaid policy.[26] West Virginia, however, has taken only incremental steps to provide a fiscally sound system of health care for its citizens and to provide easier access to health services for its widely disbursed population. The legislature has not adopted a comprehensive or coordinated policy for improving public health, and it is questionable whether the state can generate the additional revenue necessary to significantly improve rural health care in the state.

POLICY CHANGE AND THE FUTURE OF WEST VIRGINIA

State and local officials face limitations on their knowledge and ability to select policy options. These constraints are due, not to the faulty design of the state's political institutions, but primarily to the state's inability to generate the revenues necessary to implement policies that go beyond incremental, short-term, "band-aid" relief efforts to address the state's chronic unemployment and underemployment problems, to reform and improve its public education systems, and to meet the health-care needs of its people. The state legislature and governor have considered several options for policy change, some emanating from information from or demands by the federal government, as with the Medicaid policy, some from interest groups, such as the teachers' pay raise, and some from professional advisory groups, such as the Carnegie Foundation and HEAT. They designed new programs to implement incremental changes in policies in all three arenas. Clearly West Virginia's state government has the capacity to recognize policy problems and to adapt to new information about ongoing policies. However, in nearly every instance, fiscal limitations affected the implementation of policy change and the consideration of more comprehensive policy changes. The state's low per capita income, forty-ninth among the states in 1995, and the generally limited amount of wealth in the state severely limit its capacity to generate revenue. The state's tax capacity, or the "estimated capacity of each state and local government to raise revenues from a standardized, representative system of taxes," ranked forty-ninth among the states in 1991. However, the passage of additional state taxes in 1989 and the gradual reassessment of real estate values since 1990 produced a marked increase in the state's tax effort. In 1991 the state ranked eighth among the states in tax effort.[27] Yet, the tax

increase has only prevented state governmental insolvency. It has not provided the revenue necessary to address comprehensively the state's difficulties in meeting the costs of Medicaid and infrastructure development, and
it has not provided the revenue necessary to create an education system of re-
nown that might attract business and investment. It also failed to provide local governments with the revenue necessary to undertake innovative policy
initiatives.

The solution to the funding crisis for government services appears to be
the core continuing issue facing state leaders today. In an era when personal
economic comfort and popular ideology generate hostility to the public sector, when people demand something for nothing from government, and
when state and local taxes have increased, West Virginia public officials
have little incentive to generate new revenues through taxation. Also, the
traditionalist constitutional restrictions on state and local revenue creation
preclude revenue enhancement at the local level. In recent decades Washington has provided some help. The relocation of federal agencies such as the
FBI fingerprint laboratory to West Virginia, a federal decision encouraged by
the state's congressional delegation, has generated some jobs and state revenue. But if, as expected, Congress adopts policies that restrict funding for
Medicaid, welfare, and economic development, West Virginia could face
even more fiscal problems in the future. Its state and local governments
could be forced to seek funds from controversial new sources, such as casino
and riverboat gaming, and to engage in more cost cutting, which means that
employee salaries are likely to remain well below national averages and state
agencies are likely to have too few staff to effectively manage their programs. This practice already occurs to a noticeable degree in the state police,
environmental regulatory enforcement, state parks, higher education, consumer protection, and the judiciary. Consequently, the solution to the state's
policy problems is intertwined with the complexities of the politics of revenue creation. As noted in previous chapters, West Virginia has developed the
appropriate political organizations to address the public's needs, but it lacks
the resources necessary to address those needs fully, and unless there is a mi-
raculous restructuring of the state's economy, this situation is not likely to
change anytime in the near future.

CHAPTER TWELVE

Suggestions for Further Reading

There are relatively few publications on West Virginia politics. Moreover, most of them are dated or have theoretical or data collection problems. For further information, the reader should consult the notes to this book or contact the Institute for Public Affairs, West Virginia University, Box 6317, Morgantown wv 26506-6317, for copies of its recent publications.

Current Events. Extensive information on current political events is found in the *Charleston Gazette* and *Daily Mail*. An alternative source of information on current events is West Virginia Public Radio's "Dateline West Virginia" program, normally aired daily at 4:30 P.M.

General Studies and Bibliographies. Claude J. Davis, Eugene R. Elkins, Carl M. Frasure, Mavis Mann Reeves, William R. Ross, and Albert L. Sturm, *West Virginia State and Local Government* (Morgantown: Bureau for Government Research, West Virginia University, 1963) has long been the primary study of West Virginia government. Although dated, it remains an important source of information concerning the state government during the early 1960s. A. Jay Stevens, *Politics and Government in West Virginia: An Annotated and Selected Bibliography*, Publication 63 (Morgantown: Bureau for Government Research, West Virginia University, 1972), is an excellent bibliography concerning West Virginia state government. No recent bibliographical guide exists. The best general collection of state documents is in the West Virginia Collection of West Virginia University Libraries, Colson Hall, University Avenue, Morgantown.

Demographic and Economic Information. Robert Jay Dilger and Tom Stuart Witt, eds., *West Virginia in the 1990s: Opportunities for Economic Progress*

(Morgantown: West Virginia University Press, 1993), is a wide-ranging collection of scholarly studies of almost all aspects of the contemporary West Virginia economy. For data on the economy, readers should consult West Virginia Bureau of Employment Programs, *West Virginia Economic Summary*, a periodical issued monthly with employment and economic data. Older issues are compiled in West Virginia Bureau of Employment Programs, *Employment and Earnings Trends, West Virginia—1939–1990* (Charleston: West Virginia Bureau of Employment Programs, n.d.).

Demographic and social data are compiled in yearly publications from the West Virginia Department of Health and Human Resources, *West Virginia Vital Statistics*, and the West Virginia Research League, *Statistical Handbook*. Andrew Isserman, Oleg Smirnov, Terance Rephann, David Sorenson, and Elizabeth Bury, *West Virginia Population Projections by County, Age, and Sex, 1990–2020* (Morgantown: Regional Research Institute, West Virginia University, 1992), discusses projected demographic change in the state.

Political History and Political Culture. Otis K. Rice and Stephen W. Brown, *West Virginia: A History*, 2d ed. (Lexington: University Press of Kentucky, 1993), is now the standard state history, but it focuses on events in the nineteenth century and generally does not improve on the examination of nineteenth-century politics presented in Charles H. Ambler and Festus P. Summers, *West Virginia: The Mountain State*, 2d ed. (Englewood Cliffs NJ: Prentice-Hall, 1958), which is an older but still useful history of the state.

Charles H. Ambler, *Sectionalism in Virginia from 1776 to 1861* (New York: Russell and Russell, 1964), and Otis K. Rice, *The Allegheny Frontier: West Virginia Beginnings, 1730–1830* (Lexington: University Press of Kentucky, 1970), are fine scholarly studies of politics and life in antebellum western Virginia. Richard Orr Curry, *A House Divided: A Study of Statehood Politics and Copperhead Movement in West Virginia* (Pittsburgh: University of Pittsburgh Press, 1964), is the best study of statehood politics and should be supplemented by Curry's "A Reappraisal of Statehood Politics in West Virginia," *Journal of Southern History* 28 (November 1962): 403–21. Despite a heavy emphasis on class politics, John Alexander Williams, "The New Dominion and the Old: Ante-Bellum and Statehood Politics as the Backyard of West Virginia's 'Bourbon Democracy,'" *West Virginia History* 33 (1971–72): 317–407, and John Williams, *West Virginia and the Captains of Industry* (Morgantown: West Virginia University Press, 1976), describe the passage from the politics of unionists and secessionists to the politics of labor-management conflict.

Phil Conley, *History of West Virginia Coal Industry* (Charleston: Education Foundation, 1960), is an overview of a topic that deserves more comprehensive scholarly examination. David Alan Corbin, *Life, Work, and Rebellion in the Coal Fields: The Southern West Virginia Miners, 1880–1922* (Urbana: University of Illinois Press, 1981), is a valuable social history. Keith Dix, *What's a Coal Miner to Do? The Mechanization of Coal Mining* (Pittsburgh: University of Pittsburgh Press, 1988), describes change in the coal industry prior to World War II. Richard D. Lunt, *Law and Order vs. the Miners: West Virginia, 1907–1933* (Hamden CT: Archon Books, 1979), examines the labor conflicts of the early twentieth century. Curtis Seltzer, *Fire in the Hole: Miners and Managers in the American Coal Industry* (Lexington: University Press of Kentucky, 1985), offers a comprehensive overview of conflict in the coal industry to the 1980s. Joe William Trotter Jr., *Coal, Class, and Color: Blacks in Southern West Virginia, 1915–32* (Urbana: University of Illinois Press, 1990), is a fine social history of African American life in the coal towns.

Political Behavior, Elections, Political Parties, and Interest Groups. Richard A. Brisbin Jr. and Robert Jay Dilger, "Citizen Evaluations of Government in West Virginia: The 1992 West Virginia Political Survey," *West Virginia Public Affairs Reporter* 10 (1) (winter 1992): 13–17, provides the only comprehensive survey of contemporary political attitudes in West Virginia. On elections, the only contemporary compilation of information is Ken Hechler, "Financing Elections: West Virginia, the States, and the Nation," *West Virginia Public Affairs Reporter* 7 (3) (summer 1990): 1–7.

For information on efforts to control political corruption, see Michael W. Carey, Larry R. Ellis, and Joseph F. Savage Jr., "Federal Prosecution of State and Local Officials: The Obstacles to Punishing Breaches of the Public Trust and a Proposal for Reform, Part One," *West Virginia Law Review* 94 (winter 1991–92): 301–67; and Robert T. Hall, "The West Virginia Governmental Ethics Act," *West Virginia Public Affairs Reporter* 6 (1) (winter 1989): 1–7.

Intergovernmental Relations. No comprehensive contemporary treatment of this topic exists. W. W. Kaempfer, *Federal Aid in West Virginia: Its Impact on State Government*, Publication 15 (Morgantown: Bureau for Government Research, West Virginia University, 1956) is dated but useful for historical considerations. Several able studies of the Appalachian Regional Commission exist, including Michael Bradshaw, *The Appalachian Regional Commission: Twenty-Five Years of Government Policy* (Lexington: University Press of Kentucky, 1992); Steven Howard Haeberle, *The Appalachian Regional Commission: Evaluating an Experiment in Creative Federalism* (Ph.D. diss., Duke University, 1981); Donald N. Rothblatt, *Regional Planning: The Appalachian Experience* (Lexington MA: D. C. Heath, 1971); Stuart Seely Sprague, ARC: *From Implementation to Payoff Decade and Beyond* (Morehead KY: Appalachian Development Center, Morehead State University, 1986).

Constitutional Development. The Constitution of West Virginia with annotations is accessible in *The West Virginia Code*, vol. 1 (Charlottesville VA: Michie, yearly). Readers should consult the following documentary and secondary sources on its Virginia origins: Robert P. Sutton, *Revolution to Secession: Constitution Making in the Old Dominion* (Charlottesville: University Press of Virginia, 1989); *Proceedings and Debates of the Virginia State Convention of 1829–1830* (Richmond VA: S. Shepherd, 1830); Dickson D. Bruce Jr., *The Rhetoric of Conservatism: The Virginia Convention of 1829–30 and the Conservative Tradition in the South* (San Marino CA: Huntington Library, 1982); and *Journal, Acts, and Proceedings of a General Convention of the State of Virginia Assembled at Richmond on Monday, the Fourteenth Day of October, Eighteen Hundred and Fifty* (Richmond VA: W. Culley, 1851).

On West Virginia constitutions, consult Charles H. Ambler, Frances Haney Atwood, and William B. Mathews, eds., *Debates and Proceedings of the First Constitutional Convention of West Virginia*, 3 vols. (Huntington WV: Gentry Brothers, n.d.); "Constitution of West Virginia—1861–1863," in *The Federal and State Constitutions, Colonial Charters, and Other Organic Laws of the States, Territories, and Colonies Now or Heretofore Forming the United States of America*, ed. Francis Newton Thorpe (Washington: Government Printing Office, 1909); *Journal of Constitutional Convention, Assembled at Charleston, West Virginia, January 16, 1872* (Charleston: Henry S. Walker, 1872); "Constitution of West Virginia—1872," in *The Federal and State Constitutions, Colonial Charters, and Other Organic Laws of the States, Territories, and Colonies Now or Heretofore Forming the United States of America*, ed. Francis Newton Thorpe (Washington: Government Printing Office, 1909). Albert L. Sturm, *The Need for Constitutional Revision in West Virginia*, Publication 1 (Morgantown: Bureau for Government Research, West Virginia University, 1950), and Albert L. Strum, *Major Constitutional Issues in West Virginia*. Publication 21 (Morgantown: Bureau for Government Research, West Virginia University, 1961), are dated critical analyses of the West Virginia Constitution.

Legislature. The biennial edition of the *Manual of the Senate and House of Delegates*, published by the House of Delegates, contains a wealth of historical information, as well as much detail on the current members and structures of the legislature. Christopher Z. Mooney, "The West Virginia State Legislature," in *West Virginia's State Government: The Legislative, Executive, and Judicial Branches*, Institute for Public Affairs Monograph series no. 5 (Morgantown: Institute for Public Affairs, West Virginia University, 1993), pp. 1–26, is the best overview of the contemporary legislature. For further information on the contemporary West Virginia state legislature, see Patricia Bradley, "Commentary: Some Thoughts on My Experiences as a Woman in the West Virginia House of Delegates," in *Government and Politics in West Virginia*, ed. James R. Forrester (Needham MA: Ginn, 1989); David B. McKinley, "Problems and Prospects Facing the Republican Party in the House of Delegates," in *Government and Politics in West Virginia*, ed. James R. Forrester (Needham MA: Ginn, 1989); Suzanne Tewksbury, "Frasure-Singleton Student Legislative Program Manual," in *Government and Politics in West Virginia*, ed. James R. Forrester (Needham MA: Ginn, 1989).

Governor and Administration. Robert Jay Dilger, "The Governor's Office in West Virginia," in *West Virginia's State Government: The Legislative, Executive, and Judicial Branches*, Institute for Public Affairs Monograph series no. 5 (Morgantown: Institute for Public Affairs, West Virginia University, 1993), pp. 27–58, is the only contemporary evaluation of the governorship. John G. Morgan, *West Virginia Governors, 1863–1980*, 2d ed. (Charleston: Charleston Newspapers, 1980) contains descriptive information on each governor.

Budgetary and Fiscal Politics. David K. Brown, "Budgetary Realities in Aging Programs: A State Perspective" (Charleston: West Virginia Commission on Aging, 1992), and Christopher Z. Mooney, "The West Virginia State Budget Process," *West Virginia Public Affairs Reporter* 11 (1) (winter 1994): 2–16, have supplanted earlier studies like Ivor F. Boiarsky, *The Budget . . . A Management of Resources* (Charleston: Legislative Office of Public Information, 1977), and Herman Mertins Jr. and David G. Williams, *West Virginia Budgeting: Problems and Possibilities* (Morgantown: Bureau for Government Research, West Virginia University, 1971). Patrick J. Chase and Robert Jay Dilger, "West Virginia's State Taxes: A Comparative Analysis," *West Virginia Public Affairs Reporter* 8 (4) (fall 1991): 1–10, introduces the reader to West Virginia tax practices.

Judiciary. Richard A. Brisbin Jr., "The West Virginia Judiciary," in *West Virginia's State Government: The Legislative, Executive, and Judicial Branches*, Institute for Public Affairs Monograph series no. 5 (Morgantown: Institute for Public Affairs, West Virginia University, 1993), pp. 59–125, greatly extends the discussion in this book. John Patrick Hagen, "Policy Activism in the West Virginia Supreme Court of Appeals, 1930–1985," *West Virginia Law Review* 89 (fall 1986): 149–65, discusses judicial policymaking from the vantage point of political science.

County and Municipal Government. Mavis Andree Mann (Reeves), *The Structure of City Government in West Virginia*, Publication 12 (Morgantown: Bureau for Government Research, West Virginia University, 1953), and Harold J. Shamburger, *County Government and Administration in West Virginia*, Publication 6 (Morgantown: Bureau for Government Research, West Virginia University, 1952), are dated but still have valuable historical information. Dale Colyer, Anthony Ferrise, David White, and Hettiarachchige Banduratne, *Property Taxes in West Virginia*, Institute for Public Affairs Monograph series no. 4 (Morgantown: Institute for Public Affairs, West Virginia University, 1991), and David White, "The Property Tax in West Virginia: A Review and Evaluation," *West Virginia Public Affairs Reporter* 8 (3) (summer 1991): 1–12, discuss local governmental finance in West Virginia.

Policy Issues. For details on program administration by specific departments, contact the state agency for its annual report. A list of agencies and their addresses is available in the *West Virginia Bluebook*, published semiannually. Studies of public policy in West Virginia include the essays in Dilger and Witt, eds., *West Virginia in the 1990s*, cited above, and Anthony J. DeFrank and Robert D. Duval, "West Virginia in a Global Economy: The Impact of Foreign Trade and Investment," *West Virginia Public Affairs Reporter* 6 (2) (spring 1989): 1–9; Richard A. Ball, *Policy Options for Correctional Facilities in West Virginia*, Institute for Public Affairs Monograph series no. 1 (Morgantown: Institute for Public Affairs, West Virginia University, 1988), and Richard A. Ball, *Corrections in Context: Policy Strategies for West Virginia and the Nation*, Institute for Public Affairs Monograph series no. 3 (Morgantown: Institute for Public Affairs, West Virginia University, 1991) on corrections policy; Anthony J. DeFrank and Allan S. Hammock, "The Health Care Crisis and Medical Liability in West Virginia," *West Virginia Public Affairs Reporter* 7 (1) (winter 1990): 1–10; and on environmental issues, Carla Dickstein and Greg Sayre, *The Socioeconomic Impacts of Landfills*, Technical Report no. 6 (Morgantown: Institute for Public Affairs, West Virginia University, 1989), and Susan Hunter, *The Acid Rain Controversy: Policy Strategies for West Virginia and the Nation*, Institute for Public Affairs Monograph Series no. 2 (Morgantown: Institute for Public Affairs, West Virginia University, 1990).

Appalachian Politics and Society with Reference to West Virginia. Important works include: Appalachian Land Ownership Task Force, *Who Owns Appalachia? Landownership and Its Impact* (Lexington: University Press of Kentucky, 1983); Richard A. Ball, "A Poverty Case: The Analgesic Subculture of the Southern Appalachians," *American Sociological Review* 33 (December 1968): 885–95; Allen W. Batteau, ed., *Appalachia and America: Autonomy and Regional Dependence* (Lexington: University Press of Kentucky, 1983); Allen W. Batteau, *The Invention of Appalachia* (Tucson: University of Arizona Press, 1990); Bruce Ergood and Bruce E. Kuhre, eds., *Appalachia: Social Context Past and Present* (Dubuque IA: Kendall/Hunt, 1976); John Gaventa, *Power and Powerlessness: Quiescence and Rebellion in an Appalachian Valley* (Urbana: University of Illinois Press, 1980); Karl B. Raitz and Richard Ulack with Thomas R. Leinbach, *Appalachia, A Regional Geography: Land, People, and Development* (Boulder CO: Westview Press, 1984); Henry Shapiro, *Appalachia on Our Mind: The Southern Mountains and Mountaineers in the American Consciousness, 1870–1920* (Chapel Hill: University of North Carolina Press, 1978); Jack E. Weller, *Yesterday's People: Life in Contemporary Appalachia* (Lexington: University Press of Kentucky, 1965).

Notes

INTRODUCTION

1 Dawn M. Giovanni, *Forest Statistics for West Virginia—1975 and 1989*, Resource Bulletin NE-114 (Radnor PA: U.S. Dept. of Agriculture, Forest Service, 1990).

2 Donald R. Adams Jr., *Historical Analysis of Major West Virginia Statistics* (Morgantown: Center for Economic Analysis and Statistics, West Virginia University, 1986), tables 3, 4.

3 The ramp is a relative of the leek. It grows in the West Virginia mountains. See Roy B. Clarkson, William Homer Duppstad, and Roland L. Gutherie, *Forest Wildlife Plants of the Monongahela National Forest* (Pacific Grove CA: Boxwood Press, 1980), 73.

4 *West Virginia Economic Summary* (July 1994): 9; West Virginia Research League, *1991 Statistical Handbook*, 21st ed. (Charleston, 1991), 66; Brian J. Cushing, "West Virginia's Economy, 1939–2000," 41, and Clifford B. Hawley, "Demographic Change and Economic Opportunity," 47–72, both in *West Virginia in the 1990s: Opportunities for Economic Progress*, ed. Robert Jay Dilger and Tom Stuart Witt (Morgantown: West Virginia University Press, 1993).

5 West Virginia Department of Health and Human Resources, *West Virginia Provisional 1990 Vital Statistics* (Charleston: 1991), 7, 23–24.

6 U.S. Federal Bureau of Investigation, *Uniform Crime Reports for the United States* (Washington DC: Government Printing Office, 1990), 50–57.

7 Otis K. Rice, *The Allegheny Frontier: West Virginia Beginnings, 1730–1830* (Lexington: University Press of Kentucky, 1970), 21–29, 267–70; Ronald R. Lewis, "From Peasant to Proletariat: The Migration of Southern Blacks to the Central Appalachian Coal Fields," *Journal of Southern History* 55 (February 1989): 77–102; and Joe William Trotter Jr., *Coal, Class, and Color: Blacks in*

Southern West Virginia, 1915–32 (Urbana: University of Illinois Press, 1990), 63–101.

8 U.S. Bureau of the Census, *Statistical Abstract of the United States: 1991*, 111th ed. (Washington DC, 1991), 20–21, 23, 28, 34–35; and Andrew Isserman, Oleg Smirnov, Terance Rephann, David Sorenson, and Elizabeth Bury, *West Virginia Population Projections by County, Age, and Sex, 1990–2020* (Morgantown: Regional Research Institute, West Virginia University, 1992).

9 Richard Ellsworth Fast and Hu Maxwell, *The History and Government of West Virginia* (Morgantown WV: Acme, 1906); Oscar D. Lambert, *West Virginia and Its Government* (Boston: D. C. Heath, 1951); and Claude J. Davis, Eugene R. Elkins, Carl M. Frasure, Mavis Mann Reeves, William R. Ross, and Albert L. Sturm, *West Virginia State and Local Government* (Morgantown: Bureau for Government Research, West Virginia University, 1963).

10 Henry Shapiro, *Appalachia on Our Mind: The Southern Mountains and Mountaineers in the American Consciousness, 1970–1920* (Chapel Hill: University of North Carolina Press, 1978); and Allen W. Batteau, *The Invention of Appalachia* (Tucson: University of Arizona Press, 1990).

11 Bruce Ergood, "Toward a Definition of Appalachia," in *Appalachia: Social Context Past and Present*, ed. Bruce Ergood and Bruce E. Kuhre (Dubuque IA: Kendall/Hunt, 1976), 31–41; and Karl B. Raitz and Richard Ulack with Thomas R. Leinbach, *Appalachia, A Regional Geography: Land, People, and Development* (Boulder CO: Westview, 1984), 9–35.

12 Ryan-McGinn-Samples Research, "The West Virginia Poll," 13–15 March 1989, 8. The other responses were "Mid-Atlantic region" (16 percent), "the South" (15 percent), and "don't know" or no response (14 percent).

13 Helen Lewis and Edward E. Knipe, "The Colonialism Model: The Appalachian Case," in *Colonialism in Modern America*, ed. Helen Matthews Lewis, Linda Johnson, and Donald Askins (Boone NC: Appalachian Consortium, 1978), 9–31; and Emil Malizia, "Economic Imperialism: An Interpretation of Appalachian Underdevelopment," *Appalachian Journal* 1 (spring 1970): 130–37.

14 David S. Walls, "Central Appalachia: A Peripheral Region within an Advanced Capitalist Society," *Journal of Sociology and Social Welfare* 4 (1976): 238–43.

15 *Herald-Advertiser* and *Herald Dispatch, Who Owns West Virginia?* (Huntington WV: Huntington, 1974); Appalachian Land Ownership Task Force, *Addendum to Land Ownership Patterns and Their Impacts on Appalachian Communities: West Virginia*, vol. 7 (Washington DC: Appalachian Regional Commission, 1981), and *Who Owns Appalachia? Land Ownership and Its Impact* (Lexington: University Press of Kentucky, 1983).

16 Patricia D. Beaver, "Participatory Research on Land Ownership in Rural Appala-

chia," in *Appalachia and America: Autonomy and Regional Dependence,* ed. Allen Batteau (Lexington: University Press of Kentucky, 1983), 252–66.

17 David Alan Corbin, *Life, Work, and Rebellion in the Coal Fields: The Southern West Virginia Miners, 1880–1922* (Urbana: University of Illinois Press, 1981); Richard D. Lunt, *Law and Order vs. the Miners: West Virginia, 1907–1933* (Hamden CT: Archon Books, 1979); Neal R. Peirce, *The Border South States: People, Politics, and Power in the Five Border South States* (New York: W. W. Norton, 1975), 150–207; John H. Fenton, *Politics in the Border States* (New Orleans: Hauser, 1957), 82–125; and Gerald W. Johnson, "West Virginia Politics: A Socio-Cultural Analysis of Political Participants" (Ph.D. diss., University of Tennessee, 1970), 63–64.

18 Corbin, *Life, Work, and Rebellion,* 110–16; and Curtis Seltzer, *Fire in the Hole: Miners and Managers in the American Coal Industry* (Lexington: University Press of Kentucky, 1985), 62–65.

19 Seltzer, *Fire in the Hole,* 84–209.

20 It also has been called the "Subculture of Poverty Model" in David S. Walls and Dwight B. Billings, "The Sociology of Southern Appalachia," *Appalachian Journal* 5 (autumn 1977): 132; or an "Analgesic Subculture" in Richard A. Ball, "A Poverty Case: The Analgesic Subculture of the Southern Appalachians," *American Sociological Review* 33 (December 1968): 885–95.

21 Jack E. Weller, *Yesterday's People: Life in Contemporary Appalachia* (Lexington: University Press of Kentucky, 1965), 113–16, and "Appalachia: America's Mineral Colony," in *Colonialism in Modern America,* ed. Lewis, Johnson, and Askins, 47–55.

22 Ball, "A Poverty Case," 885–95; and Richard A. Ball, "New Premises for Planning in Appalachia," *Journal of Sociology and Social Welfare* 2 (1974): 92–101.

23 Stephen L. Fisher, "Victim-Blaming in Appalachia: Cultural Theories and the Southern Mountaineer," in *Appalachia,* ed. Ergood and Kuhre, 139–48; Batteau, *Invention of Appalachia,* 168–203; Lewis and Knipe, "Colonialism Model," 9–31; and Allen Batteau, "Appalachia and the Concept of Culture: A Theory of Shared Misunderstandings," *Appalachian Journal* 7 (winter 1979–80): 22–24.

24 Dwight Billings, "Culture and Poverty in Appalachia: A Theoretical Discussion and Empirical Analysis," *Social Forces* 53 (December 1974): 315–23.

25 Herbert Hirsch, *Poverty and Participation: Political Socialization in an American Sub-Culture* (New York: Free Press, 1971); Dean Jaros, Herbert Hirsch, and Fredric Fleron Jr., "The Malevolent Leader: Political Socialization in an American Sub-Culture," *American Political Science Review* 62 (June 1968): 564–75; Thomas R. Ford, "The Passing of Provincialism," in *The Southern Appalachian*

Region: A Survey, ed. Thomas R. Ford (Lexington: University of Kentucky Press, 1962), 9–34; Janet Boggess Welch, "A Study of Appalachian Cultural Values as Evidenced in the Political and Social Attitudes of Rural West Virginians" (Ph.D. diss., University of Maryland, 1984); and John D. Photiadis, *Community and Change in Rural Appalachia* (Morgantown: West Virginia University Center for Extension and Continuing Education, 1985), 85–118.

26 John Paul Ryan, *Cultural Diversity and the American Experience: Political Participation among Blacks, Appalachians, and Indians* (Beverly Hills CA: Sage, 1975); and Gerald J. Johnson, "Research Note on the Political Correlates of Voter Participation: A Deviant Case Analysis," *American Political Science Review* 65 (September 1971): 768–76.

27 Theda Skocpol and Kenneth Finegold, "State Capacity and Economic Intervention in the Early New Deal," *Political Science Quarterly* 97 (summer 1982): 260 61; Kenneth Finegold and Theda Skocpol, "State, Party, and Industry: From Business Recovery to the Wagner Act in America's New Deal," in *Statemaking and Social Movements: Essays in Theory and Society*, ed. Charles Bright and Susan Harding (Ann Arbor: University of Michigan Press, 1984), 167–69; Ann O'M. Bowman and Richard C. Kearney, "Dimensions of State Government Capacity," *Western Political Quarterly* 41 (1988): 341–62; and Beth Walter Hondale, "A Capacity-Building Framework: A Search for Concept and Purpose," *Public Administration Review* 41 (1981): 575–89.

28 Hannah Fenichel Pitkin, *The Concept of Representation* (Berkeley and Los Angeles: University of California Press, 1967), especially 209.

CHAPTER ONE

1 John W. Kingdon, *Agendas, Alternatives, and Public Policy* (Boston: Little, Brown, 1984), 3–4, 122–23.

2 Richard Orr Curry, *A House Divided: A Study of Statehood Politics and the Copperhead Movement in West Virginia* (Pittsburgh: University of Pittsburgh Press, 1964), 79–90, 100–19; and John Alexander Williams, *West Virginia: A Bicentennial History* (New York: W. W. Norton, 1976), 75–86, and "The New Dominion and the Old: Ante-Bellum and Statehood Politics as the Backyard of West Virginia's 'Bourbon Democracy,'" *West Virginia History* 33 (1971–72): 349–57.

3 Raitz and Ulack with Leinbach, *Appalachia, A Regional Geography*, 43–51.

4 Andrew Isserman and David Sorenson, "State, County, and City Population Change," *West Virginia Demographic Monitor* 1, no. 2 (February 1994): 1–3.

5 Charles H. Ambler, *A History of Transportation in the Ohio Valley* (Glendale CA: Arthur H. Clark, 1932), 185–209, 211–38, 265–318.

6 Charles H. Ambler and Festus P. Summers, *West Virginia: The Mountain State*, 2d ed. (Englewood Cliffs NJ: Prentice-Hall, 1958), 330–42; and Otis K. Rice, *West Virginia: A History* (Lexington: University Press of Kentucky, 1985), 81, 184–86, 202–3.

7 *Rand McNally 1992 Commercial Atlas and Marketing Guide*, 123d ed. (Chicago, 1992), 39; and Richard Franklin Bensel, *Sectionalism and American Political Development* (Madison: University of Wisconsin Press, 1984), 415–21.

8 Otis K. Rice, *The Allegheny Frontier: West Virginia Beginnings, 1730–1830* (Lexington: University Press of Kentucky, 1970); Alexander Scott Withers, *Chronicles of Border Warfare; or, a History of the Settlement by the Whites of North-Western Virginia, and of the Indian Wars and Massacres in that section of the State, with Reflections, Anecdotes, etc.* (Clarksburg VA (now WV): Joseph Israel, 1831); and Kenneth Keller, "What Is Distinctive about the Scotch-Irish?" in *Appalachian Frontiers: Settlement, Society, and Development in the Preindustrial Era*, ed. Robert D. Mitchell (Lexington: University Press of Kentucky, 1991), 68–86.

9 Phil Conley, *History of the West Virginia Coal Industry* (Charleston: Educational Foundation, 1960), 88–90; Crandall A. Shifflett, *Coal Towns: Life, Work, and Culture in the Company Towns of Southern Appalachia* (Knoxville: University of Tennessee Press, 1991), 67–80; Ronald R. Lewis, "From Peasant to Proletariat: The Migration of Southern Blacks to the Central Appalachian Coal Fields," *Journal of Southern History* 55 (February 1989): 77–102; and Trotter, *Coal, Class, and Color*, 63–101.

10 Rice, *West Virginia*, 64–66.

11 Rice, *West Virginia*, 67.

12 Bernard Quinn, Herman Anderson, Martin Bradley, Paul Goetting, and Peggy Shriver, *Churches and Church Membership in the United States, 1980* (Atlanta: Glenmary Research Center, 1982), 26, 297–301.

13 V. O. Key, *Politics, Parties, and Pressure Groups*, 5th ed. (New York: Thomas Y. Crowell, 1964), 228–53.

14 Richard A. Brisbin Jr. and Robert Jay Dilger, "Citizen Evaluations of Government in West Virginia: The 1992 West Virginia Political Survey," *West Virginia Public Affairs Reporter* 10, no. 1 (winter 1992): 13–17.

15 Charles H. Ambler, *A History of Education in West Virginia from Early Colonial Times to 1949* (Huntington WV: Standard, 1951), 1–65; Charles H. Ambler, *Sectionalism in Virginia from 1776 to 1861* (Chicago: University of Chicago Press, 1910); Ambler and Summers, *West Virginia*, 150–55, 164–65; Van Beck Hall, "The Politics of Appalachian Virginia, 1790–1830," in *Appalachian Frontiers*,

ed. Mitchell, 166–86; Rice, *Allegheny Frontier*, 210–34, 309–41; and Rice, *West Virginia*, 80–89, 99–102.

16 Curry, *House Divided*, 28–68, 120–30, 141–50; and Williams, *West Virginia*, 75–86.

17 Richard O. Curry, "Crisis Politics in West Virginia," in *Radicalism, Racism, and Party Realignment: The Border States during Reconstruction*, ed. Richard O. Curry (Baltimore: Johns Hopkins University Press, 1969), 80–104; Ambler and Summers, *West Virginia*, 264–77; and Henry T. Gerofsky, "Reconstruction in West Virginia," *West Virginia History* 6 (July 1945): 295–360 and 7 (October 1945): 5–39.

18 Ambler and Summers, *West Virginia*, 281–97, 376–93.

19 John Alexander Williams, *West Virginia and the Captains of Industry* (Morgantown: West Virginia University Library, 1976), 1–109, 148–87.

20 Paul Salstrom, "The Agricultural Origins of Economic Dependency, 1840–1880," in *Appalachian Frontiers*, ed. Mitchell, 261–83.

21 Kenneth R. Bailey, "The Judicious Mixture: Negroes and Immigrants in the West Virginia Coal Mines, 1880–1917," *West Virginia History* 34 (January 1973): 141–61; Corbin, *Life, Work, and Rebellion*, 1–60; and Williams, *Captains of Industry*, 110–47, 196–232.

22 West Virginia Senate and House of Delegates, *Testimony and Report of the Legislative Bribery Committee Raised under Joint Resolution No. 22* (1913).

23 Williams, *Captains of Industry*, 125–47; John Alexander Williams, "Davis and Elkins of West Virginia: Businessmen in Politics," (Ph.D. diss., Yale University, 1967), 41–61; and Williams, *West Virginia*, 115–29.

24 Corbin, *Life, Work, and Rebellion*, 87–252; Daniel P. Jordan, "The Mingo War: Labor Violence in the Southern West Virginia Coal Fields, 1919–1922," in *Essays in Southern Labor History: Selected Papers, Southern Labor History Conference, 1976*, ed. Gary Fink and Merl Reed (Westport CT: Greenwood Press, 1977), 102–43; Winthrop D. Lane, *Civil War in West Virginia: A Story of Industrial Conflict in the Coal Mines* (New York: B. W. Huebesch, 1921); Howard Lee, *Bloodletting in Appalachia* (Parsons WV: McClain, 1969); and U.S. Senate Committee on Education and Labor, *West Virginia Coal Fields: Hearings before the Committee on Education and Labor . . . , Pursuant to S. Res. 80*, 3 vols. 67th Cong., 1st sess., 1921–1922.

25 Ambler and Summers, *West Virginia*, 460–65; and Shifflett, *Coal Towns*, 112–43.

26 Ambler and Summers, *West Virginia*, 538–59; Rice, *West Virginia*, 266–87, and Williams, *West Virginia*, 171–80.

27 Keith Dix, *What's a Coal Miner to Do? The Mechanization of Coal Mining* (Pittsburgh: University of Pittsburgh Press, 1988).

28 Donald R. Adams, *Historical Analysis of Major West Virginia Statistics* (Morgantown: Center for Economic Analysis and Statistics, West Virginia University, 1986), tables 2.8, 3.2.

29 "Overview of the West Virginia Economy: 1990–1994," *West Virginia Business and Economic Review* (spring 1995): 5.

30 "Overview of the West Virginia Economy," 5.

31 Hawley, "Demographic Change and Economic Opportunity," 47–72; and Cushing, "West Virginia's Economy," 17–41.

32 Robert Jay Dilger and Tom Stuart Witt, "West Virginia's Economic Future," in *West Virginia in the 1990s*, ed. Dilger and Witt, 3–15.

33 Cushing, "West Virginia's Economy," 33.

34 Williams, *West Virginia*, 174–86.

35 Stanley J. Kloc, "Small Business in West Virginia: Trends and Strategies," 97–119, and William S. Reece, "Local Government Finance and Its Implications for West Virginia's Economic Development," 285–317, both in *West Virginia in the 1990s*, ed. Dilger and Witt.

36 Michael W. Carey, Larry R. Ellis, and Joseph F. Savage Jr., "Federal Prosecution of State and Local Officials: The Obstacles to Punishing Breaches of the Public Trust and a Proposal for Reform, Part One," *West Virginia Law Review* 94 (winter 1991–92): 301–67; Huey Perry, *They'll Cut Off Your Project: A Mingo County Chronicle* (New York: Praeger, 1972); Lester "Bus" Perry, *Forty Years Mountain Politics, 1930–1970* (Parsons WV: McClain, 1971), 81–95, 105; and Bill Peterson, *Coaltown Revisited: An Appalachian Notebook* (Chicago: Henry Regnery, 1972), 204–22.

37 Ron Hutchison, "Moore Not End of Trail for Feds," *Charleston Daily Mail*, 19 April 1990, 1A; Jack McCarthy, "Moore Sentenced to Prison, Fined," *Charleston Gazette*, 11 July 1990, 1A; and Paul Nyden, "Moore Tax Official Pleads Guilty to Felony," *Charleston Gazette*, 3 July 1990, 1A.

38 "Lobbyist Pleads Guilty to Tax Evasion Charges," *Charleston Gazette*, 6 January 1989, 3C; Ron Hutchison, "Former Lobbyist Sentenced," *Charleston Daily Mail*, 23 March 1989, 10B; Jack McCarthy, "Lobbyist Pleads Guilty as Probe into Tonkovich's Dealings Grows," *Charleston Gazette*, 1 September 1989, 1A, 6A; and Ron Hutchison, "Ex-Aide Says He Was Sacred," *Charleston Daily Mail*, 12 September 1989, 1A, 11A.

39 Barry Bernak, "A Crooked Tradition," *Morgantown Dominion-Post*, 11 July, 1990, 1D (reprinted from the *Los Angeles Times*).

40 "Manchin Testimony Showed Knowledge of Losses," *Charleston Gazette*, 19 July 1989, 6A; and "Investment Fund Found Used for Self-Promotion," *Charleston Gazette*, 21 July 1989, 6A.

41 Jack McCarthy, "Corruption Cloud Hangs over Mingo," *Charleston Gazette*, 8

November 1987, 1A, 4A; and "Ongoing Mingo Probe Examines Political Money," *Morgantown Dominion Post*, 15 February 1988, 3A.

42 Carey, Ellis, and Savage, "Federal Prosecution of State and Local Officials," 301–67.

43 Robert T. Hall, "The West Virginia Governmental Ethics Act," *West Virginia Public Affairs Reporter* 6, no. 1 (winter 1989): 1–7.

44 Lucian W. Pye, "Political Culture," *International Encyclopedia of the Social Sciences*, vol. 12 (New York: Crowell, Collier and Macmillan, 1968), 218.

45 Kingdon, *Agendas*, 122–30.

46 Daniel J. Elazar, *American Federalism: A View from the States*, 3d ed. (New York: Harper and Row, 1984), 114–22, and *Cities of the Prairie: The Metropolitan Frontier and American Politics* (New York: Basic Books, 1970), 256–80.

47 Elazar, *American Federalism*, 123–37.

48 Peter F. Nardulli, "Political Subcultures in the American States: An Empirical Examination of Elazar's Formulation," *American Politics Quarterly* 18 (July 1990): 287–315. We would like to thank Professor Nardulli for graciously providing us with the questionnaire developed by the University of Illinois Institute of Government and Public Affairs to generate data on political culture. Responses from the West Virginia sample of 517 persons were 17.9 percent individualistic, 47.6 percent moralistic, and 21.6 percent traditionalistic.

49 Elazar, *American Federalism*, 131.

50 Elazar, *Cities of the Prairie*, 262–63.

CHAPTER TWO

1 Brisbin and Dilger, "Citizen Evaluations of Government in West Virginia," 13–17.

2 Diane D. Blair, *Arkansas Politics and Government: Do the People Rule?* (Lincoln: University of Nebraska Press, 1988), 137; and Larry Sabato, *Goodbye to Good-Time Charlie: The American Governor Transformed*, 2d ed. (Washington DC: Congressional Quarterly Press, 1983), 9.

3 "Public Attitudes on Governments and Taxes," *Intergovernmental Perspective* 20, no. 3 (summer/fall 1994): 29.

4 Lester W. Milbrath, *Political Participation: How and Why Do People Get Involved in Politics?* (Chicago: Rand McNally, 1965), 19.

5 Jae-On Kim, John R. Petrocik, and Stephen N. Enokson, "Voter Turnout among the American States: Systemic and Individual Components," *American Political Science Review* 69 (March 1975): 108, 114.

6 Angus Campbell et al., *Elections and the Political Order* (New York: John Wiley,

1966), 40–62; and William H. Flanigan and Nancy H. Zingale, *Political Behavior of the American Electorate*, 7th ed. (Washington DC: Congressional Quarterly Press, 1991), 12–14.

7 Samuel C. Patterson and Gregory A. Caldeira, "Getting Out the Vote: Participation in Gubernatorial Elections," *American Political Science Review* 77 (September 1983): 686.

8 Avery Leiserson, *Parties and Politics* (New York: Alfred A. Knopf, 1958), 35; and Larry J. Sabato, *The Party's Just Begun: Shaping Political Parties for America's Future* (Glenview IL: Scott, Foresman, 1988), 5.

9 Frank J. Sorauf and Paul Allen Beck, *Party Politics in America*, 6th ed. (Glenview IL: Scott, Foresman, 1988), 12–20; Robert Dahl, *Democracy in the United States: Promises and Performance*, 4th ed. (Boston: Houghton Mifflin, 1981), 222–23; and Dennis S. Ippolito and Thomas G. Walker, *Political Parties, Interest Groups, and Public Policy: Group Influence in American Politics* (Englewood Cliffs NJ: Prentice-Hall, 1980), 1–6.

10 Clinton Rossiter, *Parties and Politics in America* (Ithaca NY: Cornell University Press, 1960), chapters 2 and 5.

11 *American National Election Study* (Ann Arbor: University of Michigan, 1992).

12 V. O. Key, *American State Politics: An Introduction* (New York: Alfred A. Knopf, 1963), 13–16.

13 Philip Nussell, "Business Needs Viable Candidates," *Charleston Daily Mail*, 10 November 1992, 10.

14 Richard Grimes, "Charleston to Regain GOP Headquarters," *Charleston Daily Mail*, 16 May 1993.

15 Robert S. Erikson, John P. McIver, and Gerald C. Wright Jr., "State Political Culture and Public Opinion," *American Political Science Review* 81 (September 1987): 801.

16 Patricia J. Detch, *West Virginia County Party Chairmen: A Profile* (master's thesis, West Virginia University, 1972), 52.

17 Fenton, *Politics in the Border States*, chapters 4 and 5.

18 Thomas R. Dye, "Party and Policy in the States," *Journal of Politics* 46 (November 1984): 1097–1116.

CHAPTER THREE

1 Jeffrey M. Berry, *The Interest Group Society* (Boston: Little, Brown, 1984); and Kingdon, *Agendas, Alternatives, and Public Policies*, 48–74.

2 Peirce, *The Border South States*, 151.

3 This chapter draws heavily on James R. Oxendale and Allan S. Hammock, "West

Virginia: Coal and the New West Virginia Politics," in *Interest Group Politics in the Northeastern States*, ed. Ronald J. Hrebenar and Clive S. Thomas (University Park: Pennsylvania State University Press, 1993), 348–66.

4 Williams, *West Virginia*, 105–9.

5 Evelyn L. Harris and Frank J. Krebs, *From Humble Beginnings* (Charleston: West Virginia Labor History Publishing Fund Committee, 1960), 19–20.

6 Homer L. Morris, *The Plight of the Bituminous Coal Miner* (Philadelphia: University of Pennsylvania Press, 1934), 86.

7 Peirce, *The Border South States*, 182; and Gerald M. Stern, *The Buffalo Creek Disaster* (New York: Random House, 1976), ix.

8 Williams, *West Virginia*, 105–9.

9 Peirce, *The Border South States*, 169.

10 John Hurd, president, West Virginia Chamber of Commerce, interview by authors, Charleston, 7 December 1987.

11 1977 data are from the clerk of the West Virginia Senate; 1993 data are from the West Virginia Ethics Commission.

12 Brent Cunningham and Paul Owens, "Chambers Most Influential at State House, Poll Shows," *Charleston Daily Mail*, 10 February 1993, 1A, 7A.

13 Clive S. Thomas and Ronald J. Hrebenar, "Interest Groups in the State," in *Politics in the American States*, ed. Virginia Gray, Herbert Jacob, and Robert B. Albritton (Glenview IL: Scott, Foresman, 1990), 150–51.

14 Joseph A. Schlesinger, "Lawyers and American Politics: A Clarified View," *Midwest Journal of Political Science* 1 (1957): 326–39; and David Derge, "The Lawyer as Decision Maker in the American State Legislature," *Journal of Politics* 21 (1959): 408–23.

15 *Martindale-Hubbel Law Directory* 7 (1988): 1005B.

16 West Virginia Business and Industry Council, *1987 Ratings and Analysis of the West Virginia Legislature* (Charleston, n.d.), 1.

17 Hurd, interview.

18 Robert T. Hall, "The West Virginia Governmental Ethics Act," *West Virginia Public Affairs Reporter* 6 (winter 1989): 6–7.

19 Phil Kabler, "Weakened Ethics Law Frustrates Commission," *Charleston Gazette* 8 January 1993, 1A.

20 Daniel Bice and Jack Deutsch, "Ethics Bill's Impact Felt at Capitol," *Charleston Daily Mail*, 1 March 1989, 1A, 7A; and A. V. Gallagher, "Ethics Law Has Curbed Unrestrained Lobbying," *Charleston Daily Mail*, 25 June 1990, 1A.

21 A. V. Gallagher, "Coal Lobbyists Called Progressive," *Charleston Gazette-Mail*, 8 March 1992, 8A.

22 Phil Kabler, "Ethics Penalties against Turnpike Official Upheld," *Charleston Gazette*, 11 March 1994, D1.

23 Paul Owens, "Insurance, Health PACs Active in '92," *Charleston Gazette*, 13 May 1993, 1A, 9A.

24 Common Cause, *Invested Interests: Money and Politics in the 1993 West Virginia Gubernatorial Election*, Research Paper (Charleston, 1993), 5.

25 Clifford B. Hawley, "Demographic Change and Economic Opportunity," in *West Virginia in the 1990s*, ed. Dilger and Witt, 47–72.

26 Aviva L. Brandt, "Environmentalists Happy with Session," *Charleston Gazette*, 12 April 1993, 2A.

CHAPTER FOUR

1 U.S. Bureau of the Census, "Government Units in 1992," Preliminary Report, *1992 Census of Governments* (Washington DC: U.S. Government Printing Office, 1992), 3–7.

2 Rice, *West Virginia*, 183, 184; and Ambler, *A History of Transportation*, 400–22.

3 Ambler, *A History of Transportation*, 134–38, 244, 416–18.

4 Daniel J. Elazar, "Federal-State Collaboration in the Nineteenth-Century United States," in *American Federalism in Perspective*, ed. Aaron Wildavsky (Boston: Little, Brown, 1967), 191–92; and Harry N. Scheiber, "Federalism and Legal Process: Historical and Contemporary Analysis of the American System," *Law and Society Review* 14 (spring 1980): 669–83.

5 Kaempfer, *Federal Aid in West Virginia* (Morgantown: Bureau for Government Research, 1956), 7–12; and Rice, *West Virginia*, 179.

6 Rice, *West Virginia*, 268.

7 Robert Jay Dilger, "The Expansion and Centralization of American Governmental Functions," in *American Intergovernmental Relations Today: Perspectives and Controversies*, ed. Robert Jay Dilger (Englewood Cliffs NJ: Prentice-Hall, 1986), 15–19.

8 U.S. Senate Committee on Environment and Public Works, *Extension of the Appalachian Regional Commission and the Title V Regional Commissions*, 96th Cong., 1st sess., 21 February 1979, 1–5, 34–82; and Michael Bradshaw, *The Appalachian Regional Commission: Twenty-Five Years of Government Policy* (Lexington: University Press of Kentucky, 1992).

9 U.S. Advisory Commission on Intergovernmental Relations, *Regulatory Federalism: Policy, Process, Impact, and Reform* (Washington DC, 1984); Joseph Zimmerman, *Federal Preemption: The Silent Revolution* (Ames: Iowa State University Press, 1991); and Timothy J. Conlan and David R. Beam, "Federal Mandates: The Record of Reform and Future Prospects," *Intergovernmental Perspective* 18:4 (fall 1992): 7–11, 15.

10 Gainer, *Analysis of Receipts and Expenditures, FY 1993* (Charleston: Office of the

State Auditor, 1993), 12; and Gaston Caperton, *Executive Budget of West Virginia, FY 1995* (Charleston: Office of the Governor, 1994), 214.

11 U.S. Advisory Commission on Intergovernmental Relations, *Significant Features of Fiscal Federalism* (Washington DC, 1992), 57.

12 Michael Barone and Grant Ujifusa, *The Almanac of American Politics, 1994* (Washington DC: National Journal, 1994), 1363.

13 U.S. Bureau of the Census, *Statistical Abstract of the United States, 1995* (Washington DC: U.S. Government Printing Office, 1995), p. 343; *West Virginia Research League, 1993 Statistical Handbook* (Charleston, 1993), 89; Gainer, *Analysis, FY 1993*, 9; and Gaston Caperton, *Executive Budget of West Virginia, FY 1996* (Charleston: Office of the Governor, 1995), xx.

14 West Virginia Code, § 29-1 (1992).

15 David C. Nice, "State Participation in Interstate Compacts," *Publius* 17, no. 2 (spring 1987): 70.

16 John G. Morgan, *West Virginia Governors*, 2d ed. (Charleston: Charleston Newspapers, 1980), 396.

17 John Hoff, executive director, West Virginia Association of Counties, interview by authors, Harper's Ferry WV, 9 October 1992.

18 Chris Miller, "State Takes Control of Logan School System," *Charleston Gazette*, 6 August 1992, 1A, 9A; and Steven J. Keith, "Logan Seizure Last Resort, Officials Say," *Charleston Daily Mail*, 6 August 1992, 1A, 9A.

19 The West Virginia Regional Jail and Correctional Facility Authority Act of 1989 changed the name of the West Virginia Regional Jail and Prison Authority to the West Virginia Jail and Correctional Facility Authority.

20 Joseph A. Clayton, Robert Jay Dilger, and Greg Sayre, "Landfills and West Virginia's Economic Development," in *West Virginia in the 1990s*, ed. Dilger and Witt, 171–94.

21 Charlene Giagola, "General Revenue Budget, FY 1995–96," *Wrap-Up: The Newsletter of the West Virginia State Legislature* (May 1995): 3.

22 David White, "The Property Tax in West Virginia: A Review and Evaluation," *The West Virginia Public Affairs Reporter* 8, no. 3 (summer 1991): 1–12; and William S. Reece, "Local Government Finance and Its Implications for West Virginia's Economic Development," in *West Virginia in the 1990s*, ed. Dilger and Witt, 285–317.

CHAPTER FIVE

1 Curry, *House Divided*, 28–85.

2 Curry, *House Divided*, 86–99.

3 "Constitution of West Virginia—1861–1863" (Article II, § 9), in *The Federal

and State Constitutions, Colonial Charters, and Other Organic Laws of the States, Territories, and Colonies Now or Heretofore Forming the United States of America, ed. Francis Newton Thorpe (Washington DC: Government Printing Office, 1909), 4014–16 [hereafter cited as *Constitutions*]; Merrill D. Peterson and Robert C. Vaughan, eds., *The Virginia Statute for Religious Freedom: Its Evolution and Consequences in American History* (Cambridge: Cambridge University Press, 1988), xvii–xviii; Charles H. Ambler, Frances Haney Atwood, and William B. Mathews, eds., *Debates and Proceedings of the First Constitutional Convention of West Virginia*, 3 vols. (Huntington WV: Gentry Brothers, n.d.); and "Constitution of Ohio—1851" (Article V, §§ 1–2), in *Constitutions*, 2924.

4 "Constitution of West Virginia—1861–1862" (Article V), in *Constitutions*, 4022–23. Compare to "Constitution of Virginia—1850" (Article V), in *Constitutions*, 3843–45.

5 "Constitution of West Virginia—1861–1862" (Article VI), in *Constitutions*, 4023–25. Compare to "Constitution of Virginia—1850" (Article VI), in *Constitutions*, 3845–49.

6 "Constitution of Ohio—1851" (Article X), in *Constitutions*, 2927–28, 4158, and "Constitution of West Virginia—1861–1863" (Article VII, §§ 1–3), in *Constitutions*, 4025–26.

7 Curry, *House Divided*, 100–35.

8 Curry, *House Divided*, 74–78, 141–52.

9 Curry, "Crisis Politics in West Virginia," 80–104; Henry T. Gerofsky, "Reconstruction in West Virginia (I)," *West Virginia History* 6 (July 1945): 295–360; and Williams, "New Dominion and the Old," 349–57.

10 *Journal of Constitutional Convention, Assembled at Charleston, West Virginia, January 16, 1872* (Charleston: Henry S. Walker, 1872); Henry T. Gerofsky, "Reconstruction in West Virginia (II)," *West Virginia History* 7 (October 1945): 5–39; and Williams, "New Dominion and the Old," 365–73.

11 Article I, § 2, on states' rights was added by motion on 13 March 1872; see *Journal of Constitutional Convention*, 167–68.

12 Stephen Skowronek, *Building a New American State: The Expansion of National Administrative Capacities, 1877–1920* (Cambridge: Cambridge University Press, 1982).

13 *Walter v. West Virginia Bd. of Educ*, 610 F. Supp. 1169 (S.D.W.Va. 1985), following *Wallace v. Jaffree*, 472 U.S. 38 (1985).

14 Except for every fourth year after 1973, when the legislature would convene to open election returns, adjourn, and reconvene on the second Wednesday of February.

15 Strum, "Development," 91–92.

16 W. W. Kaempfer, *The Board of Public Works: West Virginia's Plural Executive* (Morgantown: Bureau for Government Research, West Virginia University, 1957), 7–19.

17 *United States v. Darby*, 312 U.S. 100 (1941), and *Brown v. Board of Education*, 347 U.S. 483 (1954) and 349 U.S. 294 (1955).

18 On residency requirements see *Dunn v. Blumstein*, 405 U.S. 330 (1972); on military voting see *Carrington v. Rash*, 380 U.S. 89 (1965).

19 *Reynolds v. Sims*, 377 U.S. 533 (1964).

CHAPTER SIX

1 Alan Rosenthal, "The Legislative Institution—Transformed and at Risk," in *The State of the States*, 2d ed., ed. Carl Van Horn (Washington DC: Congressional Quarterly Press, 1993).

2 The legislature convenes on the second Wednesday in February in years following a gubernatorial election.

3 Beth Bazar, *State Legislators' Occupations: A Decade of Change* (Denver: National Conference of State Legislatures, 1987).

4 James David Barber, *The Lawmakers: Recruitment and Adaptation to Legislative Life* (New Haven: Yale University Press, 1965).

5 Katrina L. Schochet and David M. Hedge, "Redistricting in West Virginia" (Morgantown: West Virginia University, n.d.).

6 Alan Rosenthal, "A Vanishing Breed," *State Legislatures* (November/December 1989): 30–34.

7 Burdett Loomis, "Trends, Cycles, and Endgames: Legislative Implications of Political Time" (paper presented at the Midwest Political Science Association, Chicago, 1991), 9–10.

8 Christopher Z. Mooney, "Measuring U.S. State Legislative Professionalism: An Evaluation of Five Indices," *State and Local Government Review* 26 (1994): 70–78.

9 John Burns, *The Sometimes Governments* (New York: Bantam Books, 1971), 107.

10 Mavis Mann Reeves, *The Question of State Government Capability* (Washington DC: Advisory Commission on Intergovernmental Relations, 1985), 81.

11 Council of State Governments, *The Book of the States, 1994–95*, (Lexington KY, 1994, 157.

12 Donald L. Kopp, ed., *Manual of the Senate and House of Delegates: 70th Legislature, 199–92* (Charleston: West Virginia House of Delegates), 368–70.

13 American Society of Legislative Clerks and Secretaries, *Inside the Legislative Process* (Denver: National Conference of State Legislatures, 1988), 62.

14 American Society of Legislative Clerks and Secretaries, *Inside the Legislative Process*, 62–64.

15 James R. Oxendale Jr., "Membership Stability on Standing Committees in Legislative Lower Chambers," *State Government* 54 (1981): 126; and Kopp, *Manual*, 283–85, 368–70.

16 William J. Keefe and Morris S. Ogul, *The American Legislative Process: Congress and the States*, 7th ed. (Englewood Cliffs NJ: Prentice-Hall, 1989), 48–49.

17 Council of State Governments, *Book of the States*, 166.

18 Burns, *Sometimes Governments*, 161–67; Reeves, *State Government Capability*, 90–92.

19 Alan Rosenthal and Rod Forth, "The Legislative Assembly Line: Law Production in the American States," *Legislative Studies Quarterly* 3 (1978): 265–91.

20 Council of State Governments, *Book of the States, 1994–95*, 148–53.

21 Alan Rosenthal, *Legislative Life* (New York: Harper and Row, 1981), 256.

22 Rosenthal, *Legislative Life*, 314.

23 Rosenthal, *Legislative Life*, 317.

24 Council of State Governments, *Book of the States, 1994–95*, 164–66.

25 Kopp, *Manual*, 283, 268.

26 West Virginia Legislative Auditor, *Digest of Enrolled Budget Bill: Regular Session of the Legislature of West Virginia* (Charleston: Office of the Legislative Auditor, 1991).

27 *Common Cause v. Tomblin*, 413 S.E. 2d 358 (W. Va. 1991).

CHAPTER SEVEN

1 Robert Jay Dilger, *National Intergovernmental Programs* (Englewood Cliffs NJ: Prentice-Hall, 1989); John Kincaid, "From Cooperative to Coercive Federalism," *The Annals* 509 (May 1990): 139–52; Joseph F. Zimmerman, *Federal Preemption: The Silent Revolution* (Ames: Iowa State University Press, 1991); Timothy Conlan, "And the Beat Goes On: Intergovernmental Mandates and Preemption in an Era of Deregulation," *Publius* 21, no. 3 (summer 1991): 43–58; and Timothy J. Conlan and David R. Beam, "Federal Mandates: The Record of Reform and Future Prospects," *Intergovernmental Perspective* 18, no. 4 (fall 1992): 7–15.

2 Sabato, *Goodbye to Goodtime Charlie*, 1–5.

3 George Weeks, "A Statehouse Hall of Fame," *State Government* 55, no. 2 (spring 1982): 67–69, 71–73.

4 Ann O'M. Bowman and Richard Kearney, *The Resurgence of the States* (Englewood Cliffs NJ: Prentice-Hall, 1986); and Thad L. Beyle, "Governors," in

Politics in the American States, 5th ed., ed. Virginia Gray, Herbert Jacob, and Robert B. Albritton (Glenview IL: Scott, Foresman/Little Brown, 1990), 201–51.

5 Beyle, "Governors," 201–51; and Mavis Mann Reeves, "The States as Polities: Reformed, Reinvigorated, Resourceful," *The Annals* (May 1990): 83–93.

6 Bowman and Kearney, *Resurgence of the States*, 47–75.

7 John G. Morgan, *West Virginia Governors*, 2d ed. (Charleston: Charleston Newspapers, 1980), 366–67.

8 Council of State Governments, *The Book of the States, 1992–93* (Lexington KY: Council of State Governments, 1992), 33–35.

9 Beyle, "Governors," 201–51; and Council of State Governments, *Book of the States, 1992–93*, 33–35.

10 "State Officials Ask Legal Immunity for 1987 Investment Fund Loss," *Charleston Gazette*, 23 September 1992, 3A; Jack Deutsch, "Brotherton Sets Impeachment Trial Guidelines," *Charleston Daily Mail*, 23 May 1989, 1A; and A. V. Gallagher, "Manchin Closes Out Long Career," *Charleston Daily Mail*, 8 July 1989, 2A.

11 Jeffrey Bair, "Amendments Face Battle," *Charleston Daily Mail*, 28 August 1989, 5A; and Mark W. Kelley, "Amendment Offers Citizens Path to Better Government," *Charleston Gazette*, 30 August 1989, 1A.

12 Sabato, *Goodbye to Goodtime Charlie*, 198–201; and Bowman and Kearney, *Resurgence of the States*, 65–68.

13 Morgan, *West Virginia Governors*, 188–550. In West Virginia, the constitutional qualifications for office are that the governor must be at least thirty years old, a state citizen for at least five years, a legal resident of West Virginia, a U.S. citizen, and a qualified voter.

14 Morgan, *West Virginia Governors*, 277–333.

15 Ron Hutchinson, "Moore Pleads Guilty; Prison Term Possible," *Charleston Daily Mail*, 8 May 1990, 1A, 9A; and Bill Poovey, "Moore Turns Himself In, Awaits Job Assignment," *Charleston Daily Mail*, 8 August 1990, 1A, 9A.

16 Morgan, *West Virginia Governors*, 208–75, 334–550.

17 Morgan, *West Virginia Governors*, 365–450.

18 James K. Conant, "Executive Branch Reorganization in the States, 1965–1991," in Council of State Governments, *Book of the States, 1992–93*, 64–73.

19 Brent Cunningham, "Are the Secretaries Really Super?" *Charleston Daily Mail*, 29 November 1991, 1A, 9A.

20 Martha W. Weinberg, *Managing the State* (Cambridge MA: MIT Press, 1977), 58; and Bowman and Kearney, *Resurgence of the States*, 47–75.

21 Beyle, "Governors," 180–221; and National Governors' Association, "The In-

stitutionalized Powers of the Governorship," *States Services Management Notes* (June 1987): 14–17.

22 Thad L. Beyle, "The Institutionalized Powers of the Governorship: 1965–1985," *Comparative State Politics Newsletter* 9, no. 1 (February 1988): 23–29.

23 Beyle, "Institutional Powers," 23–29.

CHAPTER EIGHT

1 Patrick J. Chase and Robert J. Dilger, "West Virginia's State Taxes: A Comparative Analysis," *West Virginia Public Affairs Reporter* 8, no. 4 (fall 1991): 1–10; and U.S. Advisory Commission on Intergovernmental Relations, *RTS 1991: State Revenue Capacity and Effort* (Washington DC, 1993), 132.

2 Office of the Governor, *Executive Budget, Fiscal Year 1996: Budget Detail* (Charleston, 1995).

3 Office of the Governor, *Executive Budget, Fiscal Year 1996.*

4 Allen Schick, "An Inquiry into the Possibility of a Budgetary Theory," in *New Directions in Budget Theory*, ed. Irene S. Rubin (Albany: SUNY Press, 1988).

5 Herman Mertins Jr., and David G. Williams, *West Virginia Budgeting: Problems and Possibilities* (Morgantown: Bureau for Government Research, 1971), chapter 2; and Claude J. Davis et al., *West Virginia State and Local Government* (Morgantown: Bureau for Government Research, 1963), chapter 10.

6 Council of State Governments, *The Book of the States: 1992–93*, 351.

7 Allen Schick, *Budget Innovations in the States* (Washington DC: Brookings Institution, 1971); and Ira Sharkansky, "Agency Requests, Gubernatorial Support and Budget Success in State Legislatures," *American Political Science Review* 62 (1968): 1220–31.

8 Schick, *Budget Innovation*, chapter 6.

9 Marcia A. Howard and Laura L. Shaw, *Budgetary Processes in the States* (Washington DC: National Association of State Budget Officers, 1989), 15.

10 David K. Brown, "Budgetary Realities in Aging Programs: A State Perspective," (Charleston: West Virginia Commission on Aging, 1992), 5.

11 Beyle, "Governors," 224.

12 In a year following a gubernatorial election year, the budget is presented to the legislature thirty days after the second Wednesday in January to allow the (potentially) newly elected governor time to put his or her stamp on the proposal.

13 Henry J. Raimondo, "State Budgeting in the Nineties," in *The State of the States*, 2d ed., ed. Carl E. Van Horn (Washington DC: Congressional Quarterly Press, 1993).

14 M. E. Mowery, Alison Patient, and Debra Graham, "Brief of Respondents in the

Supreme Court of Appeals of West Virginia: Common Cause v. Tomblin,'' unpublished; *Common Cause v. Tomblin*, 413 S.E. 2d 358 (W.Va. 1991).

15 Brown, "Budgetary Realities."

16 Reeves, *State Government Capability*.

CHAPTER NINE

1 Richard A. Brisbin Jr., "The West Virginia Judiciary," in *West Virginia Government: The Legislative, Executive, and Judiciary* (Morgantown: West Virginia University, Institute for Public Affairs, 1993) expands the discussion in this chapter.

2 *West Virginia Judicial Personnel System Manual* (Charleston: Supreme Court of Appeals, 1990).

3 *Mayer v. Ferguson*, 327 S.E. 2d 409, 412 (W. Va. 1985).

4 Mail survey conducted by the authors.

5 Ted Philyaw, director, Administrative Office of the Supreme Court of Appeals, interview by authors, Charleston, 12 March 1991.

6 John Paul Ryan, Alan Ashman, Bruce D. Sales, and Sandra Shane-DuBow, *American Trial Judges* (New York: Free Press, 1980), 90–97.

7 John A. Rogers, Public Defender Services, interview by authors, Charleston, 6 January 1992; "West Virginia Public Defender Services Public Defender Corporations," January 3, 1992; and West Virginia Public Defender Services, "Annual Report, Fiscal Year 1990-'91."

8 Penelope Crandall, assistant airector, Administrative Office of the Supreme Court of Appeals, interview by authors, Charleston, 11 February 1992.

9 Martha Hill, director, Child Advocate Office, interview by authors, Charleston, 7 January 1992.

10 *State ex rel. Walker v. Giardina*, 294 S.E. 2d 900 (W. Va. 1982).

11 The Judicial Investigation Commission is composed of two circuit judges appointed by the West Virginia Judicial Association, a magistrate appointed by the West Virginia Magistrates Association, a family law master appointed by the West Virginia Family Law Master Association, two lawyers appointed by the West Virginia State Bar, and three lay persons selected by the governor.

12 Norman Oder, "Behind the Rhetoric: Philosophies Clash in Supreme Court Race," *Charleston Gazette-Mail*, 17 April 1988, C-1; Norman Oder, "Spending Gaps Narrowed between High Court Candidates," *Charleston Gazette*, 5 May 1988, 6D; and "Primary Race Contributions Listed," *Charleston Daily Mail*, 10 June 1988, 8A.

13 West Virginia judges are prohibited by the Code of Judicial Conduct (Canon 5)

from soliciting or accepting campaign funds, but they are allowed to establish committees to secure and manage the expenditure of campaign funds and to obtain public statements of support for their candidacy; West Virginia Code, Court Rules, 621–22 (1994).

14 Author interviews with Justice William T. Brotherton Jr., Charleston, 11 February 1992; Chief Justice Thomas E. McHugh, Charleston, 7 January 1992; Justice Richard Neely, Charleston, 16 December 1991; Justice Thomas Miller, Charleston, 16 March 1992; and Justice Margaret Workman, Charleston, 11 February 1992.

15 West Virginia Supreme Court of Appeals, "Statistical Activity, 1989 Executive Summary" (unpublished), and "Docketing System, Statistical Summary for 1990" (unpublished).

16 Thomas K. McQuain Jr., deputy clerk of the Supreme Court of Appeals, interview by authors, Charleston, 12 March 1991.

17 Interviews with the justices, Supreme Court of Appeals.

18 Interviews with the justices, Supreme Court of Appeals.

19 Council of State Governments, *The Book of the States, 1990–91 Edition*, 204–5; and Melinda Gann Hall, "Opinion Assignment Procedures and Conference Practices in State Supreme Courts," *Judicature* 73 (1990): 209–14.

20 West Virginia Code, § 51-1-4a (1994).

21 Allissa Bailey, "Inside the Legal Ethics Process," *West Virginia Lawyer* 4: 3 (1990): 6–8; "Innovative Program Brings in over a Quarter Million Dollars to Fund Legal Services for the Poor," *West Virginia Lawyer* 2 (1988): 5; "IOLTA—Interest on Lawyers Trust Accounts," *West Virginia Lawyer* 3, no. 4 (1989) 6–7; Thomas R. Tinder, "IOLTA—A West Virginia Success Story," *West Virginia Lawyer* 4, no. 5 (1990): 6; and Thomas R. Tinder, executive director, West Virginia State Bar, interview by authors, Charleston, 7 January 1992.

22 Interviews with the justices, Supreme Court of Appeals; Philyaw, interview; and Tinder, interview.

23 West Virginia Code, Court Rules, "Constitution, By-Laws and Rules and Regulations of the West Virginia State Bar," 646–77 (1994); Allissa Bailey, "Inside the Legal Ethics Process," *West Virginia Lawyer* 4, no. 3 (1990): 6–8; and Tinder, interview.

24 John Patrick Hagan, "Policy Activism in the West Virginia Supreme Court of Appeals, 1930–1985," *West Virginia Law Review* 89 (1986): 152.

25 This is the Uniform Commercial Code, Article 2. See Vincent P. Cardi, "The Experience of Article 2 of the Uniform Commercial Code in West Virginia," *West Virginia Law Review* 93 (summer 1991): 735–858.

26 *Johnson v. Tsapis*, 413 S.E. 699 (W. Va. 1991).

27 *Thomas v. La Rosa*, 400 S.E. 2d 809 (W. Va. 1990).

28 *Murredu v. Murredu*, 160 W. Va. 610 (1977); and *Garska v. McCoy*, 167 W. Va. 59 (1981).

29 *Hendershot v. Handlan*, 162 W. Va. 175 (1978).

30 *McGuire v. Farley*, 370 S.E. 2d 136 (W. Va. 1988).

31 *Western Maryland Rwy. v. Goodwin*, 167 W. Va. 804 (1981); *Armco, Inc. v. Hardesty*, 303 S.E. 2d 206 (W. Va. 1983), reviewed on other grounds, 467 U.S. 638 (1984); and *Webb v. Fury*, 167 W. Va. 434 (1981).

32 Thomas B. Miller, "The New Federalism in West Virginia," *West Virginia Law Review* 90 (1987): 51–65.

33 On schools, compare *Pauley v. Kelly*, 162 W. Va. 672 (1979), to *San Antonio Ind. School Dist. v. Rodriguez*, 411 U.S. 1 (1973). On sentences, compare *State v. Buck*, 314 S.E. 2d 406 (W. Va. 1984), and *Wanstreet v. Bordenkircher*, 166 W. Va. 523 (1981), to *Rummel v. Estelle*, 445 U.S. 263 (1980). On access to hearings, compare *State ex rel. The Herald-Mail Co. v. Hamilton*, 165 W. Va. 103 (1980), to *Gannett Co. v. DePasquale*, 443 U.S. 368 (1979). On alcohol, compare *State v. Zegeer*, 296 S.E. 2d 873 (W. Va. 1982), to *Powell v. Texas*, 392 U.S. 514 (1968).

34 *Bradley v. Appalachian Power Co.*, 163 W. Va. 322 (1979); and "Symposium on *Bradley v. Appalachian Power Co.*—West Virginia Adopts Comparative Negligence," *West Virginia Law Review* 82 (1980): 473–550.

35 *Morningstar v. Black and Decker Mfg. Co.*, 162 W. Va. 857, 875–92 (1979).

36 *Blankenship v. General Motors Corp.*, 406 S.E. 2d 781 (W. Va. 1991).

37 *Mandolidis v. Elkins Industries*, 161 W. Va. 695 (1978).

38 *Pauley v. Kelly*, 162 W. Va. 672 (1979).

39 *State ex rel. Board of Education v. Rockefeller*, 167 W. Va. 72 (1981).

40 *Jefferson Cty. Bd. of Educ. v. Jefferson Cty. Educ. Ass'n.*, 393 S.E. 2d 653 (W. Va. 1990); *Meadows on behalf of Prof. Emp. of WVEA v. Hey*, 399 S.E. 2d 657 (W. Va. 1990).

41 *In re 1975 Tax Assessments against Oneida Coal Co.*, 360 S.E. 2d 560, 565 (W. Va. 1987).

42 *Allegheny Pittsburgh Coal Co. v. County Commission of Webster County, W. Va.*, 109 S. Ct. 633 (1989).

CHAPTER TEN

1 West Virginia Code, §§ 7–1 to 7–20.

2 Stephen Zoeller, director, County Commissioners' Association of West Virginia, interview by authors, Charleston, 2 March 1993.

3 Rodney Pyles, Monongalia County assessor and president, West Virginia Assessors Association, interview by authors, Morgantown, 4 March 1993.

4 *State ex. rel. Summerfield v. Maxwell*, 148 W. Va. 535 (1964).

5 John Hoff, executive director, West Virginia Association of Counties, interview by authors, Charleston, 25 May 1993.

6 John W. Horne, Monongalia County surveyor, interview by authors, Morgantown, 1 March 1993.

7 West Virginia Department of Tax and Revenue, *Coal Severance Tax: Consolidated Budget Report, Fiscal Year Ending June 30, 1995* (Charleston, 1993).

8 West Virginia Department of Tax and Revenue, *Coal Severance Tax*; and Andrew Isserman, Oleg Smirnov, Terance Rephann, David Sorenson, and Elizabeth Bury, *West Virginia Population Projections by County, Age, and Sex, 1990–2020* (Morgantown: Regional Research Institute, West Virginia University, 1992), 13.

9 Claude J. Davis et al., *West Virginia State and Local Government* (Morgantown: Bureau for Government Research, 1963), 445.

10 West Virginia Department of Tax and Revenue, *Coal Severance Tax.*

11 West Virginia Department of Tax and Revenue, *Coal Severance Tax.*

12 "Carry over Carey," *Dominion Post*, 14 January 1993, 4A.

13 *Elrod v. Burns*, 427 U.S. 347 (1976).

14 "Political Spoils," *Charleston Gazette*, 25 February 1993, 4A.

15 Mavis Andree Mann (Reeves), *The Structure of City Government in West Virginia* (Morgantown: Bureau for Government Research, West Virginia University, 1953), 2.

16 Holmes, ed., *West Virginia Blue Book, 1994* (Charleston: R. R. Donnelley, 1994), 690–768.

17 Richard H. Leach and Timothy G. O'Rourke, *State and Local Government: The Third Century of Federalism* (Englewood Cliffs NJ: Prentice-Hall, 1988), 188.

18 West Virginia Department of Tax and Revenue, *Coal Severance Tax.*

19 "Special Governments Eclipsing Cities, Towns," *Charleston Gazette*, 2 February 1993, 8C.

20 U.S. Dept. of Commerce, "Government Units in 1992," in *1992 Census of Governments* (Washington DC: U.S. Government Printing Office, 1992), 6, 7.

21 U.S. Dept. of Commerce, "Government Units in 1992," 7–8.

CHAPTER ELEVEN

1 Robert Jay Dilger and Tom Stuart Witt, "West Virginia's Economic Future," in *West Virginia in the 1990s*, ed. Dilger and Witt, 3–6.

2 David R. Martinelli and Ronald W. Eck, "West Virginia's Transportation Infrastructure: Conditions, Trends and Implications for Economic Growth," in *West Virginia in the 1990s*, ed. Dilger and Witt, 195–201.

3 Clifford B. Hawley, "Demographic Change and Economic Opportunity," in *West Virginia in the 1990s*, ed. Dilger and Witt, 63–65.

4 Joseph A. Clayton, Robert Jay Dilger, and Greg Sayre, "Landfills and West Virginia's Economic Development," 171–94; Robert Jay Dilger, "Clean Water and Its Implications for Economic Development in West Virginia," 149–70; and Susan Hunter, "The 1990 Clean Air Act: Immediate and Long Term Impacts on West Virginia," 123–47; all in *West Virginia in the 1990s*, ed. Dilger and Witt; and Susan Hunter, *The Acid Rain Controversy: Policy Strategies for West Virginia and the Nation*, Policy Monograph Series no. 2 (Morgantown: Institute for Public Affairs, West Virginia University, 1990).

5 Hawley, "Demographic Change," 48–53.

6 Fanny Seiler, "Tax Credits Drain $110 Million from State," *Charleston Gazette*, 12 February 1993, 1A.

7 Paul Nyden, "Super Tax Credits Cost State Millions but Few Jobs Created," *Sunday Gazette-Mail*, 7 March 1993, 3B.

8 "Giveaway Mess," *Charleston Gazette*, 10 March 1993, 4A.

9 Seiler, "Tax Credits Drain $110 Million from State," 1A.

10 Sharon Lewis, West Virginia Department of Education, interview by authors, Charleston, 1 February 1995.

11 Trina Kleist, "19 Counties to Walk Out," *Charleston Gazette*, 14 February 1990, 1A; "Marockie Cancels School," *Charleston Gazette*, 15 March 1990, 1A; and Mark J. Coyle, "'Frustrated' Teachers Wait to See Results," *Charleston Gazette*, 3 August 1990, 1C.

12 Meg Thomas, "Student Services Office: License Program Works," *Morgantown Dominion Post*, 30 March 1989, 6A; and Jennifer Bundy, "Court Upholds Dropout License Law," *Charleston Daily Mail*, 30 November 1990, 1A.

13 Mary Wade Burnside, "State's Spending Less on Higher Education," *Charleston Gazette*, 5 December 1989, 5A; Ken Ward Jr., "College Faculty Still Lose Ground," *Charleston Gazette*, 30 July 1991, 1C; "State Higher-Education Spending Totals $39.3 Billion This Year," *Chronicle of Higher Education*, 25 October 1989, A 21; and "State Professors Earn Less Than National Average," *Charleston Daily Mail*, 21 April 1992.

14 Therese Cox, "College System Needs Overhaul," *Charleston Daily Mail*, 6 February 1989, 1A, 11A.

15 Patty Vandergrift, "Senate OKs Reorganization of Higher Education," *Charleston Gazette*, 31 March 1989, 1A.

16 Sue Morgan, "Education Savings Proof of No Bureaucracy, Governor says," *Charleston Gazette*, 4 November 1989, 12A; and State College and University System of West Virginia, *West Virginia Higher Education Report Card, 1992* (Charleston: Department of Education, 1992).

17 A. V. Gallagher, "New Law Ensures Higher-Ed Pay Raises," *Charleston Gazette*, 13 May 1993, 1A.

18 West Virginia Department of Health and Human Resources, *Provisional 1990 West Virginia Vital Statistics* (Charleston: Department of Health and Human Services, 1991), 2, 23–24; "Unhealthy-Lifestyles Study Ranks State Highly," *Charleston Gazette*, 18 February 1993, 5B.

19 Saundra K. Schneider, "Governors and Health Care Policy in the American States," *Policy Studies Journal* 17 (1989): 911–26; and Saundra K. Schneider, "Intergovernmental Influences on Medicaid Program Expenditures," *Public Administration Review* 48 (1989): 756–63.

20 Fanny Seiler, "States's Medicaid Bills $68 Million Behind," *Charleston Gazette*, 23 May 1989; and Daniel Botch, "State Plans to Extend Medicaid Coverage Time," *Charleston Daily Mail*, 20 July 1989, 1A, 15A.

21 "Health Funds for Neediest Face Big Cuts," *Charleston Daily Mail*, 25 November 1992, 1A, 13A; T. J. Simoneaux, "Medicaid Compromise Reached," *Charleston Gazette*, 21 May 1990, 1A; and A. V. Gallagher, "House OKs Medicaid Bill," *Charleston Sunday Gazette Mail*, 23 May 1993, 1A.

22 Phil Kaber, "State Appears Winner of Major Health Grant," *Charleston Gazette*, 20 June 1991, 1A; Fanny Seiler, "Lawmakers Demand Details of Rural Health Program," *Charleston Gazette*, 2 October 1991, 1A, 8A; and State College and University System of West Virginia, *West Virginia Higher Education Report Card*, 251–74.

23 Dawn Miller, "Theories on Accidental Death Rate Vary," *Charleston Gazette* 11 September 1991, 1A, 8A; and West Virginia Commission on Aging, *Annual Report 1989* (Charleston, 1989).

24 West Virginia Health Care Planning Commission, *For the Health of West Virginia: A Report to the Governor and the Legislature* (Charleston, 1991).

25 Paul Owens, "Officials Pledge Support for Health Care Reforms," *Charleston Daily Mail*, 6 January 1992, 6B; Dawn Miller, "Health-Care Reform Plan Would Coordinate State Policies, Programs," *Charleston Gazette*, 4 March 1993, 1C; and Anthony J. DeFrank and Allan S. Hammock, "The Health Care Crisis and Medical Liability in West Virginia," *West Virginia Public Affairs Reporter* 7, no. 1 (1990): 1–10.

26 Deane Neubauer, "Hawaii: The Health State," 147–72, and Howard M. Leich-

ter, "Rationing of Health Care: Oregon Comes Out of the Closet," 117–46, both in *Health Policy Reform in America*, ed. Howard M. Leichter (Armonk NY: M. E. Sharpe, 1992).

27 Advisory Commission on Intergovernmental Relations, *1991 State Fiscal Capacity and Effort* (Washington DC, 1993).

Index

In the Politics and Governments of the American States series

Alabama Government and Politics
By James D. Thomas and William H. Stewart

Alaska Politics and Government
By Gerald A. McBeath and Thomas A. Morehouse

Arkansas Politics and Government: Do the People Rule?
By Diane D. Blair

Colorado Politics and Government: Governing the Centennial State
By Thomas E. Cronin and Robert D. Loevy

Illinois Politics and Government: The Expanding Metropolitan Frontier
By Samuel K. Gove and James D. Nowlan

Kentucky Politics and Government: Do We Stand United?
By Penny M. Miller

Maine Politics and Government
By Kenneth T. Palmer, G. Thomas Taylor, and Marcus A. LiBrizzi

Michigan Politics and Government: Facing Change in a Complex State
By William P. Browne and Kenneth VerBurg

Mississippi Government and Politics: Modernizers versus Traditionalists
By Dale Krane and Stephen D. Shaffer

Nebraska Government and Politics
Edited by Robert D. Miewald

Nevada Politics and Government: Conservatism in an Open Society
By Don W. Driggs and Leonard E. Goodall

New Jersey Politics and Government: Suburban Politics Comes of Age
By Barbara G. Salmore and Stephen A. Salmore

North Carolina Government and Politics
By Jack D. Fleer

Oklahoma Politics and Policies: Governing the Sooner State
By David R. Morgan, Robert E. England, and George G. Humphreys

South Carolina Politics and Government
By Cole Blease Graham Jr. and William V. Moore

West Virginia Politics and Government
By Richard A. Brisbin Jr., Robert Jay Dilger, Allan S. Hammock, and Christopher Z. Mooney